Meet Wally Street

The Reason You're Stupid

I0030504

0929

By:
Richard Allison Johnson
The Introverted Advisor

Copyright © 2014 Richard Allison Johnson

All rights reserved.

ISBN - 10: 0615894518
ISBN - 13: 978-0615894515

Dedication

I dedicate my book to my good friend Wally Street. I probably would not have a job, if it wasn't for Wally and all his shenanigans.

[This page intentionally left blank]

Acknowledgement

I acknowledge that if you are currently doing business with banks, insurance companies and Wall Street firms for your financial advice, then, unfortunately, you are doing business with Wally Street. As you will soon realize by reading this book, getting your financial advice from Wally Street is a very stupid thing to do. Very stupid indeed.

Thanks to my daughter Rudi for her illustration of Wally Street. Thanks to my wife Natalie for her help with this book and for being my wife for the last 26 years. Thanks to my son Marshall for being all knowing and all powerful and explaining to me what the heck is going on in Game of Thrones.

Thanks to my business partner Stan Rosenthal and his wife Donna for sharing their wisdom, experience and expertise.

Thanks to my baseball buddies Gregg Rollins, Jimmy Scott and Randall Guard for knowing what it means to be a true friend and the Arkansas Diamonds, Houston Yankees and Savannah Tropics teams and players.

Thanks to my late father Hillman E. Johnson for his quips and jokes interspersed throughout the book.

Thanks to the many family and friends whose names that I didn't mention and who will probably get their feelings hurt because of it. Besides, we would be here all day if I had to list them all and nobody really gives a flip anyway.

And finally, a special thank you goes out to all my readers who will soon forgive me for calling them stupid.

Table of Contents

Introduction

You may be wondering why I am calling myself "The Introverted Advisor." It's simple really. I am an introvert.

I think I have pinpointed the reason that I am so introverted. I grew up with a father that was six foot six inches (6'6") tall and he was very intimidating. He yelled and cussed a lot at the most mundane things. You did not want to spill a glass of milk around him, because he would let you have it. Don't get me wrong. I loved my dad, but when you are around someone that is 6'6" tall, plus yells and cusses a lot, then you tend to become quiet and introverted. This is what happened to me.

Being introverted and also being in sales is not a good combination. To make up for this glaring shortfall, I have taken the path of staying on top of things by being educated. This is self-education that I am describing. I have always loved to read and with the internet, books, magazines and other forms of education, it is easier than ever to become self-educated. Of course, you cannot do everything on your own. You need a mentor here and there and I have had several, including my dad.

It is totally ridiculous how introverted I am. Sometimes it is hard for me to reach out to people, because of my introverted nature. The thought of beating on doors, or glad handing at networking events makes me cringe. My dad used to call networking "shaking hands and patting fannies." He was a funny guy and I will pass along more of his famous quips throughout the book.

I once was a member of a financial services trade organization for at least eight years. I regularly attended their meetings, but never once received a referral from an attorney, or CPA. I cannot blame it on the organization or its members. It was my own fault, because of my introverted nature.

Even when I was in this group, most of the topics that were discussed and presented were rarely ever over my head. That is unless it was some topic on litigation. Then, I have to admit that I do not know much in that area. Most of the time however, I already knew all about the subject being presented. That sounds egotistical I know, but in reality, it shows the effort that I have made to stay on top of things. I am proof positive that you can be introverted and a little bit egotistical at the same time.

Perhaps, I can make up for this glaring weakness of being afraid to speak up and network with people by writing this book. Being afraid to talk about your weaknesses is a weakness in itself. It is better to be open and honest with people rather than try and deceive them into believing that you are someone that deep down inside you are not.

This is what I am doing here in this Introduction. I am exposing one of my major weaknesses for all the world to see. I wanted you to know that I am an introvert, but very extroverted when it comes to writing a book. As you are reading this book, you may think to yourself, "Wow, Rick. You sure have strong opinions." That is certainly true. I do have strong opinions, especially when it comes to people being taken advantage of by the big Wall Street revenue generating machine.

In order to get my story out there, I have written this book targeted primarily at people "who need to be taken to the woodshed," or, as my dad used to say, "We need to have a come to Jesus meeting." This is where you need something like a hickory switch to your rear end to get your attention, because most of you are woefully unaware of how badly you are being treated by banks, insurance companies and Wall Street firms. My aim is to fix that for you. For your sake, let's hope that I am successful.

As you are reading this book, you must realize that I can be a little condescending at times. Well maybe, a lot more than a little. That will be my hickory switch. In addition, I may even use a few politically incorrect cuss words. Sorry, but I am not a politically correct kind of guy. Fair enough?

This book is voluminous for sure. However, I wrote it with the intention that you can use it as a sort of "review-as-needed" reference book. Keep in mind that with most of the subjects that I describe throughout the book, I am only scratching the surface. There is significantly more to the story.

There is something in the book for pretty much all demographics. Young and old. In addition, there are chapters targeted to both the middle class and the affluent. The over-riding theme of the book, however, is targeted to the people who get their financial advice from banks, insurance companies and Wall Street firms. Sadly, that covers pretty much the large majority of you which is about 85% of America.

Another theme of the book is the fact that I believe that you will be immensely better off using the proper professional to help you. Specifically, this means *independent* registered investment advisers, Estate Planning attorneys, Elder Law attorneys and CPA's. The things that I am adamantly opposed to are you investing on your own, (you're not qualified, even if you think you are,) using Wally Street, (the reason you're stupid,) using an online legal document firm, (dumb with a capital "D") and preparing your taxes yourself, (you cannot be serious,) especially when your financial situation demands a qualified CPA.

Also, when you come across the quotes that I have placed throughout the book at the beginning of each chapter, then I want you to take a moment to reflect on what those quotes mean. You should find them inspirational, educational and funny in some cases.

Further, at the end of each chapter, I will summarize the key points that I want you to remember. Some of these key points will make you laugh, too.

The last chapter of this book is My Personal Story. This chapter will help you to understand who I am as a person, the challenges that I have faced in my life, and finally how I have overcome those challenges. In addition, you will understand why I believe what I believe. Further, if you have been through some tough times, then perhaps you can look at me as someone who has had it worse than you. This might make you realize what I have learned from my challenges. Specifically, you can always find other people who have had a tougher time than you. Hopefully, by realizing this fact, then this will help you keep moving forward with a promising outlook on life.

One more thing. I know it is hard to believe, but I am not flawless. It is very possible that something in the book might be inaccurate, because of changes in tax law, or because simply that I didn't do enough research. However, I have done my best to insure that this is not the case. Again, instead of just relying on this book, I would prefer that you rely on the corresponding professional for advice whether that be an *independent* registered investment adviser, an Estate Planning attorney, an Elder Law attorney, or a CPA.

Thank you again for buying this book. I really appreciate it. If you purchased this as an eBook, then you will automatically get my updates as they occur. Welcome to your journey of self-discovery. If after reading this book you choose to follow my advice, then you will experience major self-improvement without a doubt. That's a fact, Jack.

Richard Allison Johnson *aka* Richard Mark Allison
The Introverted Advisor

Chapter One

Meet Wally Street

"We are what we repeatedly do. Excellence, then, is not an act, but a habit."

~ Aristotle

[This page intentionally left blank]

Meet Wally Street

Wally Street is a made up character that I invented to showcase the financial advice offered by financial advisors who work for banks, insurance companies and Wall Street firms. *Wally* Street could work for a bank, an insurance company, a Wall Street firm, or perhaps all three.

Wally Street is a man who does things by the rules of the game. You see, it is a game to Wally. He has a creed that he lives by and that creed is to generate revenue for his firm and himself. Your needs are sadly missing from his creed.

Wally has to produce revenue to keep his job. His revenue target is $250,000 a year or more. This means that he has to sell you products that generate lots of commissions and fees. Don't be fooled. He does not work in your best interests.

You may scoff at what I am telling you. Your Wally Street would never treat you like a revenue source, or so you would think. He always remembers your birthday. He invites you to client appreciation events. Perhaps, he even gives you "free" tickets to sporting events. In your mind, he is an all-around good guy.

We had a Wally Street here locally that took everyone to the Super Bowl every year and paid for everything. He called on DEA and FBI agents no less. The guy ended up being a Ponzi schemer. Once they figured that out, they went after him. He killed himself before they could catch him. If DEA and FBI agents can be scammed by a Ponzi schemer, then so can you.

We had a female Wally Street here locally that sold high interest car loans and paid her investors a high rate of interest, minus her commission of course. Not only did she charge them a commission on their investment, she took their entire investment, too! The victims were mostly the elderly who were in investment clubs. This Ponzi schemer infiltrated their investment club and ingratiated herself with the members. These victims believed that this Wally Street was a financial guru. She was a guru all right. A Ponzi scheme guru.

Your Wally Street might be a nice person and probably is in fact a nice person. However, the business model under which he operates is the major factor in his quest to take your money. In the following chapter, I am going to describe the products that Wally Street routinely sells to his victims, or excuse me, I meant "clients."

Here is my agreement with you as the reader:

If you have bought any of the products described in the next chapter, then you will have to admit that you have indeed been a victim of Wally Street.

After you have discovered that you have been a victim, then you have a choice.

1. **Do you become a victim over and over again?**
2. Or, do you make the bold step to make a change, regardless of how much your Wally Street seems to be a genuine good person? This may be very hard for you, but it would absolutely be the smartest choice.

I realize that most people like their version of Wally Street and would never even think of leaving them. However, there is something inherently wrong with the business models of banks, insurance companies and Wall Street firms. As long their main focus is to generate revenue, then you would be a fool to do business with them. Of course, I do not expect you to believe me at this point, because you have no reason to believe me right now. However, by the time I get through with you, then you will be agreeing wholeheartedly with me, if you have any sense at all. If not, then you get what you deserve. That is a harsh statement I know, but you need to hear it. The fact that your version of Wally Street is a nice person has nothing to do with the business model under which he operates. It is the business model that is the root of the problem. You must understand this critical point.

You have heard it said, "The definition of insanity is doing the same thing over and over again and expecting a different result." If you keep doing business with your version of Wally Street, then you will continue to get taken advantage of by his company's business model. There is not any doubt whatsoever of this fact.

Hold on to your seats boys and girls. You are about to embark on a journey of self-discovery and it is not going to be pretty.

Chapter Summary

What did we learn in this chapter?

- We learned that even DEA and FBI agents can be scammed by Ponzi schemes.
- We learned that Wally Street can be a man or a woman and also a Ponzi schemer.
- Rick is trying to tell us that our financial advisor is just like Wally Street, but we at this point are not convinced.
- We think that we are too smart to be fooled by the likes of a Wally Street.
- We will soon learn that we are way too confident.

Notes

Chapter Two

Wally's Products

"Whatever is received is received according to the nature of the
recipient."

~ Thomas Aquinas

[This page intentionally left blank]

Wally's Products

Wally, as you can imagine, is all about making money. In order to make money, he has to sell the right products. The right products are the ones that pay the most commissions.

1. Variable Annuities
2. Non-Publicly Traded (BDC's) or Real Estate Investment Trusts (REIT's)
3. UIT's or Unit Investment Trusts
4. Stepped Up CD's
5. Structured Products
6. Private Placements
7. Promissory Notes
8. Regulation D Offerings
9. Exchange Traded Notes (ETN's)
10. Precious Metals
11. Floating Rate Bank Loan Mutual Funds
12. Class "A" Shares Mutual Funds
13. Class "B" Shares Mutual Funds
14. Class "C" Shares Mutual Funds

I'll go over these products one by one, so you know which ones to avoid.

[This page intentionally left blank]

Variable Annuities

The main way that banks, insurance companies and Wall Street firms take people's heads off is via this animal and I do mean animal.

The Variable Annuity (VA).

Generally, Variable Annuities have lots of expenses. A bare bones VA has expenses of about 2.5% according to Morningstar®. Wally loves to add on riders to his VA's that he sells. These additional riders can cost anywhere from 0.50% to as much as 1.00% per rider! So, it is very possible to be sold a VA with expenses in the 3 – 4% range. Now, you do not have to be a smart person to figure out that if you are being charged 3 – 4% right off the top, then it makes it hard to make any money. Wally knows this, too. That is why he *always* wants to slam you into 100% stocks when you buy a VA. If Wally puts you in something that only had an expected return of 4%, then you would never make any money on your VA. This is why Wally is almost always aggressive with the investment choices that he (don't make me laugh) "recommends" for his victims. Excuse me, I meant to say clients.

I wonder. Did Wally tell you that he makes 6 – 10% in commissions on a VA sale? Most of the time, he just says, "sign here." Ever wonder why Wally wants to put so much of your money in VA's? Now you know. A couple of hundred thousand ($200,000) in VA's and Wally is making somewhere in the neighborhood of $12,000 to $20,000 depending on the VA that he sells. That is a lot of money. At least it is to me. Wally earned every penny of that $12,000 to $20,000 too by saying "sign here." It takes a lot of skills and training to say "sign here," so you should have no trouble paying Wally that kind of commission. Apparently, up to $2,500 per letter by saying "s-i-g-n h-e-r-e."

Oh, by the way, did you know that you will have a surrender charge period of at least ten years? That is if you live in Florida. In other states, it could be fourteen years or longer.

Please help me out a little bit here. Explain to me how buying a product with expenses that could be north of 3% per year, that you are stuck in for at least ten years, while Wally makes off with 6 – 10% in commissions, how does this benefit you? I am struggling to understand how a product whose sole existence is to generate revenue for Wally World and Wally Street, how does this benefit you, the client?

Sadly, I do not think you can give me a good answer to that question. As a result, I think I will move on. Don't worry however. I will intersperse more of my thoughts on Variable Annuities throughout the book. I am nowhere near through discussing them.

Non-Publicly Traded REIT's/BDC's

Everyone has heard about Ponzi schemes. Did you know that Non-Publicly Traded REIT's (NPT REIT's) or Business Development Companies (BDC's) as they are sometimes called are designed just like a Ponzi scheme? It is true. This is how it works.

1. You give them your money.
2. They take 11 -13% right off the top for expenses.
3. They pay you back your principal as an income stream.

This is exactly how Ponzi schemes work! That's a fact, Jack. You cannot argue with my three points above. This is exactly, and I mean exactly how Ponzi schemes work.

There is no secondary market to speak of with these NPT REIT's. Oh, don't get me wrong. They will tell you that there is a market for them. Yes, there is a market, but it is about 70% of what you put in it. For example, if you put in $100,000, then right after your deposit, if you want to sell it, then you can maybe get 70% back. Does that sound like a secondary market to you? Not to me.

Imagine if you bought a stock and soon after you buy it, it is now worth 70% of what you paid for it. You would be livid if that happened to you. Wally has no conscious when it comes to selling these NPT REIT's and I mean no conscious whatsoever.

I met an 86 year old man recently who had $400,000 worth of these NPT REIT's. Why do you think that is? Because it pays the Wally Street who sold them, 8.5% commissions! Let's see. $400,000 times 8.5% commission equals $34,000 in commissions to Wally.

Oh by the way, the 86 year old man had a wife who lived in the local assisted living center. He came to see me for an Elder Law attorney recommendation, because he was going to have to start paying for her care and he wanted to know what he could do. You see, her Long Term Care Insurance was running out soon. The sad truth is that he was going to have to foot the bill after that happened. Even sadder was the fact that the $400,000 in NPT REIT's was not liquid!! In addition, he was going to have to take a big loss to get to his money!

Now imagine his request for money from the NPT REIT. Because of the liquidity restrictions, he might be able to get 70% of his money. After all, the managers of the NPT REIT take 11 – 13% right off the top as soon as the money is invested. Then, the managers of the fund have to find someone who wants to buy a secondary market NPT REIT. The potential buyer of this "investment" will not want to pay full price for it. They will only buy it if they get a bargain. In case you do not know, assisted living centers can cost $3,000 to $4,000 per month. The elderly gentlemen will probably request a withdrawal of $50,000. Unfortunately, because he has to go to the secondary market, he may have to liquidate around $71,000 worth of his NPT REIT shares to get the needed $50,000.

The bottom line is that he will lose about $21,000 in shares ($71,000 - $50,000) in order to get to his own money. Keep in mind that he has to do this each year his wife is in the assisted living center. Further, the assisted living center was pressuring the elderly gentlemen to move his wife to the nursing home, which will cost $6,000 to $8,000 per month. Sadly, she was going to have to make this move very soon. That means he will need a bigger withdrawal from his NPT REIT.

This elderly gentlemen had no trouble paying $34,000 in commissions to Wally Street for the Non-Publicly Traded REIT's, but he thought the Elder Law attorney's fully disclosed fee to get him out of the mess was too much. (More on Elder Care later in the book.)

[30]

Hey, I wonder. I wonder if Wally told him that he was making $34,000 in commissions. Further, I wonder if he told him about the liquidity restrictions, too. What do you want to bet that Wally quickly glossed over those items when he sold these NPT REIT's to this elderly man?

This guy was in a heap of trouble because of a Wally Street who sold him this crappy, inappropriate product. The guy was in his eighties for goodness sakes! As they say on ESPN®, "Come on, man!"

Oh, by the way, this is all perfectly legal for Wally Street. Legal, but certainly unethical. This is the Wall Street machine that I want to stop ladies and gentlemen.

One of the guys who sold this man the NPT REIT's even had a radio show for a while. Guess what he was promoting on his radio show?

Non-Publicly Traded REIT's!

I cannot believe that his broker/dealer compliance department actually approved this guy to be on the radio hawking these Non-Publicly Traded REIT's. Either his compliance department or the radio station finally wised up and kicked him off the air. Perhaps, he just hit a cold streak and could not pay the radio station their bill anymore. I'm not sure which of the three it was, but thankfully he is no longer on the radio.

The sad truth is that this elderly gentlemen will lose thousands upon thousands of dollars by not letting the Elder Law attorney help him. The nursing home bill is not going to go away. In the end, instead of paying for an Elder Law attorney, he decided that he would rather give the nursing home owner his money instead. It was not a very good decision on his part. Hopefully somewhere down the road he wised up and went to an Elder Law attorney for help. Every month that he waits it is going to cost him $6,000 to $8,000 which is money he could have saved with an

Elder Law attorney. I guess he could always go to Wally for help, because Wally is always looking out for him, isn't he? After all, Wally is the one who sold him the Non-Publicly Traded REIT's in the first place. I am sure he has a solution.

Another one of Wally's sales pitches revolving around these Non-Publicly Traded REIT's is the fact that:

"Someday, they will take this REIT public and you will reap the rewards."

My responses and questions for Wally are the following:

- Excuse me Wally, but you can buy *Publicly* Traded REIT's that are listed on the NYSE any day of the week without the 8.5% commissions and with full liquidity where I can get my money in as little as 3 days.
- Why do you have to wait 10 to 12 years for the privilege with *your* Non-Publicly Traded REIT?
- Also, doesn't the firm that is selling this Non-Publicly Traded REIT already have several Publicly Traded REIT's that are listed on the NYSE?
- If so, then why do I need to put so much money into your Non-Publicly Traded REIT?

Wally would be squirming in his seat if you asked him these questions. The truth is that Wally just wants to rake your ass over the coals and nail you with as big of a commission as possible by selling you this crap. That was one of my hickory switches by the way.

The next time Wally tries to sell you a Non-Publicly Traded REIT/BDC, run as fast as you can in the opposite direction. Run fast. Run very, very fast.

UIT's or Unit Investment Trusts

This product is purely a Wall Street firm's invention. When these first came about, CD rates were very high, like 6%. Wall Street firms were having trouble competing against those type of CD rates. So, what they did was invent the UIT. These UIT's are basically a pool of investments that have a maturity date, as Wally would say, "They mature just like a CD." I'm serious. Wally would say this all the time when he was selling these UIT's.

At first, these UIT's were kind of simple. They simply bought the 30 Dow Jones Industrial Average stocks, then stuck a one year maturity date on them and presto! Now you have a UIT. All you had to do was hold onto your UIT until maturity and you would get the return of the DJIA. Good or bad, I might add.

By the way, Wally got paid 4.95% commission for selling you a UIT when these first came out. The even better part for Wally is when it matured, it automatically rolled over for another year. You guessed it. Wally gets another 4.95% commission when it rolled over. Pretty nice product design, don't you agree? Well, it is for Wally anyway. Wally can make 4.95% per year as long as you keep rolling that UIT over each year. Sweet!

What did you get? You got a UIT man! Isn't that great? It is great except for the fact that you do not know what the hell is in a stinking UIT. Can you lose money in a UIT? Yes. If the DJIA goes down, then you lose money. Are there liquidity restrictions with a UIT? Yes. If you want to sell a UIT early, then you have to sell it on the open market. Further, if the DJIA has gone down since you bought it, then you might have to sell it at a discount. Think about the reverse. Even if the DJIA went up, the secondary market buyer may think that the market is too high and not want to pay too much for your UIT. Either way, regardless if your UIT is up or down based on the DJIA, then you may have to sell it at a discount. Who would really look at your UIT as something that they absolutely just had to have? Let me answer that for you. No one. It is a piece of crap investment. Although, Wally would disagree with me.

Look at it this way. Supposed you thought the UIT buying the Dow Jones Industrial Average was a good thing and you did not mind paying the 4.95% commission. Instead, take $100,000 and buy the actual 30 stocks in the DJIA. Assuming a commission of $8.95 per trade, you would pay $268.50 to buy all 30 stocks. Interesting. Let's factor this out. $268.50 divided by $100,000 investment equals 0.2695%. Let's round this off to 0.27%. Now, let's compare. 4.95% to 0.27%. Which is better for you as the investor? Which is better for Wally Street?

Okay. Okay. That was misleading on my part. I forgot to add back the cost to sell those 30 DJIA stocks. This would double the 0.27% to 0.54%. Whooped-de-frigging-do! I still beat the dog do-do out of Wally Street's UIT which is 4.95% versus buying and selling the 30 stocks yourself that only costs 0.54%.

I got you on this one, didn't I? You cannot wiggle out of this one. You need a UIT like you need a hole in the head. That hickory switch can sting.

Look, with the UIT, you have liquidity, but at a price. When you buy the DJIA stocks, you can sell them anytime that you like. You are not at the mercy of some broker/dealer who is shopping your crappy UIT at an inopportune time to sell it.

Wally Street's broker/dealer has figured out that some people are getting wise to this UIT fiasco. As a result, out of the goodness of their heart I might add, they have discounted their UIT commissions. They dropped them from 4.95% down to 2.95%. Isn't Wally Street's broker/dealer nice? That was so nice of them to do that. They are saving you 2% in UIT commissions!

Okay. I get it. Now, I have to go back to my trusty HP 12C calculator and re-figure the differences. A 2.95% commission versus 0.54% in trading commissions. Looky there! I still win!

Don't be fooled into believing that Wally Street's broker/dealer is going to take this lying down. They will get more creative than ever with UIT's. Except now, they will call them "Structured Products." Don't jump ahead, but I will describe these in the upcoming pages.

[This page intentionally left blank]

Stepped-Up CD's

Here comes another invention of Wally Street's brokerage firm:

The Stepped-Up CD.

This is similar to a CD with built in interest rate escalations. The problem for Wally Street's brokerage firm was when interest rates were low, they had to come up with a way to attract investors. People who routinely buy CD's were their target market. The way these worked is that they might pay 2% in year one, 3% in year two and 4% in year three. The problem was that you could buy a one year CD from a bank at 3%, so why would you buy something that starts out paying 2%? Wally Street was taught to say, "It averages 3% over the whole time period."

Wally Street's brokerage firm got real creative with these Stepped-Up CD's. They switched from paying a flat interest rate to paying what the market did. I know what you are thinking. "You mean like a UIT?" Yes. Excellent my avid student.

Someone that I know was sold one of these. Notice I said "sold" one of these. Nobody ever wakes up one day and says, "You know, I think I want to buy me a Stepped-Up CD today." After they bought it, they came sheepishly complaining to me that they had bought it. They thought perhaps that they should not have bought it. They wanted my opinion of it, after the fact of course.

Here is my standard answer:

It is a piece of crap investment.

I wonder. Why do people choose to allow themselves to be "sold" products that benefit Wally instead of themselves? This is a choice that they make. They make the choice that their version of Wally Street is a good guy and he is real smart and all, so he must be recommending something good for me.

Further still, why do they always ask me about these piece of crap investments after they are sold one by Wally? I guess it never occurred to anyone to ask me _before_ you make that decision. They always come to me when they have already been taken to the cleaners.

Don't be such a push-over when Wally is trying to sell you a Stepped-Up CD.

Structured Products

Here go those Wall Street guys again. Here is another one of their inventions:

The Structured Product.

You know that boring old UIT with just the DJIA in it? Well, unfortunately it is not sexy anymore. How about a commodities structured product that invests in agriculture, oil and gas, or precious metals? Or perhaps one that invests in master limited partnerships, natural gas pipelines and shipping containers? Oh, let me tell you, these Wall Street guys went crazy on this one. There are now so many different Structured Products out there today that it will make you dizzy.

You see, people soon figured out that they could buy a mutual fund or an Exchange Traded Fund that invested in the DJIA and not pay that hefty 2.95% UIT commission every year. This sent the Wall Street firms into a panic. They had to find a way to attract investors, so they simply complicated the daylights out of things and invented Structured Products. Their goal was to create investments that you cannot replicate anywhere else like the "21 Month Buffered Return Enhanced Note." Say what? See what I mean? How are you going to replicate that investment? You can't. That is why *you have to* buy the Structured Product, because you cannot get it anywhere else. That is the sales pitch you will likely hear anyway.

Boy, I would love to be a fly on the wall listening to Wally Street trying to sell the "21 Month Buffered Return Enhanced Note."

My questions would be, "Why 21 months? What is a buffered return? What is an enhanced note?" I guarantee you that Wally Street doesn't have a clue.

I also guarantee you that if you drill down inside the "21 Month Buffered Return Enhanced Note," then you will find that you can probably replicate it for about 0.54%. However, you will not do that, because you "trust" your advisor's advice to be in your best interests.

I got you again, didn't I? You are starting to doubt Wally Street aren't you? That hickory switch is starting to sting a little bit, isn't it? Well, I have just scratched the surface my friend. I have a lot more convincing to do to get you to do an about face. You are only in the first semester of this course.

Never buy anything that you do not fully understand! Better yet. Don't buy a Structured Product from Wally

Private Placements

Red flag alert! Red flag alert! Almost all investments that turn out to be Ponzi schemes originate as a bogus Private Placement.

I know of another advisor who didn't have a lick of sense. When I call him an advisor, please understand that I am using that term very loosely. In reality, he was just another Wally Street.

Anyway, this more experienced Wally Street had a buddy who wanted to open a restaurant. These two imbeciles got together and devised a scheme to raise money for this restaurant via a Private Placement. The advisor sold this "investment" to a bunch of unsuspecting investors. In fact, people lined up to buy this Private Placement, because they were offering 12% interest on it. What a deal!

For the life of me, I still to this day do not understand why people would fall for that garbage, but they still do. Day after day after day. They line up to get ripped off. If only they had read this book first.

The advisor's restaurateur buddy had a little trouble making his restaurant succeed. I was totally shocked. It's hard to believe, isn't it? His buddy also did not like having to pay payroll taxes. Instead he liked all the perks that came with being a restaurateur. Things like his new house, his new Lamborghini, his new girlfriend that he had to keep up and so on.

The problem developed when the guy didn't pay any payroll taxes. The investors had to step in and pay it. That's right. The investors who invested in this Private Placement had their investments seized by the IRS in order to pay the back payroll taxes and penalties. The final IRS tally was over $800,000 in back taxes and penalties. Needless to say, they never got any, that's right, they never got any of their money back. Their Private Placement assets were gone like the wind.

Do you think they ever thought that was possible when they put their money into that Private Placement? All they thought about was that fictitious 12% interest, believe me. I cannot say that I feel all that sorry for them. In fact, I do not feel the least bit sorry for them. They were stupid. That's right. I said they were stupid. They let greed dictate their investment choices.

These kind of people will gladly give an interview on television and tell all about how they were duped. The sad truth is that they were not duped. They were greedy and stupid, which is a terrible combination when it comes to investing.

Don't be greedy and stupid, then you won't get duped!

Promissory Notes

Promissory notes are not worth the paper they are printed on. Promissory notes are basically a promise to pay someone back. That's it. That is all there is to them. There is nothing guaranteed about them. Let me dumb it down for you.

"The people who want your money and who want to sell you a Promissory note will most likely never pay you back, plus there is a 100% chance that you are talking to a Ponzi schemer."

If you put your money in a Promissory Note, then there is a high likelihood that you will be investing in a Ponzi scheme. You can kiss your money good-bye in all probability.

Are you doubting me? Okay then, go find me ten people who have invested in a Promissory Note *and* who actually profited from their investment. I'll be here waiting for your list. In the meantime, I will move on.

Some Promissory Notes have a rate of interest that they will pay, like 12% while others just let you share in the capital gains of their investment idea. The Promissory Note could be for anything under the sun like land development, a restaurant, or a shopping center. The sky is the limit with Promissory Notes. They can literally be used for anything. Odds are that the Promissory Note is for someone else's new Lamborghini.

Promissory Notes are not regulated like a publicly traded stock or mutual fund. They kind of fly under the regulatory radar. You normally find out about them after the investor has been fleeced. Do you want to get fleeced? If not, then do not buy any Promissory Notes.

Promissory Notes are also structured just like a Ponzi scheme. They take your money, skim a bunch off the top for Lamborghini's, or excuse me, I meant to say management expenses, then they pay you back your own principal. Well, they pay you back your principal for a little while, until they spend it all. Interesting. That sounds just like a Ponzi scheme.

By the way, if you have bought into a Promissory Note and wonder why you are not getting paid any more, then more than likely it is because you bought into a Ponzi scheme. If you need help trying to figure out what is going on with your Promissory Note, then give me a call.

Hopefully, you were smart enough to stay away from Promissory Notes.

Regulation D Offerings

Regulation D offerings are really Private Placements. These Regulation D offerings allow companies to sell the securities of their company without having to register with the SEC.

The rules are that:

1. There can only be one offering.
2. Disclosures must be provided.
3. There can be no general solicitation to the public.
4. The securities that are sold must contain restrictions against being sold for one year.
5. The securities in most cases, must be sold to accredited investors.
6. The securities can be sold to non-accredited investors in some cases, but it is limited to 35 of those non-accredited investors.

An accredited investor is by definition someone with a $1,000,000 plus net worth excluding their primary residence and who makes north of $200,000 per year for each of the last two years.

There are three rules associated with Regulation D offerings.

These are:

1. Rule 504 which says the company can raise no more than $1,000,000 in a 12 month period and they must be from _only_ accredited investors.
2. Rule 505 which says the company can raise no more than $5,000,000 in a 12 month period from an _unlimited_ number of accredited investors, but no more than 35 non-accredited investors.

3. Rule 506 which says the company can raise an *unlimited amount of funds* from accredited investors, but are limited to 35 investors who are non-accredited.

Now, imagine if a couple of guys, who were a little smarter than most, started a corporation and they decided to do a Regulation D Offering to fund their venture. These smart guys were real estate pros. They have been in the real estate business for years. They come to you and want to give you a piece of the action! They are going to give you stock in their company. Yippee! Only you have to hold onto it for at least a year, before you can sell it. These two guys have this great idea to develop a shopping center and they are working with Wal-Mart to be the anchor of their shopping center. Sounds great, doesn't it? Man oh man. They are going to make money hand over fist and lucky you, you get to own part of it with them!

Didn't you read the offering memorandum? You see that Regulation D stock you bought is like way down the food chain. The guys who sold you that really own the company, not you. Your stock is actually a B class of the company's stock without any voting rights.

Those guys get to skim a bunch of money off the top of the Regulation D funds, since after all, it was their great idea to do the shopping center in the first place. As luck would have it, that Wal-Mart anchor deal fell through. After a year, all they have is a nail salon and a sub shop, but they are working on it. Meanwhile, your couple of hundred thousand is sitting there languishing away waiting on these two guys to sell out the shopping center. Who knows how long that will take without an anchor like Wal-Mart?

That first year went by pretty fast and now your restricted stock is now available for you to sell. Who are you going to sell it to? Remember, the shopping center just got built during that year and they only have a sub

[46]

shop and a nail salon as tenants so far. What do you think your B class non-voting rights stock is worth? I hate to tell you this, but it is not worth anywhere near $200,000, especially after they skimmed a bunch off the top for "management expenses."

Regulation D Offerings are just a little bit more sophisticated way of taking your money away from you. My advice is to stay far away. Even sophisticated real estate investors lose money in deals that are similar to the one I described above. Just because you are an accredited investor, doesn't mean you are smart. In fact, it may mean just the opposite if you invest in a Regulation D offering.

[This page intentionally left blank]

Exchange Traded Notes (ETN's)

Although some Exchange Traded _Funds_ providers would like you to believe that Exchange Traded _Notes_ are the same as Exchange Traded Funds, they in fact would be lying about that. ETN's have a lot of issuer risk to them. If the issuer gets into financial difficulty, then you could risk losing your entire ETN investment. "No, say it isn't so Rick."

Do you mean that these ETN issuers are banks? There has never been a bank have financial difficulty has there? Of course, I am being facetious.

ETN's are actually _Promissory Notes_ issued by banks. Yikes! Promissory Notes. Oh, no!

ETN's do not hold any underlying securities. What? That's right. They do not hold any stocks within the ETN. What you are buying are derivatives from the bank's traders. Can you say "London Whale?"

With ETN's, banks make derivative bets, buy futures and options on an index and give you the result of their successes or failures. So, even though you think you are buying an ETN based on the Agriculture Sector, what you are really doing is buying the Agriculture expertise of the ETN issuer. In other words, you are making a bet on their ability to correctly buy derivatives, hedges, futures and options in the Agriculture market. Can you do that? If not, then why invest in something that you have absolutely no idea how it really works? I promise you. Even if you think you know how an ETN works, you are wrong.

You're not going to tell me how you "trust" your Wally Street again are you? I hope not.

[This page intentionally left blank]

Precious Metals

How many Gold and Silver commercials have you seen lately? The financial television shows are filled with them. They want you to buy gold coins and gold bullion, or silver coins and silver bullion. You can even put these in your IRA's! Of course, you have to let those guys hold your precious metals for you. You see, you cannot hold gold coins in your house if they are a part of your IRA. You have to have a custodian for that. It is the IRS' rules. Also, there is a custodian fee for holding your gold, too.

The problem with Precious Metals are many. It is dead money if the precious metals do not go up. They pay no dividends. You generally have to pay a premium over the spot price to buy the metals and a discount to sell them. Some dealers are more unscrupulous than others. Some charge 1% and others say no dealer fees. Even when they say no dealer fees, then they can still make money. All they have to do is adjust the spot price to any time period that meets their objective. For example, gold closed at a high yesterday and you want to buy today. They make you pay for your gold at yesterday's closing price. It is down today, so they make the spread. Guess what? That spread can be more than 2% sometimes in a day.

We have all heard the stories about some eccentric old dude who passed away and they discovered a boatload of gold coins in his house. This is great if it was your uncle and you are the last surviving heir. However, very few of us would ever get this lucky.

My thoughts on Precious Metals is to look for alternatives. You can buy an Exchange Traded Fund that buys Gold or Silver or both and you do not have to pay any mark up or mark down, other than the bid and ask spread. Plus the cost to get in or out is like $8.95 per trade. That is as opposed to 1% per trade. If you invest $100,000 in gold bullion or coins, then 1% is $1,000 versus $8.95 for an ETF. In addition, if you own one of these ETF funds, then they can be sold pretty easily. Unless you are a coin collector and enjoy the hobby, then I would probably just go with Exchange Traded Funds instead of buying the actual Precious Metals.

If you are dead set on buying Precious Metals, then be careful buying over the phone or Internet. I would rather you walk into a Coin Shop and buy from someone local. Even then however, you still have to be careful. You need to know the spot price at that moment and then figure out what the Coin Shop's mark-up is, plus any additional fees. In other words, you need to know what you are doing. Imagine that. An investor who actually knows what they are doing, as opposed to one who "trusts" Wally Street.

Also, in case you did not know, you can buy directly from the U.S. Mint. You need to check their web site for details. It is located at http://www.usmint.gov. They have gold coins and silver coins listed right there on their web site and the prices, too.

Here is what really ticks me off about the gold and silver promoters. It is their advertisements. Imagine if I were to say on television something like this, "The ABC Mutual Fund is going way up in value and you had better get some of it. Experts predict the ABC Mutual Fund will triple in value over the next couple of years." If I ran an ad like that, then every regulator on the planet would be breathing down my neck.

In addition, you have all these actors who are promoting gold and silver on television. These are in effect testimonials. I cannot under any circumstances use testimonials, but the gold and silver promoters can do it all day long. Is that fair? I don't think so. There is even a Wall Street firm that is stretching the limits with a well-known actor who is doing their commercials. To me, this is a testimonial and against the rules.

[52]

Gold and silver promoters can say whatever the hell they want to say. Why in the name of Sam Hill is this allowed? Where does it say in the regulations that an IRA promoter, who happens to also be a gold and silver promoter, tell me where does it say that they can say these things? If they can say them, then why can't I? Not that I wanted to, but it doesn't seem fair to me. They are Wally Street trying to get you to invest your IRA money with them, are they not? If so, then why the hell do they get a loophole? I try to get people to invest their IRA with me, but I do not embellish, lie and exaggerate in the process like these guys do. Yet I, the regulated one, cannot say much of anything in advertisements. These gold and silver promoters can say pretty much anything unchecked. It doesn't make any sense to me.

Perhaps our fine friends who are securities regulators might just want to rethink this loophole. I guess these gold and silver guys have the securities regulators conned into believing that gold and silver are not securities. That is pure BS. Sorry, but I am not politically correct.

The Department of Labor (DOL) may be about to upset the apple cart. They have proposed a rule that "anyone offering an IRA account must be a fiduciary." If they are a fiduciary, then they will not be able to do exaggerated advertisements and testimonials any longer. The SEC and state regulators would be on them like stink on a June bug.

It looks like the DOL is going to get this rule in place to stop these shenanigans from continuing. The DOL has proposed a rule in April of 2015 to make anyone giving investment advice to a plan, plan fiduciary, plan participant, beneficiary or IRA or IRA beneficiary will be a fiduciary. The ERISA rule is 2510.3-21 and the Internal Revenue Code is 4975(e)(3) are exactly the same. The DOL was real smart about this rule in that instead of focusing on labels like stockbroker, insurance agent or investment adviser, they instead said the rule is based on your activities.

[This page intentionally left blank]

Floating Rate Bank Loan Funds

I hate these things with a passion. I have seen so many misrepresentations of this product from Wally that it is not even funny. Wally routinely sells this product as an inflation hedge. Here is Wally Street's sales pitch:

"When interest rates go up, then this fund benefits."

On the surface that sounds good and unfortunately, that is all that most people need to hear to give their approval to buy it. However, as with anything involved in investing, you should at least educate yourself enough to understand the product, because this one can be very dangerous.

Floating Rate Bank Loan Funds invest in bank loans. When interest rates go up, so do loan rates, therefore the supposed attraction according to our friend Wally Street. However, that fact depends on continued money flow. When interest rates go up on home loans, most people don't like it. Therefore, they choose not to borrow. It is a simple supply and demand thing. If rates are too high, then demand for loans will decline. The exact same thing happens with commercial loans. If rates are too high, then people will not borrow as much. This in turn means that continued money flow declines and the bank has less loans to offer. Got it?

The mutual fund families will buy these bank loans for their Floating Rate Bank Loan portfolios and hold them. Here is my issue with these type of products. In a word, liquidity. I am a big believer in liquidity. Some of these funds are not very liquid.

Think about a typical loan at a bank for commercial property. The loan may be for fifteen years depending on the project. Suppose you invested in one of these Floating Rate Bank Loan funds. After a year and a half, you suddenly need some money. The mutual fund has not received anything but the payments on their loans, so they do not have a big chunk to return to clients. In fact, they restrict access to the money. With some of these funds, you can only sell a small percentage of your shares at certain windows of time per year. What if you needed money today, but you have to wait until the end of the next quarter before you can get your money? Does this sound good to you?

Read this sample disclosure about a Floating Rate Bank Loan fund's risks:

"An imbalance in supply and demand in the income market may result in valuation uncertainties and greater volatility, less liquidity, widening credit spreads and a lack of price transparency in the market. There can be no assurance that the liquidation of collateral securing an investment will satisfy the issuer's obligation in the event of nonpayment or that collateral can be readily liquidated. The ability to realize the benefits of any collateral may be delayed or limited. Investments in income securities may be affected by changes in the creditworthiness of the issuer and are subject to the risk of non–payment of principal and interest. The value of income securities also may decline because of real or perceived concerns about the issuer's ability to make principal and interest payments. Investments rated below investment grade (typically referred to as "junk") are generally subject to greater price volatility and illiquidity than higher rated investments. As interest rates rise, the value of certain income investments is likely to decline. Bank loans are subject to prepayment risk. Investments in foreign instruments or currencies can involve greater risk and volatility than U.S. investments because of adverse market, economic, political, regulatory, and geopolitical or other conditions. Changes in the value of investments entered for hedging purposes may not match those of the position being hedged. No Fund is a complete investment program and you may lose money investing in a Fund."

I couldn't have said it better myself. Here is another problem with these Floating Rate Bank Loan funds. If a bank loans money at 6% and interest rates spike up quickly, as they have historically been known to do, then new loans may be made at 7%. Therefore, a 6% loan is worth less than a 7% loan. If you as the fund holder demand payment, the bank has already handed the fund company the loan. They bank is totally out of the picture. It is the fund company's problem now.

If there is a run on Floating Rate Bank Loan funds, then the mutual fund company puts it out in the marketplace. Generally, these loans are considered low investment grade to junk in the marketplace. By the way, did you know that? That's what I thought.

Why would anyone want to buy that mutual fund company's 6% loan when they can get 7%? They will not do it, unless they discount the price of their 6% loan to make it equivalent to a 7% yield.

Discount means "lose money" just in case you don't know.

Also, if you read the sample verbiage above, then you will have noticed that if there is a rush to the exits with this fund and everyone wants to sell, then this presents a *major*, not minor problem. The principal on these will fall precipitously as a result of a rush to the exits. I have seen it happen. It can get really ugly.

You may be wondering how I have seen it happen. Wally Street's clients always come to me after the fact. I read their account statements and listen to them lament about how they got ripped off by Wally Street. This is how I see it happen.

Generally, nobody tells you all this when you buy these funds. You only find out about it afterwards when it becomes a problem. My advice is to not reach for yield with these funds and stay far, far away from them.

Class "A" Shares Mutual Funds

True confession. I sold these in the past myself when I was in Wally World. That was a long time ago. Why? Because, I had to keep my job and put food on the table. The same exact reason Wally Street has to sell them.

In Wally World, it is all about generating revenue. Wally has to generate revenue to keep his job and put food on the table. The broker/dealer has to have revenue to survive. Where do you fit into that equation? You are the poor sap who buys Wally's products!

There is no reason whatsoever that you <u>have to have</u> a class "A" shares mutual fund from any broker/dealer. Period. Don't tell me it is because of the fine money managers at the mutual fund company, either.

I saw a recent comparison of mutual funds that showed the assets under management of class "A" shares funds compared to no load funds. The sales of class "A" shares funds were 400% higher than that of the nearest competing no load fund. What does that tell you? It should tell you that reps (Wally Street) who work for broker/dealers (Wally World) are selling the crap out of these funds. Proof positive that it is all about generating revenue.

Did you wake up one day and say, "Gee, I think I will buy a class "A" shares mutual fund that benefits my friend Wally Street and his broker/dealer and not me."? No, you didn't, because you were sold the fund based on some insane premise that it was good for you.

Wally Street and his brokerage firm are ripping you off!

That hickory switch can sting, can't it?

This is why you need to do business with an _independent_ registered investment adviser that has no affiliation with a bank, insurance company or Wall Street firm. That would be someone like me, by the way.

Independent registered investment advisers have no incentive to sell you mutual funds. Specifically, they do not get a commission on the securities that they recommend. Instead, they show you a fully disclosed fee. In addition, they develop a plan and a process for your investments that is designed in your best interests.

More on the differences between Wally Street and independent registered investment advisers later. You are still in class and you still have a lot to learn.

Class "B" Shares Mutual Funds

This originally was the mutual fund industry's answer to competing with no load mutual funds. They designed these class "B" shares so that there was "no upfront charges." Sounds great, doesn't it? You probably didn't get a lot of time spent by Wally telling you about the 6% penalty during the first six years. I'm sure Wally quickly glossed over that issue when he sold it to you.

The expenses on equity class "B" shares mutual funds tend to average about 1.94% for the Large Cap Growth category, according to Lipper®. I know of a few mutual fund companies that offer several growth funds with expenses as low as 0.10% or even lower.

Let us calculate that difference, shall we? 1.94% minus 0.10% equals 1.84%. This means on average, you are paying 1.84% too much for a class "B" shares growth mutual fund. Yet, Wally Street and his brokerage firm are selling these "like beer on a troop train." Plus, you are stuck in it for six years, but I know you don't mind since Wally is such a good friend of yours.

Odds are that you own one or have owned one before today. Tell the truth. Come on. Admit it. There now. Doesn't that feel better? It is part of your learning process. You are going in the right direction, but we are not there yet.

Another thing I do not like about these class "B" shares mutual funds is their illiquidity. These funds have a declining surrender charge that can start as high as 6% in the first year and decline 1% per year until it finally reaches no surrender charges.

Here is the problem. Wally doesn't explain this very well or you forget about it. When it comes time to needing some money, then it is at this point that you realize or remember about the surrender charges. Instead of selling out and taking the penalty, you will instead wait it out. The problem with waiting it out is that you will be over paying 1.84% per year in expenses while you are waiting. In addition, there is a high likelihood that the fund is a crappy fund, too. Therefore, you will be over-paying in expenses and keeping a crappy fund to boot. Neither of those choices are good for you.

Liquidity is by far the most important thing in investing. If you do not learn a thing from this book, at least make a lifetime vow to never invest in anything that is not fully liquid. By fully liquid, I mean that you can sell it and get your money without penalties in as little as three business days, if not sooner. Wouldn't that be nice?

Did I mention that when you buy class "B" shares mutual funds that Wally can make between 4 and 5%? Again, how is that good for you? The truth is that it is not. The mutual fund industry, in conjunction with the broker/dealer industry (Wally World) has sold you this can of worms. Or, is it snake oil?

Year after year, you have been "taught" how to buy investments from these "professionals" (i.e., Wally Street.) The only thing professional about the way they do business is that they are very good at pulling the wool over people's eyes.

Class "C" Shares Mutual Funds

Can it get any worse with the different share classes of mutual funds? I am afraid so. Enter the class "C" shares. When people started getting screwed with class "B" shares, then the mutual fund industry and the broker/dealers got scared of the backlash and invented the class "C" shares. People who owned class "B" shares complained loudly when they needed liquidity and found out the ugly truth of those pesky surrender penalties as high as 6%. As a result, Wally Street's brokerage firm reluctantly gave in and stopped promoting the class "B" shares. Don't get me wrong, they still sell the class "B" shares. They just quit promoting them heavily to their field force of Wally Streets who sell them.

The class "C" shares only have a one year surrender penalty of 1%. After one year, then you are home free. No more penalties. Sounds great, doesn't it? Well not so fast. The same growth fund expenses for class "B" shares applies to class "C" shares. You would be over-paying about 1.84% on average per year when you buy a class "C" shares growth fund, according to Lipper®.

By the way, Wally gets 1% per year for selling you that crappy "C" shares mutual fund that has 1.84% more in expenses than you should be paying. Of course, don't forget, he is always looking out for you. At least that is what you are trying to tell me. Sorry, but I'm not buying it.

Explain to me how over-paying 1.84% in annual fees helps you again? Go ahead. I am listening.

Chapter Summary

What did we learn in this chapter?

- Liquidity is king.
- Low expenses are very, very important.
- Variable Annuities have expenses generally north of 3%, long term surrender charges and are invested by Wally who has limited portfolio management skills.
- Non-regulated investments may end up being a Ponzi scheme.
- Non-Publicly Traded REIT's or Business Development Companies (BDC's) as they are sometimes called are a bad alternative compared to Publicly Traded REIT's.
- Promissory Notes are very likely to be a Ponzi scheme.
- Private Placements and Regulation D offerings may end up being a Ponzi scheme, or at the very least, a very poor performing investment with a lot of risk and liquidity restrictions.
- Investments like Floating Rate Bank Loan funds have complex risks that need to be fully understood in advance.
- Class A, B and C shares mutual funds have commissions and high expenses and there is no good reason why we just have to have one.
- Wally Street sells complicated, illiquid investments that benefit him, not you.

Chapter Three

Wally's Tools of the Trade

"Facts are stubborn things; and whatever may be our wishes, our inclinations, or the dictates of our passions, they cannot alter the state of facts and evidence."

~ John Adams

[This page intentionally left blank]

The Financial Plan

Wally Street has it made. He has his own Financial Planning department! Isn't that wonderful? Wally doesn't even have to create his own financial plans. His Financial Planning department does it for him! Wally must be a big shot. I wish I had a Financial Planning department.

Here is what is confusing to me. Broker/dealers want Wally to be a CFP®, or a ChFC® and the like. Yet, when it comes to designing a financial plan, they cannot do it without the approval of the Financial Planning department and also their Compliance department. My question then becomes, are they really Financial Planners? In my opinion, no. Although, I am sure that Wally would disagree.

Let me get this straight. My financial planner says he can do a financial plan for me, for which he charges somewhere around $2,000 and maybe even as high as $5,000 or more? Yes, this is really what Wally Street's brokerage firm charges, but don't forget your financial plan is _special_. Wally is looking out for you, remember? It was prepared by the Financial Planning Department!

You mean to tell me that Wally Street doesn't even prepare my Financial Plan? Where is that Financial Planning Department anyway? They must be in Manhattan, thus their reason for charging so much for a financial plan. The truth is most of them are in Manhattan.

The people in the Financial Planning Department have absolutely no idea who you are or what you are all about. You may be thinking, "Yes, but Rick, I filled out their form." Don't jump ahead, but I will explain more about that form in the next section in this chapter, "The Investment Questionnaire."

Think of it this way. When you are talking to a friend and you recommend a CPA or an attorney to them, can you really relay to that CPA or attorney the full details of your friend's financial situation? If that is doubtful, then how can your financial planner relay the information about you personally to their Financial Planning Department? You never thought of it that way, did you?

The CPA or attorney may take the information you give them and get a general idea about your friend. However, what they really prefer is to sit down face to face with your friend. Don't you agree? Think about it.

Imagine if you tried to be in the middle between your friend and the CPA or attorney. All information had to flow through you. Your friend could never meet the CPA or attorney. The only way they got their information was from you. How solid would the CPA or attorney's advice be as a result? It would only be as solid as the information that you relayed to them. Right again, Mr. Rick.

What if you left out some important details, because your main goals are to sell products that generate revenue? Do you think that a CPA or attorney would agree to give advice under such a scenario? I doubt it. Yet, this is precisely how financial planning works in Wally World. It is all designed by Wally Street's brokerage firm to sell you products. See the "Wally Products" list in a prior chapter just in case you forgot.

Most broker/dealers use a few different software firms for their financial plans. I called these financial plans "63 pages of crap." That is what they are precisely. They may look real fancy with lots of charts and graphs, but the reality is that once you get it, you will look at it once or twice, then stick it in a drawer never to be seen again. Then, one day down the road you will stumble across it and wonder if it is worth keeping. In the end, it will get shredded and you will grumble that you paid $2,000 to $5,000 for "the damn thing."

There is a way to receive a Financial Plan. Get it from an independent registered investment adviser like me who charges a fair fee and who doesn't have a vested interest in any of the investments recommended by the Financial Plan.

Wally always has a vested interest in the products recommended by his financial plan. Never forget it, either.

[This page intentionally left blank]

The Investment Questionnaire

Just the sound of that is impressive, isn't it? The Investment Questionnaire! It has a French sounding ring to it.

I wrote about this in my last book, but it is worth repeating since it is a tool of the trade.

Investment Questionnaires are designed to sell products. The questions you find on these forms have a way of arriving at a destination that favors the broker/dealer and our friend Wally Street.

Some of the questions are CYA questions. The broker/dealer likes to cover their rear and ask questions like:

- *What is your risk tolerance?*
- *What is your time horizon?*
- *What are your investment objectives?*

Even our firm has to ask these questions, but it is because the regulators believe that Wally World and independent registered investment advisers are the same. They are totally different however, even if our fine regulator friends do not know it.

My experience with dealing with almost two dozen different state regulators has taught me that they all have diametrically opposed opinions. I had one state say nothing about our questionnaire and another demand more questions added. So, if you wonder why certain questions like these above and others are in our Investment Advisory Agreement, it is because some regulator told us to put them in there. Blame them. Not me.

I would like to drill down and examine these questions one by one. Let's take the first one. "What is your risk tolerance?" Give me an answer to that question. Take your time. Go ahead. I'll give you a moment to think about it.

If you had to answer that on your own, then you might say something like "I am risk adverse or I am conservative." If you are younger and know it all, (yes I am being facetious) then you might say "I can handle risk. I'm aggressive. I need to grow my money."

The broker/dealers and regulators I might add, do not like your answers. They can't have you running around <u>explaining</u> your answers. That would only complicate things. They want you to choose from a few choices like:

- *Very Conservative*
- *Conservative*
- *Moderate*
- *Moderately Aggressive*
- *Aggressive*

Pick one that you believe is appropriate in describing your risk tolerance. Now, tell me what it means. Further, tell me how being a *"Conservative"* investor translates into an investment plan. Let's assume that ten different people chose *"Conservative"* as their risk tolerance. What do you expect Wally Street and his broker/dealer to recommend? Ten different portfolios? No way, Jose. It works the same way as the Financial Planning Department. Everything is systemized.

You see, the broker/dealer cannot have all these ten thousand plus reps running around willy-nilly giving out all kinds of <u>*different*</u> advice. If ten people are conservative, then the branch manager is going to say, "Wally, sell this and that and put them in the Conservative Portfolio."

Odds are that all ten conservative clients are going to be sold the same thing! For evidence that this is true, see the previous list of Wally's Products in the prior chapter that I suggested that you stay away from. Damn it man. I got you again, didn't I?

More than likely, if you have an account or two with a broker/dealer, then you probably own some of the investments on that list like class "A" shares mutual funds, Non-Publicly Traded REIT's/BDC's, Variable Annuities and Unit Investment Trusts. Come on. Tell the truth.

Ding, ding, ding, ding. Is that light bulb going off yet? Are you figuring out this game that you did not know you were a participant in? These broker/dealers are playing a game and that game is to take your money and generate revenue that benefits them. That's a fact, Jack.

Let's look at another question. "What is your time horizon?" Think about that for a minute. Now answer the question.

Suppose you are 55 years old. What is your time horizon? You think to yourself, "Well, let's see. People in my family tend to live to around 80 years old, therefore my time horizon must be 25 years." So, you blurt out to your trusted advisor and friend Wally Street "twenty-five years." Wally jumps for joy when you say that because, he can lock up your money for ten years, no problem at all. After all, you said 25 years. So, selling you a Variable Annuity with a 10 year surrender charge is not a problem. Don't you see? You said you could handle 25 years! Ten years is a piece of cake. Wally Street is home free. He has got it in writing, too!

This question is designed to get you to admit in writing a time horizon longer than the products that these broker/dealers sell. Almost everyone has at least an assumed 10 year time horizon except the people who are already eighty years old. Generally, believe it or not, these broker/dealers can sell you a Variable Annuity at age 85. That's right. They can stick

[73]

you in a product with a shortened but still long surrender charge at age 85. By virtue of you having attained the ripe old age of 85, instead of a 10 year surrender charge, you get a 3 year surrender charge. Lucky you.

Of course, Wally will tell you about the death benefit features of the Variable Annuity and how your heirs will inherit it with a step up in basis. Your heirs get that step up in basis anyway no matter what you invest in you big dummy. Wally is good at confusing you, especially if you are 85 years old.

You see when you get older, Wally Street has no problem killing you off. Wally is getting his commission. He knows that your life expectancy is short. Wally does not even know your adult children. Wally will worry with that later on, after you die. All that matters is this sale Wally has staring him in the face. Everything else is an easy objection to overcome.

The third question in my list is "What are your investment objectives?" Same exercise. Think about it and answer the question.

Without guidelines, then you might need a little assistance. Pre-defined answers like:

- *Income*
- *Income & Growth*
- *Moderate Growth*
- *Moderately Aggressive Growth*
- *Aggressive Growth*

Again, we have similar answers on our form, primarily because a regulator told us to put it on our form.

Let's examine this further. What if two different broker/dealers have similarly defined categories? Broker/dealer A has an *Income objective* and broker/dealer B, also has an *Income objective*. Remember, you are the one who choose the objective, so you cannot argue with it. You put it in writing.

Suppose broker/dealer A's *Income* portfolio has 60% bonds, 35% stocks and 5% cash. Suppose broker/dealer B's has as its *Income* portfolio 50% bonds, 30% stocks, 10% real estate, 5% commodities and 5% cash. Which portfolio matches your investment objective? You chose *Income* as your investment objective, so that is what you received.

Obviously, it makes a difference in which broker/dealer or Wally Street that you chose. You will end up with one or the other's *Income* portfolio. As far as Wally is concerned, he and his brokerage firm have given you the right portfolio based on your answer to <u>their</u> Investment Questionnaire.

Wait a minute. Didn't the question ask "What is <u>your</u> investment objectives?" Yes it did, but you see, your needs don't factor into this solution. You get what the broker/dealer believes is an *Income* portfolio, like it or not and perhaps one that is inappropriate for your situation, too.

Some broker/dealers get a little creative with their Investment Questionnaires. They ask you to pick a number for your risk tolerance between 1 and 10. Go ahead. Pick a number. What did you pick? Just for fun, let's say you picked five. Now, tell me how five translates into your risk tolerance. Go ahead. I can wait. Take your time. This is so much fun!

Do you see how pointless this exercise is? Yet, regulators demand questions like these be completed on every client. I'm not against regulators mind you, it is just that I don't think they have ever really _critically_ thought about adding another question to an Investment Questionnaire. Critically being the key word in that sentence.

Some in Wally World make things a little more challenging with their questions. They have questions on their questionnaires like these:

Question # 1

Suppose you have a hypothetical portfolio of $200,000. Being invested has its rewards. For long term potential gains, you have to accept fluctuations in the value of your account. Please pick a range that represents your acceptable risk level. Pick a range number from the Range Choices below.

Range Choice	Upside	Downside
1	$210,000	$190,000
2	$220,000	$180,000
3	$230,000	$170,000
4	$240,000	$160,000

Question # 2

Suppose that the day you invested with our firm the market declined and continue to do so for a prolonged period. At what point would you want to sell out of all of your positions? Choose one:

- _5% decline_
- _10% decline_
- _15% decline_
- _20% decline_
- _More than a 20% decline_

How will you answer these questions? I have no idea, but I assume that you would make choices for both. If this scenario actually played out and let's suppose that on the day you filled out this questionnaire you chose the $220,000 upside to $180,000 downside. How will you really react when it heads south towards $180,000? That drop to $180,000 is a ten percent (10%) decline on paper.

Investing has emotions that flair up when you are losing money. Believe me. After 27 plus years in business, I know this for a fact.

Are you really going to just sit there and watch your account drop $20,000? That is $20,000 dollars! That is real money, man! That is more than your grandparents probably made in a year. That is 10% on $200,000. Twenty-thousand dollars gone in the blink of an eye!

Most likely, you will blame your financial advisor for making bad investment choices for you. You will look for another Wally Street who works for a bank, an insurance company or a Wall Street firm and repeat the process all over again. I have seen it happen over and over again.

Perhaps, the one to blame is the one who keeps turning to Wally Street for "advice."

The truth is that you will react based on the money lessons that you have learned over the years. In particular, money lessons that you learned from your parents and grandparents. One thing is for sure. You will not base your decisions on whether to get out of the market on some choice you made on some stinking investment questionnaire that you completed months ago. If this is true, then what is the real point of the investment questionnaire? The point is to sell you an *Income* portfolio, so you will buy "Wally's Products" that I listed in a prior chapter. Got it?

Finally, I am making some headway with you.

Chapter Summary

What did we learn in this chapter?

- Wally's financial planning department does not know diddly about you.
- Investment questionnaires prepared by Wally's company has to be looked upon with a lot of skepticism.
- Your risk tolerance cannot be accurately known in advance of a market decline.
- A long term time horizon plays right into Wally's hands to sell you illiquid products.
- Your investment objectives cannot be adequately determined by picking from a handful of Wally's company prepared choices.
- You will not know how much of a decline you can accept until after you have experienced a big decline.

Chapter Four

Wally Loves Seniors

"Life is ten percent what happens to you and ninety percent how you respond to it."

~ Lou Holtz

[This page intentionally left blank]

Wally Loves Seniors

My fictional friend Wally Street loves seniors. Why? Because seniors are always looking for more income. Most seniors remember CD rates in the good old 6% range. You didn't need to ever invest in the stock market when you were getting an FDIC insured CD of 6%. Those were the good old days. However, today it is a totally different story. CD rates are under 1%. In fact, in today's Wall Street Journal, a one year CD is 0.15%. Can you believe it? Did you ever think you would see the day when this would be true?

Seniors grew up expecting simple rates of returns. They like guarantees and high yields. The only problem is that today, this is not available like it was in the past. Even the seniors who ventured out on the risk scale and bought bonds recently are affected. These seniors have found that even bonds are paying really low interest rates. As a result, seniors like going to seminars to see what Wally has to offer. Wally is real good at attracting seniors to his seminars. All he has to do is buy a list and send out the invitations and lo and behold, seniors show up like clockwork. Wally is good at blowing smoke up senior's skirts to get them to show up for an appointment. The seniors feel guilty about that free lunch, so they figure they owe Wally an appointment at the very least.

Wally loves getting an appointment with seniors, because they are the easiest group of people to sell. You see, all Wally has to do is quote a high interest rate and seniors are hooked. Saying "sign here" never worked better than it does with seniors.

If you are a senior, then do not worry about those bad old CD rates. Wally has a solution for you. In fact, Wally can guarantee you a 12% return with his Promissory Note. Or, if you don't like that, then he can show you his Private Placement where you will make a boatload of cash.

[This page intentionally left blank]

Fixed Annuities

Insurance companies have enjoyed success over the years selling fixed annuities. When CD rates were 6%, then fixed annuities were also around 6%. The major difference was that fixed annuities were tax-deferred. So, their taxable equivalent yield was even higher than CD's. Therefore, it was easy for insurance companies to sell fixed annuities. You see, it was a little harder to sell seniors on the nuances of Variable Annuities, so most seniors were easy targets for fixed annuities. Wally's sales pitch was:

"It pays just like a CD, except it earns tax-deferred interest. Therefore, it is better than a CD on an after-tax basis."

This worked fine for seniors when interest rates were higher, but the last few years, the sale of fixed annuities has ground to a halt, or a trickle. Today's fixed annuity rates are down to around 2 or 3%. Seniors are a little smarter than most people when it comes to fixed annuities. You see they bought a bunch of them when rates were up around 6% and watched as their annual renewal rate went down to 2%. When they wanted out, that was when they found out about those pesky surrender charges. So, they waited 10 years until they were gone. All the while mind you while their money was languishing away at the insurance company. Now, seniors are educated. They now realize that getting 2% and locking their money up for another ten years in surrender charges is not a good idea. It took them awhile, like ten years, but they finally figured it out.

Nothing is ever static in the insurance industry. As my dad used to say, "That was the old deal. This is the new deal." Another thing my dad would say about insurance companies is that "they change products like I change underwear." Sadly, he was 100% right about that.

[83]

When the flow of fixed annuity money ground to a halt, insurance company actuaries knew that they had to come up with some new products to attract funds. Enter the Fixed Indexed Annuity.

Fixed Indexed Annuity

I have to admit that I like the design of these products. You can never lose money on these annuities. They have a floor of either 0% or 1% that they guarantee. Well that doesn't sound all that great, but stay with me here. I will explain.

Fixed indexed annuities are kind of a hybrid product. They have a return of an index like the S&P 500® without the downside risk. If the S&P 500® made 20%, then perhaps you made 15%. That is a typical return you might have made when the caps and participation rates were that high.

When they first came out, these products were simple. You typically had a fixed indexed annuity with a 15% cap and a 100% participation rate. This means if the S&P 500® made 20%, then your return was capped at 15% with a 100% participation rate. The insurance company kept the difference. You were credited with 15%. It was that simple.

It is not so simple any more. With some insurance companies, that 15% cap is down to 3%. That 100% participation rate is down to 87.5%. This means that if the S&P 500 makes 20%, then you get 2.625%. Come again? 2.625%? Huh?

By the way, insurance companies always build into their policy legalese that they can lower their current caps and participation rates. Generally, however, you find this out after you buy the fixed indexed annuity. Wally can be a little vague about explaining caps and participation rates. You see, he doesn't want to get into all that confusing stuff. It might spoil his sale.

When these first came out, there was just one choice. You bought a fixed indexed annuity with a one year point to point return based on the S&P

500®. Today, you can buy fixed indexed annuities based on all kinds of strategies. You can find monthly averaging, one year point to point, two year point to point and so on. In addition, there are multiple choices of indices that these products are based on, in addition to the S&P 500®.

The monthly averaging option, when it first came out, had about a 2% monthly cap. This meant that if the S&P 500® made more than 2% in a month, then all you got was 2%, because of the cap. That is when you also had a 100% participation rate. Today, most of the monthly averaging caps are down around 0.50% with 87.5% participation rates. As my dad would say, "That was the old deal. This is the new deal."

Insurance companies like to say that they are the best and to hell with all the rest. If you do business with a Wally Street who works for an insurance company, then this is going to be the answer you get. Wally will tell you how great his fixed indexed annuity is and there is none better than his fixed indexed annuity.

If you are looking at options where you will not lose money and you want to potentially make returns better than CD's, then you may want to consider these products. However, you should never do business with a one company agent on these products. You need an independent advisor who doesn't represent just one insurance company.

Further, you have to realize that there will be years that the product will return the minimum guarantee of 0% or 1%. Take a look at the last decade. There were several years where the S&P 500® lost money. If you owned a fixed indexed annuity based on that index, then you would have made the minimum 0% or 1% during those years. That is not a bad alternative when you think about it. It is certainly way better than losing 20% by being 100% in the stock market in that Variable Annuity Wally sold you.

Things to know about Fixed Indexed Annuities before you buy:

- The Crediting Method
  - Annual, Bi-annual, or Monthly.
- Minimum Guarantee
  - 0% or 1% or some other figure.
- Index Participation Rate
  - 100%, 90% or 87.5% or some other figure.
- Cap Rate
  - 2%, 2.5%, 3%, 3.5% or some other figure.
- Fixed Interest Rate Option
  - The alternative option inside the annuity that allows you to get out of the indexed option and just go with a straight declared interest rate such as 2% or 2.5%.
- Market Value Adjustment
  - This is not good on a Fixed Indexed Annuity unless interest rates are in a free fall. We've already had the free fall, so you missed out. I don't like any Market Value Adjustment (MVA) annuities in a rising interest rate environment. It is just another way to get screwed.
- Bonus or Additional Interest
  - This is where the insurance company gives you a first year bonus for investing with their company. The surrender charge will be the longest you can get with a bonus. The surrender charge can be as high as 14 years in some states.
- Penalty Free Withdrawal Benefits
  - 10% free withdrawal.
  - Long Term Care benefit.
  - Home Health Care benefit.
  - Terminal illness benefit.

Like I mentioned early, I am not against these products at all. They are guaranteed not to lose money, plus they do not have any expenses either. For a portion of your portfolio to segregate as your safe money, then this might just fit the bill. However, I prefer that you buy them from an independent and experienced insurance agent, not Wally Street. One that explains everything about the product to you so there are no surprises. Wouldn't that be nice?

If Wally Street wants to put every dime you have into Fixed Indexed Annuities, then that ought to be a red flag in and of itself. Once again, this would be proof positive that Wally is not looking out for you. A truly ethical insurance professional knows not to do this to you, because of liquidity needs if nothing else. It is those unethical bastards that you have to watch out for. In most cases, these unethical Wally Streets are not independent registered investment advisers. Although, they will call themselves everything under the sun to imply their expertise. Things like financial advisor, financial planner, wealth manager, Vice-President of Investments and other misleading terms. Most of the time, they are just a plain old insurance agent.

These fixed indexed annuities fall in between a regular fixed annuity and a more risky Variable Annuity on the total return scale. However, the major difference is that you make can make more than a regular fixed annuity without any of the downside risk of a Variable Annuity. It is considered a hybrid insurance product. In other words, the fixed indexed annuity is in the middle in regard to expected returns. As long as you do not think you are going to get "stock market returns without the risk" (Wally's sales pitch), then you will be okay.

Chapter Summary

What did we learn in this chapter?

- We learned that Wally has an income solution for seniors that benefits him more than you.
- We found out the hard way about annual renewal rates on fixed annuities that tend to be lower than the first year rate.
- We finally figured out what a cap rate was and how cap rates are not guaranteed.
- In addition, we found out about participation rates and how they can be lowered at the insurance company's direction.
- We will always remember my dad's saying when it comes to insurance companies. "That was the old deal. This is the new deal."

[This page intentionally left blank]

Chapter Five

Stay Obtuse or Be Smart

"When you arrive at a fork in the road, take it."

~ Yogi Berra

[This page intentionally left blank]

Stay Obtuse or Be Smart

You have a choice. You can continue to stay obtuse, or change your ways. The problem is that you don't know what you don't know, because Wally Street has you fooled big time. You have been brain washed into believing that Wally Street is looking out for you. That is your critical mistake. Wally Street is not looking out for you! Never believe that!

Now, I am going to ask you to think _critically_ about this subject. Don't just blow off what I am telling you without really thinking hard about it.

This is your proof:

Revenue quotas.

A revenue quota is what Wally Street has to produce each and every year to keep his job. At most Wall Street firms, this revenue quota is $250,000 per year. However, the payout rate for Wally Street is between 30% and 40%. Let's pick the middle number of 35%. We know Wally Street is a veteran with lots of experience. That is why you "trust" him.

In order to net $250,000 per year in revenue, Wally Street has to produce $250,000 in commissions or fees. Go ahead. Take out your calculator and multiply $250,000 times 35%. You will get $87,500 which is what poor old Wally is making at a minimum by meeting his revenue quota. It is kind of hard for Wally to buy all those nice suits, drive those fancy cars and take you to the Super Bowl on $87,500 a year. Therefore, he is a very good salesman. He usually has no problem cracking his revenue quota.

Wally Street has to see a lot of people to hit that bogey. Let's drill down on this some more, shall we? Let's assume that Wally is a good salesman and he closes a little over four people a month. By closing I mean sells approximately four people per month. We will round this off to fifty people per year. Fifty people per year divided into $250,000 equals $5,000. Wally needs to average, on each person he sells, $5,000 in commissions or fees in order to meet his revenue target quota.

You are probably thinking:

"There is no way I would let Wally Street sell me stuff that generates $5,000 in commissions for him."

Sorry my fine friend. You are not as smart as you think.

Why do you think Wally Street only likes to do business with people who have at least $250,000 or more? Did you get your accounts assigned to the call center, because you don't have the $250,000 minimum? Damn it man. I got you again, didn't I?

Wally sells products that generate commissions. In fact, his goal of $5,000 worth of commissions per "client" is so darn easy for him. He can get $5,000 out of most anyone he comes across. It is a piece of cake to Wally.

Suppose a typical client of Wally Street has $300,000 to invest. Ponder this typical Wally Street client scenario. This will be Wally's "advice."

Wally's Advice

	Amount Invested	Commissions Earned	Commission Percentage
Variable Annuity	$100,000	$7,000	7.00%
Non-Public REIT	$ 50,000	$3,750	6.50%
UIT's	$ 50,000	$1,450	2.95%
Municipal Bonds	$ 50,000	$1,000	2.00%
Mutual Funds	$ 50,000	$2,875	5.75%
Totals	$300,000	**$16,075**	

Wally needed to make $5,000 and he made **$16,075**. This is how Wally does it. He sells products that generate revenue so he can keep his job.

He has to do this or he loses his job!

Let me repeat that. He has to do this <u>or he loses his job</u>. Ask yourself, if you had to produce results to keep your job, then would you? You would if you wanted to keep your job. What if you knew the game was rigged and it was fairly easy, because of the Wall Street revenue generating machine to generate $250,000 per year? That is a pretty easy target my friend. You are probably thinking to yourself, "No wonder my financial advisor dresses in high dollar suits, drives a fancy car and is so willing to buy me lunch." Wally, my dear friend can afford it, thanks to you.

Now imagine, if Wally sold 50 people and he made on average $16,075 per "client," instead of his goal of $5,000. He would be generating $803,750 in revenue and making $281,312.50 for himself at a 35% payout rate. Not bad for old Wally.

An *independent* registered investment adviser who looks out for your best interests and does not have a revenue quota would charge $3,750 the first year for their advice. I know what you are thinking. "Rick, you charge that every year where with Wally Street, I only pay that $16,075 once." Partially true, but you need to think critically about what you are getting in exchange for that "advice." Plus, you are forgetting the fact that Wally will be *looping back around* to sell you a new and better Variable Annuity in the future. You cannot be naïve enough to believe that Wally will only sell you products that make him money once and never sell you another product again. That would be foolish to believe. Further you are skipping over the fact that if you left Wally after the first few months, then it still cost you $16,075, plus surrender charges that may be in the thousands. Not to mention the lack of liquidity you would have with Wally.

If you left an independent registered investment adviser after a few months, then you would only be charged for those months. This breaks down to $312.50 per month compared to Wally's hit 'em a big lick $16,075 and the additional thousands lost in surrender charges.

Read on my avid pupil. I have faith that you will eventually come around to my way of thinking.

Wally sold you a Variable Annuity with a 10 year surrender charge. After your 30 day free look, it will cost you 10% in the first year to get out of it. On a $100,000 investment, that is $10,000 dollars! With some VA's, it can cost you 14% to get out of it in year one.

Wally sold you a Non-Publicly Traded REIT which has no secondary market and is illiquid for at least 10 to 12 years. There is a high probability that you will lose money on it, too. You might get $40,000 of your original $50,000 investment back if you are lucky. After 12 years!

Most often, as your Non-Publicly Traded REIT is failing and the general partners have fleeced you for all they can get, then they roll up your investment into another Non-Publicly Traded REIT. As a result of buying this crappy thing, you later find out that you are rolled into a different crappy thing. Did you know that this could happen? Oh, I see, Wally forget to mention it to you. By the way, this roll up might delay your chance to get what is left of your principal back from 10 to 12 years to perhaps 14 to 16 years. I wonder. Did Wally Street tell you about that possibility? Wally tends to be a little vague on details.

Also, Wally sold you some UIT's that he will want to roll over each year and make another 2.95% commission on. Oh, by the way, you may lose money if you want to sell these early. You do not even know what is in these stinking UIT's, much less why you own them.

Wally sold you some municipal bonds with long maturities of generally twenty to thirty years. These bonds will get creamed when interest rates go up. If you want to get out of them, then you will have to sell them at a discount. How much will you lose on these? A good bet is at least 10%.

[97]

Wally sold you some mutual funds that have high expenses including 12b-1 fees that pay him a little commission each year. You paid 5.75% upfront on these funds, but leave it to Wally to squeeze some more money out of you with these annual 12b-1 fees. In addition, the annual expenses on Wally's recommended mutual funds are generally 0.75 – 1.00% *per year* higher than comparable Exchange Traded Funds (ETF's).

Let's tally this up. You have $100,000 in a Variable Annuity that you are stuck with for ten years, because of the surrender charges. Oh, I almost forgot. The expenses on it, because of the riders, is over 3% per year. That's easily $3,000 per year, plus Wally pocketed $7,000 in commissions or more. Oh yeah. You will have to pay $10,000 to get out of it after 30 days and perhaps more depending on what state you are in.

Don't forget either that Wally slams everyone in 100% stocks in the Variable Annuity. Remember, he has to overcome that 3% in annual expenses. He cannot do that being conservative. With an aggressive mix, when the market goes down, guess what, it might lose 10 to 20%.

Wally is not watching your Variable Annuity every day. Wally does not have the time. Remember he has that revenue quota to hit. For goodness sakes, he cannot sit around watching your Variable Annuity go up and down. How silly of you to think that way.

Guess what you will do when your Variable Annuity loses 10 to 20% and you realize that in order to sell out, you will lose $10,000 in surrender charges? You will grumble a bit and keep the damn thing. You will not lose 20 to 30% to get out of it. However, you will tell your friend Wally Street to make it more conservative. Your expected return will dip down to probably in the 3 to 4% range. Not enough, unfortunately, to compensate for the annual expenses of 3%. Now, tell me again, why did you buy this Variable Annuity?

The Non-Publicly Traded REIT paid Wally 6.5 – 8.5% in commissions, but you get no liquidity for 10 to 12 years and the distinct possibility that you will lose your money and get rolled up to boot. Oh by the way, the REIT sponsor took 11 to 13% right off the top for expenses, so you start out that amount in the hole. Read the prospectus if you do not believe me. It is right there in black and white. While you are reading that prospectus, I want you to think about what a good guy Wally is to you, too.

Come on now. I need you to think *critically*. If you take $50,000 and skim 11 to 13% right off the top, then your REIT has to overcome that, before you make a cent. This means you are $5,500 to $6,500 in the hole, right off the bat. By the way, the income that you are getting is a return of capital. This means that they are giving you back the money that you put in. Remember, I said these were structured just like a Ponzi scheme.

Yes, I know what you are thinking, "Wally would never sell me a bad investment." Wally Street told you that this Non-Publicly Traded REIT was a good investment. Wally is full of "stuffing" like a Thanksgiving turkey.

Taking out my trusty HP 12C calculator, I find that to grow $44,500 ($50,000 minus 11% of the top) back to $50,000 in 12 years it is going to take an 8.13% return. This means that to get your original $50,000 dollars back that you had to wait 12 years for the possibility, then you need to make 8.13% on your investment. That doesn't mean making a return! This is just to get your principal back! Also, the income being paid to you is your principal! Damn it man!

In order to make a 10% return, this is the return Wally Street told you it would make, it is going to take a return of 14.84%. Of course you know real estate never goes down. It always goes up. Forget about what just

[99]

happened in the last five years. "That was an anomaly," Wally would tell you.

What does a Non-Publicly Traded REIT invest in again? Real estate. A 14.84% return (each and every year) is a sure fire bet in real estate, isn't it? Wally said it was anyway.

The UIT's, unfortunately, you are stuck in. That is unless you want to sell at a loss. Wally will convince you to roll over your UIT's every year, so he can make another 2.95% in commissions. If you want to sell early, then you will have to discount your UIT in order to get anyone to buy it. Whatever you do, don't try and sell it when the market is down, because you will get even less. When do most people want to sell? You guessed it. When the market is down that's when. Why are you paying that 2.95% commission again? Help me to understand it. I can't quite figure out why that is good for you. Oh yeah. I almost forgot about that "21 Month Buffered Return Enhanced Note" that you can only get from Wally.

In regard to the municipal bonds, it really depends on the greed factor with your brokerage firm. The reason they like to sell long maturity muni bonds is because they can mark them up more! They can mark them up to as high as 5% legally. So, I am being real conservative saying they only fleeced you for 2%. More than likely, they got you for more than 2%. The longer the maturity, the more they can fleece, or excuse me, legally charge you. Wally did not tell you that, did he? Surprise. Surprise. Oh by the way, when interest rates go up and you want to sell, you are going to have to discount your muni bonds most likely in order to get someone to buy them. Don't forget it will be an inopportune time to sell, too.

You have to discount a lot when you do business with Wally Street.

That means lose money in case you are confused. Odds are the spike in interest rates will happen before you know what hit you. Ten percent or more will disappear from your principal in a flash. That would be another $5,000, by the way.

Those mutual funds Wally sold you, you know, the ones that you paid $2,875 in commission on, well at least you can sell those without a commission. However, tell me why you paid that $2,875 in commissions in the first place and *overpaid* roughly 0.75 – 1.00% per year in expenses? Especially when you could have paid expenses of 0.25% or less on a portfolio of ETF's without those same commissions. Please tell me why. I am having a hard time understanding your justification.

Now, come on! Tell me how all this stuff that Wally Street sold you is looking out for your best interests. You have half of your money locked up for 10 years or more in Variable Annuities and Non-Publicly Traded REIT's.

Half of it!

Why? Why on earth would you ever agree to that? Let me repeat that. You sat there in the beginning and actually agreed to lock up half of your money for ten years or more. Why? Please tell me why would you do such a thing?

You have a UIT that you bought only to benefit Wally, not you. You have municipal bonds that you paid no telling what kind of markup on which will lose principal guaranteed when interest rates rise and you will have to discount to sell them. You bought high commission and high expense mutual funds? For what? Rather, for whom? Oh, yeah. Wally Street is a nice guy and you can "trust" him. I almost forgot.

Now, please justify to me how you paying Wally Street over $16,000 in commissions for his "advice" and locking up half of your money, please tell me how that benefits you?

Here is your choice. Stay stupid or do business with an *independent* registered investment adviser who looks out for you. Trust me. It is not a tough decision once you think *critically* about it.

Every time, almost without fail that I look at a statement from a Wally Street type financial advisor, I see Variable Annuities, Non-Publicly Traded REIT's/BDC's, UIT's, Municipal Bonds, and class "A" shares mutual funds. Why? Because, that is where the money is you big dummy!

Remember what I told you about <u>thinking critically</u>? Wally Street has a revenue quota and he is going to meet that target come hell or high water. He wants to get it from you! If you allow this to continue, then you are stupid. There. I said it. The cold blooded truth. I have seen estimates that eighty-five percent of the investors out there do business with the likes of a Wally Street! This means that there is an 85% chance that you are one of them, too.

All you have to do is look at your own account statements for proof.

If you own any Variable Annuities, Non-Publicly Traded REIT's/BDC's, UIT's, muni bonds or class "A" shares mutual funds, then congratulations. You are one of Wally Street's "clients." Now, go look in the mirror. Convince yourself of what a good guy Wally Street is to you. Can you still do it? I doubt it now that you have thought about it *critically*.

Independent registered investment advisers on the other hand will put you in a portfolio of ETF's with expenses as low as 0.25% per year and the best part is that you have full liquidity! You can get at your money within 3 business days! Not 10 to 12 years like Wally Street's crappy "investments."

My question then becomes:

How long are you people going to stay torpid and put up with this?

It is estimated that eighty-five percent of you are doing business with Wally Street! Now I want you to think critically again. If 85% of you are doing business with Wally, then you can see what I am up against. Wally would have you believe that his firm has market penetration of 85%, because their advice is so good for you. No, my dear friend. That is not the case. The reality is that they have a marketing machine with millions and millions of dollars *that has convinced you* that they are doing things in your best interest. The sad reality is that you are a fool if you believe them.

In addition, Wally World donates a lot of money to politicians to keep everything status quo. Politician's pockets are full of Wally World money. It is all publicly available information at www.opensecrets.org. Look it up if you don't believe me. Wally World has no trouble squashing a peon like me behind the closed doors of a politician's office. Even if this book ends up as Amazon® bestseller, it might only reach a small percentage of Americans. Wally World and Wally Street have nothing to fear from me.

Smoke ought to be coming out of your ears by now. It is okay if you want to put the book down for a few minutes to call me for an appointment. If you don't call me, at least call a totally independent registered investment adviser.

Your "trusted" friend Wally Street will tell you that he is also a registered investment adviser. Don't be fooled. He is not independent. He works for a bank, an insurance company or a Wall Street firm. <u>He still has that same revenue target</u>. Wally is going to hit that revenue target, or he will lose his job. That revenue target is the major factor in skewing the playing field. Oh, by the way, you are the one being played.

Chapter Summary

What did we learn in this chapter?

- We found out about Wally's revenue quotas.
- We found out how easy it is for Wally to fool us with his advice and achieve his revenue quota.
- We found out why we do not ever want to buy a loaded down with fees, commissions and surrender charges Variable Annuity.
- We learned the truth about Non-Publicly Traded REIT's and why we would be an idiot to ever buy one.
- We learned that Wally generally likes to lock up half or more of our money so he can fleece us for more commissions.
- We learned the real truth of why we have those municipal bonds with long maturities.
- We understand the difference between an independent registered investment adviser and Wally's version of a registered investment adviser.
- Sadly, we learned that we are one of the 85% being played by Wally Street.

Notes

Chapter Six

Wally is My Water Boy

"We are all born ignorant, but one must work hard to remain stupid."

~ Benjamin Franklin

[This page intentionally left blank]

Wally is My Water Boy

By now, you may be wondering what real advice looks like. Well, sit tight. I will tell you, but first you need to know what makes me qualified to tell you more than your friend Wally Street.

I obtained my insurance license to sell life, health, disability and annuities in 1984. I got my CFP® in 1992, my CMFC®, CASL® and RFC® came after that. I obtained my real estate agent license in 2006.

Before I knew better, I once held the Series 7, 9, 10, 24, 63 and 65 licenses. I have worked as a Registered Principal (Independent Branch Manager) for independent broker/dealers and as a Branch Manager II for Charles Schwab & Co. Inc. I started in the securities business in 1988.

Your typical Wally Street may hold a Series 7, 63 and maybe a 65. That's it. Some don't even have a Series 7. They instead get the lesser Series 6. Most Wally Street types hold an insurance license. Very few Wally Streets hold a real estate license. Very few Wally Streets have ever been Branch Managers and if they are, then most likely they are not in personal production. They are telling Wally Street what to sell to you.

Most Wally Streets are looking to pass the least amount of tests possible. The last thing they want to do is take another test. They do not like those continuing education requirements either.

My background is varied and extensive. I've been in the financial services business a long time. Over 27 years in fact. Over thirty if you start counting when I got my insurance license. Is your version of Wally Street a former NYSE Branch Manager? I supervised option trades in my branch at Schwab. Does your Wally Street know enough about options to supervise options trades? I seriously doubt it.

Is your version of Wally Street a real estate agent? It would be a plus if they were a real estate agent, but odds are that Wally is not one.

When I tell you that I know what I am doing, then you would be wise to believe it. You cannot look at me as if I was just another financial advisor like Wally Street. Although, I get a lot of people who compare me to Wally all the time. A typical Wally Street does not have anywhere near the background that I do.

If you treat me as if I am just another Wally Street, then odds are I will not do business with you. I will let you continue do business with the likes of Wally Street. Yes, it is true. I am the one interviewing you and trying to decide if I want to take you on as a client. I'm not being arrogant about it. Rather, I am being smart.

If you are tired of getting taken to the cleaners by Wally Street, then I can help you more than you can ever imagine. However, you have to meet my ideal client profile.

> *I only want to work with people who are critical thinkers, who have moral values that are important to them, who believe in working with someone who looks out for their best interests and who does not mind paying a reasonable fee for their advice.*

You still may be questioning what I have to offer, so I will fill the rest of this book with some of my best advice ideas. Truth be told, I did not think of all of these ideas. Some of these ideas have become popular on their own, or by other professionals. In the following pages you will find some advice that you have not ever seen before. Something I like to call, real advice, or advice in your best interests.

Chapter Summary

What did we learn in this chapter?

- Wally is Rick's water boy when it comes to experience and dedication.
- The author is significantly more qualified than your typical Wally Street.
- Rick does not like it when he is thought of a just another Wally Street.
- Independent registered investment advisers like the author do not just take anybody as their client.

Notes

Chapter Seven

Your Core Values

"Achievement of your happiness is the only moral purpose of your life, and that happiness, not pain or mindless self-indulgence, is the proof of your moral integrity, since it is the proof and the result of your loyalty to the achievement of your values."

~ Ayn Rand

[This page intentionally left blank]

Your Core Values

Life Planning is an area that I did not invent. Other thought leaders did. Life Planning is about asking questions to elicit passion and critical thinking.

Let's face it. When you go to a financial advisor like Wally Street, he is going to ask to see copies of your account statements, make you fill out an investment questionnaire, and then make his recommendations. He will recommend Variable Annuities, Non-Publicly Traded REIT's/BDC's, UIT's, Municipal Bonds, and class "A" shares mutual funds. It does not matter what you put on that investment questionnaire. You are getting some amount in each of the foregoing products, like it or not.

Life Planning questions are designed to make you think. Here are some popular Life Planning questions:

- If you had one year left to live, how would you spend it?
- What does that tell you about what you enjoy and what you have a passion for?
- If you had enough money to do whatever you wanted, what would you do?
- If you knew you were going to be highly successfully in your career, what job would you pursue today?
- What would you like to tell your children and grandchildren about what you accomplished in your career?
- How will you explain to them what career you chose?
- What would you want your children and grandchildren to know about you that perhaps they do not know today?
- If you had enough money to do whatever you wanted in retirement, then what would you do?

- If you had enough money to take your whole family on a trip, where would you take them and why?
- If you could volunteer your time or money to your favorite charity, what charity would that be and why?

These are just a sampling of some Life Planning questions that make you sit back and think critically. You may be thinking "what does this have to do with investing?" It has everything to do with it, because you have to determine your core values. Your investments should match your core values.

Wally Street doesn't care what you will tell your grandchildren, where you want to travel in retirement or your favorite charity. The Wally World commercials make a pretty convincing attempt at conveying that they care about you. In fact, they know about Life Planning, too. In order to compete with independent registered investment advisers, they told their advertising firms to project the image of a caring firm. It is all a ruse. You are still buying products from Wally Street no matter how good their commercials make you feel. Remember, Wally has to sell you products, so he can hit his revenue quota.

A good financial advisor takes the time to understand your core values. A good financial advisor wants to know your passions, your charitable inclinations and your career successes. A good financial advisor wants to know things like what you want to do in retirement and where you like to travel. Wally, on the other hand, wants to tell you about how great his products are for you. He will pretend to care, but never forget he is always trying to hit that revenue quota.

Exercise

Take the Life Planning questions above and write down your answers or type them on your word processor if you prefer. Either way, take the time and do it. This exercise will clear your mind of the clutter of life. You just might re-focus on the more important things. Your core values.

Chapter Summary

What did we learn in this chapter?

- We learned what Life Planning is and how those questions make us re-focus on what is truly important to us.
- We learned about our core values.
- We found out that an investment questionnaire is no comparison to a Life Planning questionnaire.
- We learned that Wally's focus will be on products, not on core values.

Chapter Eight

Loans Can Be Good

"The truth is more important than the facts."

~ Frank Lloyd Wright

[This page intentionally left blank]

Loans Can Be Good

The American dream is to own our own home. The way you do it is what is important. This may seem strange to say, but in most cases, you never want to pay off your house. You want to have a mortgage all of your life, preferably one with the least amount of money committed to it and where you refinance it often.

For proof, let's go back in time to 2006. You just bought a house for $250,000. Today that house is worth probably $175,000. If you paid that house off, then you lost $75,000. That is real money. Gone. Poof. Up in smoke. Further, you lost out on using that $250,000 to earn money elsewhere. Plus, you lost out on tax deductions for the mortgage interest.

If you took out a 30 year mortgage in 2006, then your house payment might have been around $1,400 per month. Most of that was tax deductible on Schedule A of your tax return, if you itemized deductions. So, even paying that $1,400 from 2006 until today, you came out way ahead.

I know what you are thinking. Your parents bought a house for $40,000 and it is worth about $120,000 today. That was the old deal. This is the new deal. Haven't you heard of "The New Normal"? Just because your parent's house grew in value, does not mean that yours will. I am asking you to _think critically_ again now. Truthfully, in the last five years, has your house gone up, down or stayed sideways? You see. No matter how you answered that question, in all likelihood, it is not going to be the same as your parent's house. More than likely, even if it has gone up, it has not tripled in value or something similar. It probably has maybe just made it back to break even. Clean off you glasses man. You are not seeing the real picture.

I bought my house that I am living in now in 2002 for $244,700. Today, houses in my neighborhood that are built exactly the same are going for around $295,000. Taking out my trusty HP 12C calculator, I find that for the eleven year holding period, that is a return of 1.71%. I am one of the lucky ones. If I were to have paid off my house back in 2002, instead of taking out a loan, then all I would have made would have been 1.71% on that $244,700. Hopefully, you are getting that "my house is going to make 5% a year" stuff out of your head.

Here is another real world example. When I first got married, we were able to assume the loan of a couple who had a house that we could afford. It was around $500 a month. The neighborhood was big and growing. Lots of young couples were moving into it. We lived there for ten years. The house originally cost $60,000. We ended up with $68,000 after closing costs. (I'm ball parking it here. Don't beat me up over exact numbers.) We walked away with $8,000 when we sold it. We made a 1.25% per year return on it for that ten year period. If we would have paid it off, then we would have made the same 1.25% per year return. Except the major difference is that the $60,000 we used to pay off the house was only going to earn us that 1.25%. Of course, being a young married couple there was no way we could have paid off that house anyway.

You may be thinking, but you had to pay the mortgage for those 10 years. You're right. $500 a month for ten years is guess what? $60,000. The difference is that instead of paying $60,000 all at once in the beginning, I spread it out over ten years.

In year one, by paying the mortgage, I had $54,000 invested elsewhere earning _more than_ 1.25%. In year two, I had $48,000 invested elsewhere earning _more than_ 1.25%. Do you see how this works? Subtract out the $500 a month mortgage each year which is $6,000 a year. We started with $60,000, but after year one we are down to $54,000. A 5% return on

$54,000 is $2,700. It is a little easier to make 5% investing, than it is with real estate. After you take off another $6,000, then we are down to $48,000. Interest on that is $2,400. On $42,000 it is $2,100. On $36,000 it is $1,800. On $30,000 it is $1,500. After only five years, you have earned an extra $10,500. But wait. There is more to consider. Now, don't beat me up you CPA's out there by overanalyzing my explanation.

What really happens is after one year, you have $54,000 to start year two and then you add the approximate $2,700 that you earned from year one. This makes the start of year two actually $56,700. Then, you earn 5% on that amount and carry that forward. So, you exceed the extra $10,500 even more with compounding the earnings. Plus don't forget the itemized deductions tax savings. You also need to factor in the tax savings on top of the 5% earnings. You know how mortgages work, don't you? All of it is interest in the early years. This works to your advantage.

Most of your mortgage payments in year one are tax deductible. For simplistic sakes, let's assume 90% of your mortgage payment is deductible and you are in the 25% tax bracket. That works out to about $315 per month that is saved in taxes. You add that $315 per month to the $56,700 you have invested at 5% at the start of year two. That kicks that up another $3,780 making the start of year two actually $60,480. Now you are earning 5% on that amount which is $3,024. The second year starts with $60,480 in your side fund, but you subtract out the $6,000 and you have $54,480 to invest to start year three. You see how this works? After the first year, it cost the difference between $60,000 and $60,480, which means _you made_ $480 or $40 a month to live in that house! Compare that to $60,000 lost opportunity, if you paid off the house.

You have to live somewhere and most of us cannot live somewhere for nothing. Making $480 the first year is pretty good to me. Even if you have paid off your house, you are not living in it for free. The money that you have tied up in your house is probably just sitting there stagnant, or perhaps mildly growing at 1.25%. Don't you see? You are losing your opportunity costs to earn a better return elsewhere when your house is paid off. Not to mention the tax savings. Okay Kemosabe?

Everyone thinks that they have to get rid of their house payment. It may be appropriate in some cases, but in most cases it is not. If you paid off your house with the $60,000, then you lost other investment opportunities for those funds. You also lost tax deductions for the mortgage interest. After ten years, I would have made 1.25% on that $60,000 period, if I paid my house off. This is not an efficient use of money when I could have made more than that investing it elsewhere.

Alternatively, by having the mortgage, even with paying the mortgage payment plus interest, you still come out ahead. Don't forget. You also had the tax deductions for the mortgage interest for those ten years on top of the compounded 5% earnings that you earned elsewhere. Refinancing every 5 years or so tends to make this work even better, because it keeps the deductibility of your mortgage interest at its highest. Now, you should be able to see how a mortgage might actually be better for you.

Every situation is different and I know that, but you need to really think critically about a lot of different factors before you decide to pay off a mortgage. Specifically, consider the other possible uses of that money that might make a better return. Especially if you are buying an older house _without_ a lot of potential for growth in value. In addition, do not forget how important the tax deductions can be.

Whatever you do, don't tell Wally that you _are not_ paying off your house. He will want you to buy a Variable Annuity with the money.

Chapter Summary

What did we learn in this chapter?

- Paying off a mortgage may not be such a good idea after all.
- There is such a thing as opportunity costs that is lost when you pay off a mortgage.
- Tax deductions for mortgage interest and a side fund reinvestment account can be better than paying off the mortgage, especially where there is limited real estate growth potential of the house you are paying off.

Notes

Chapter Nine

Private Banking

"Outstanding leaders go out of their way to boost the self-esteem of their personnel. If people believe in themselves, it's amazing what they can accomplish."

~ Sam Walton

[This page intentionally left blank]

Private Banking

There are some concepts based on loaning yourself money and paying yourself just as if _you were the bank_. This is where you utilize a whole life insurance policy as your own private bank.

This concept has several different names, depending on who is promoting it. I don't want to get into naming the names, because I don't want to imply that one name or one particular concept is better than another. In my humble opinion, they are all similar as far as the concept is concerned. The difference is the whole life policy being used for the concept.

Here is how it works. First, you over-fund a whole life insurance policy. You want to cram as much cash as you are legally allowed to into this policy for 5 to 7 years. This one fact will knock most people out of the capability of doing it. Most people cannot cram ten, twenty or thirty thousand a year or more into a whole life insurance policy.

In order to make this concept work, then it is that kind of money that you are going to need to cram into it. After all, if you only put $1,000 per year in a whole life policy, then how are you going to be able to buy a car for $35,000 in 5 years? You cannot. This is why it takes boo-coo amounts of money to make this concept work.

Here is the concept in a nutshell. Cram as much money into a whole life policy as you can. After you have done that, then when you need a new car for example, you simply borrow it out of your whole life insurance policy. However, the major difference is that you make the "car payment" back to your life insurance policy instead of the bank for 5 years. You set the term of the loan and the interest rate for the loan. You are paying yourself, because you are the "bank." You have to stick to the schedule and pay it back. No cheating.

Here is the major attraction with this private banking concept. By paying off the car loan via your whole life insurance policy, you are getting the loan principal back plus interest. If you borrowed from a bank, the bank would be getting the loan principal plus interest.

By paying your life insurance policy back, you are eliminating the loan you took out for the car. In other words, you are replenishing your cash value in the life insurance policy. You are paying yourself interest. In addition, you are earning interest on the money in the policy. The whole life policy is earning interest and you are making interest by charging yourself interest to buy the car. A double benefit in effect. Further, the earnings are tax-deferred.

The insurance company is still crediting your cash value, too. Even though you have taken some money out, they will still give you credit for the amount borrowed. It is in the contract. It is a little hocus pocus, but it works something like this:

If you borrow cash from the policy, then the insurance company will charge you 8%. However, they will credit you 6%, thus your net loan charge is 2%.

See what I mean about hocus pocus? Why the hell don't they just charge the 2% and be done with it? Beats me.

Further, there are some life insurance companies that tell you they have zero cost loans. Instead of a 2% net loan, you can get a 0% loan. Remember what my dad said about insurance companies? "That was the old deal. This is the new deal." In regard to 0% loans, those are generally not contractually guaranteed. They are the _currently declared_ rate that the insurance company puts out there in the market place to attract clients. Although, I will admit that some companies do guarantee a 0% loan rate. With this concept however, you need to know for sure.

Wally probably will not mention the fact that the 0% loan rate that you were expecting, you will probably not get. Further, Wally might fail to tell you that you have to wait 10 years to get that 0% loan rate. That is right. You may have to wait a full ten years to qualify for that 0% net loan rate.

Picture this scenario. You pay into the policy for 5 years and you are ready to buy a car. You borrow from the account and find out that you are not getting that 0% loan rate that Wally told you about. What happened? You see, Wally did not mention that the 0% loan rate doesn't kick in for 10 years. You either wait another 5 years to buy that car, or buy it in 5 years, then pay that additional 2% on top of what you are going to charge yourself in interest. Damn it man. That stinking Wally Street is starting to piss me off.

Sometimes, these insurance companies don't have fixed loan rates. Instead they have what is known as variable loan rates. Variable loan rates are based on current market rates and go up or down. Here is the problem with these variable loans and this private banking concept that Wally is promoting.

If you borrow money out of your policy and interest rates begin an upward rise in rates, then your loan costs will also rise as a result.

If your policy only returns 3% and the loan cost for that year is 6%, then you are losing a net 3% in that year on the loaned funds.

Consequentially, be aware of variable loans involving life insurance policies, especially with this concept. They can upset the apple cart if you take loans. Wally will tell you to take a loan rather than a withdrawal.

Let's dive into this concept a little deeper. The whole life policy chosen for this concept is very important. Not just any whole life policy will work. There is one company that I know of that has a whole life policy with a unique rider on it. The rider is a 100% cash rider. Which means it acts like it is a separate account that just holds cash. There are no insurance charges or expenses that comes out of it. Those expenses come out of the regular whole life premium that you pay. So, what you have is two buckets with this whole life policy. One bucket is for the actual death benefit. This is where you pay the premiums for that death benefit. The other bucket is strictly a pure cash rider account. There are no insurance charges against this pure cash rider account. Everything that goes into that second bucket acts as if it was your own private bank account, except it is tax-deferred. That is a good thing, by the way.

Let's look at an example. Do not beat me up on the numbers here, but this is roughly how it works. Suppose you like the concept and you could put $20,000 per year into one of these whole life policies for five years. The whole life policies are designed so that you put the minimum death benefit with the highest premium that you can legally drop into the policy. In this example, that would be $20,000 per year.

Our whole life policy might have a death benefit of say $424,567, for example. Why the weird number? Because the insurance company software calculates the maximum death benefit for a policy with a scheduled premium of $20,000 per year. Whatever the minimum death benefit is, then that is what it is as far as this concept is concerned.

The whole life premium ordinarily, without this concept and rider, might be $6,000 per year. However, with the concept, then $20,000

[132]

minus the $6,000 means that $14,000 per year is going into your private bank tax-deferred rider account. Again, I am over-simplifying things here for explanation purposes.

Suppose you did pay the $20,000 for 5 years before you bought a new car. You will have netted $14,000 per year times five years, (not counting the earnings) or roughly $70,000 or so. You can easily buy a $35,000 car by taking a loan from the policy by the fifth year, or sooner if desired.

Assuming a five year loan at 5% interest, then your monthly payment would be $657.75 per month. You pay this amount back into your policy for the next 5 years. You will have paid back into to your whole life policy $44,917.55 according to my trusty HP 12C calculator. That is a profit of $9,917.55 that goes to you instead of your local bank, plus you are getting the $35,000 principal back, too.

Let's evaluate this concept after the loan. You have basically used your excess cash flow to fund the whole life policy. You borrowed $35,000 from yourself (your whole life policy) and you paid a monthly loan payment of $657.75 back into your whole life policy. At the end of the loan term, you have paid back $44,917.55. You have a gross return of 5%, but don't forget the 2% loan charged by the insurance company. So, you netted 3%. Okay. You did earn money every time that you made the $657.75 monthly payment. Plus it was tax-deferred growth, so your after-tax return, depending on your tax bracket probably was close to 5%. All in all, you came out smelling like a rose.

The concept promoters have tools to show how this approach is better than borrowing from a bank or credit union. Some of the software on this is pretty impressive. One of these concept promoters wanted over $3,000 a year for their software. Why do they charge so much? Because, they know that the commissions payable to a life insurance agent who sells one of these $20,000 cases will more than cover their software costs. Therefore, they know they can get away with it.

The concept is good. It works and it is beneficial for some people. It is for those who have the excess cash flow to cram a bunch of money, and I mean a bunch, into a whole life policy and use it for their own private bank. If you can put $10,000, $20,000 or more into a whole life insurance policy, then call me. I will be glad to help you get your own private bank up and running. Oh by the way, I hope you don't mind if I make a little insurance commission while I am at it. Full disclosure upfront.

There is one thing to watch out for if you do not use me for this concept. Some insurance agents, (notice that I didn't say financial advisors, because they are not financial advisors) will suggest that you take out a home equity line of credit for five years to fund the whole life insurance policy, then after five years take a withdrawal and pay off the home equity line of credit.

Here is the problem. Wally Street and the companies who sell these special whole life insurance policies project a current dividend rate in the 7 or 8% range. Historically, they almost never meet that range. Usually, they are around 2 – 3% lower than what they currently project. Therefore, Wally is going to show you an illustration at the higher (funny money) projection. Wally will try and get you to pull out the maximum that you can from your house. He will tell you:

"If you die, then the insurance death benefit will be there to pay off the home equity line of credit. If you live, the whole life insurance cash values will be there to pay off the home equity line of credit. It is a win-win situation, either way."

True on the first part, but not necessarily true on the second part.

[134]

Suppose, Wally showed you a 7.5% dividend projection, but it only actually paid 4.5% which is more realistic. Let's use my $100,000 example. Remember, I said in my earlier example, if you paid $20,000 per year into this policy for five years, then about $6,000 of it would be for the life insurance itself. The difference of $14,000 per year would go into the cash rider. Multiply this payment stream of $14,000 for five years and you have $70,000. My trusty little HP 12C calculator tells me that $70,000 times a 4.5% return over five years grows to $80,036.48. That is about $20,000 short of the $100,000 you borrowed.

Wally conned you into pulling out $100,000 out of your home equity and probably got you to put that into a Single Premium Immediate Annuity with a 5 year payout to pay the whole life insurance premium. By the way, I hope you do not mind if Wally earned a little commission in the process of selling you that Single Premium Immediate Annuity.

At the end of five years, you have a $100,000 home equity line of credit outstanding for which you have been paying the interest on for five years, too. At 6%, this would be $6,000 per year. In addition, Wally probably finagled the whole life insurance illustration to show you how your $100,000 will be there in five years. However, my trusty little HP 12C says that only $87,416.28 will be in that rider account, if all your dreams were to come true and the life insurance company actually did pay that 7.5% dividend rate. Fat chance.

Let's see. You have paid $6,000 per year in interest on the home equity loan which is $30,000. Even with Wally's rosy illustration you only have $87,416.28 in that cash rider. Net-net, you end up with $57,416.28 after five years. Yet, the problem is that you still have that $100,000 home equity line to pay off, but you cannot just yet. So, you will have to wait one more year to get the cash rider account up over $100,000. That is assuming you get the full 7.5% dividend rate each of those years. Even when you get the $100,000 in the cash rider however, you still have had to pay $6,000 per year in home equity interest. Personally, I do not see how you ever can catch up.

Maybe, just maybe Wally will tell you to pay the interest out of the whole life insurance policy. "Oh, I see," said the blind man. However, this means that I have to pull out my little trusty HP 12C calculator again. Dad gum it!

You mean if I use the cash rider to pay the home equity interest, then instead of $14,000 going to the cash rider, I will only have $8,000 going to it? Yes, sir. That is correct. This means it will take 9 years to grow that net $8,000 per year into $100,000, so I can then pay off the home equity loan. Oh by the way, that is at the rosy dividend rate of 7.5% for those nine years. If it averages the 4.5% more realistic rate, then it will take 10 years.

Here is the final evaluation of this rosy idea. You put $20,000 per year into a whole life insurance policy. You borrowed $100,000 from your house to do it. You paid the interest on the home equity line from the cash rider account which means a net $8,000 per year was left to grow back to the $100,000 needed to pay of the home equity line. At 7.5% interest, (don't make me laugh) your cash rider grew to $105,176.70 at the end of 9 years. You take out $100,000 from your cash rider and you are left with $5,176.70 to buy your $40,000 car. Come again?

If you do not add any more money to the whole life insurance policy, it will only take another 29 years to grow that $5,176.70 into $40,000 so you can buy that brand new car! That is 29 years on top of the 9 years that it took you to get to this point. So, that is a total of 38 years to reach $40,000 with the home equity line of credit idea Wally Street presented you.

All you have done is helped Wally Street make a big commission. The private bank idea using whole life insurance is best for people with excess cash flow and lots of it. It is for those who can afford to keep funding the policy for 5 to 7 years. It is a good idea if you can afford to do it. *Just do not do it with a home equity loan*.

For example, if you are a highly paid professional and you can slam $30,000 or more into a whole life policy with a cash rider, then it is a great idea. You can use the cash rider later on to be your own private bank and it will work great for you. In fact, it will be fantastic for you.

Alternatively, you may have some other assets that you could transfer into your private bank whole life policy for the next 5 to 7 years. If so, then you have a way to fund your private bank without affecting your cash flow.

One last point to remember is that it is an awful idea and I mean awful, if you use a home equity line of credit to pay the whole life insurance premiums. Got it? Good.

As my dad would say, "You are like an Airedale dog. You are a whole lot smarter than you look."

Chapter Summary

What did we learn in this chapter?

- Private banking with life insurance is for people with a lot of excess and steady cash flow.
- There are a lot of Wally Streets running around out there touting this private bank concept.
- Insurance company loans are hocus pocus and there is a difference between a declared loan rate and the loan rate guaranteed in the policy.
- Zero interest rate loans may not kick in for 10 years, if at all.
- We learned that variable loans are an unknown and can negatively impact life insurance cash values.
- Whole life dividend projections almost never come true.
- Lower whole life dividends can delay our ability to use our private bank.
- Borrowing from a home equity line of credit to fund our private bank is a stupid thing to do.
- If done right, the private bank idea with life insurance can be a good thing.
- Rick can help you with your own private bank.

Chapter Ten

Get Some Life Insurance

"Large skepticism leads to large understanding. Small skepticism leads to small understanding. No skepticism leads to no understanding."
~ Xi Zhi

[This page intentionally left blank]

Get Some Life Insurance

One of my favorite quips by my dad, who was a very successful life insurance agent, was when he said, "Don't make it a sad day for everybody." What he meant was at least *somebody* at your funeral will be happy.

Another one of his favorite quotes was, "Don't you want your poor wife to be able to shop at all the best stores?" He would try and shame them into realizing that their wife was spending money at the best stores now. He would further add, "You can't possible leave her in the position that she has to start going to Wal-Mart instead of Dillard's or Nordstrom to buy clothes!" Nothing against Wal-Mart mind you as they are a fine company.

My dad sold a lot of life insurance making light of death. Sometimes when one of his clients would pass away, he would say, "I got to go throw dirt in somebody's face today."

I know you've heard this one before, but my dad actually had a friend and client who was a funeral director. Every time he saw him he would call him "The last guy to ever let you down."

I had two fathers. You can read more about my story at the end of this book, but I wanted to point out how life insurance can be properly used to benefit your family with both of my fathers as examples.

My real father, Bill Allison, died when I was a senior in high school. He didn't have much life insurance. He had three young kids, not counting me, who he was responsible for at the time. At the age of 39, he probably figured that he didn't need much life insurance. His wife was a housewife. Suddenly, she was thrust into the role of being the family breadwinner. She was a wonderful mother and did the best that she could under the circumstances. However, some life insurance would certainly have made her life a lot easier. None of her kids had college degrees and it was not their fault either. She simply could not afford it without the life insurance.

This little speech is for the men out there.

> Life insurance is for the people that remain after your death dummy. None of us know when we will die, but we will all die. The way to make sure that your wife doesn't have to get a job, especially in this job environment, is to buy some damn life insurance! You don't have a hair on your rear end, if you don't buy at least $500,000 worth of death benefit, especially if you have young kids. Term insurance for a young guy is nothing. There is no excuse for not having it. None at all!

Ladies, this applies to you.

> Most people who are married today are two income families. They need both spouse's incomes to make ends meet. If your family needs your income to make ends meet, then think what a burden you would put on your spouse, and kids for that matter, if something were to happen to you. The house might have to go. They might have to move to a different cheaper neighborhood where the schools are not as good. The college education for your kids might have to go by the wayside. It is simply not a pretty picture.

Hopefully, I have convinced you of the importance of life insurance. If not, here is another story.

My dad Hillman Johnson, the life insurance salesman, died when he was 57 years old of cancer. He had life insurance. My mom never had to worry about keeping her house. She never had to worry about how she was going to pay bills. She never had to worry about what she was going to eat. She never had to worry about buying Christmas presents for her grandchildren. The life insurance gave her peace of mind that she would be okay.

It is bad enough to lose a spouse. You don't want to compound the problem by not having any life insurance for your surviving spouse. Quit thinking of yourself for a minute and think about your surviving family instead. You have to think of the life insurance premium like a utility bill. Just pay it and be done with it.

The best way to buy life insurance is from an independent life insurance agent. Although big, well known insurance companies are good solid companies, you might be better off going to an independent agent who is able to shop your case. What is the big, well known life insurance agent going to sell you? A big, well known life insurance policy which is not a bad thing in and of itself, but is there a better alternative? How will you know unless you shop your case? What if you are rated up? If you go to a one company agent, then you are stuck with their solution.

Further, if you do have any minor health issues, your independent agent can shop it with other carriers to get you the best underwriting rates.

I have sold life insurance from 1984 until today. I know how these companies operate. If you have any little impairment, you can bet your bottom dollar they will rate you at a higher premium. Especially, <u>if they know that you are doing business with only their company</u>! Think about that for a second. It makes sense, doesn't it?

Not too long ago, I wrote a case on a client who had a little impairment. I told him that we would shop it, if it came back rated. Sure enough, they came back with a small rating. I dropped that company and went to another one for this client and they _were not_ rated at that new company. The client saved a lot in rating costs by shopping the policy with an independent agent. That would be me, by the way.

I learned from my dad. Whenever a life insurance company tried to rate one of his clients, he would get madder than a hornet. He used to call them up and say, "Send me my shit." (Sorry for the profanity, but if you knew my dad, then you would understand.) To my dad, what he meant to say was "send me the medical records so I can shop it with another insurance company." This was in the pre-HIPAA era when privacy rules were not so strict. Every single time he had to shop it, he always was able to get a better offer for his clients. Every time without fail. _Always_. It pays to shop. Wally does not want you to shop his life insurance recommendation for you. He wants you to "trust" him and pay the extra policy rating charges. Remember, his company is the "best."

Some life insurance companies make bad investment decisions and are too aggressive on their life insurance policies. When they realize it, then they freeze up and try to rate anyone with a minor impairment like high blood pressure or high cholesterol. If you as the client are going to Wally who is representing one of these companies, then guess what you are getting? A rated up insurance policy. This costs you more money.

This is Wally Street from the insurance company prospective. Wally would have you believe that his product is the best out there and his company is the best out there and there is no need to go anywhere else. Yep. That's my friend Wally Street. No different from the Wally working at the local bank, or the Wally working for the Wall Street firm. Their _modus operandi_ is all the same.

[144]

Independent agents are worth their weight in gold, in my opinion. Especially, if they have been around since 1984 or longer. I wonder. Where can you find someone like that?

Chapter Summary

What did we learn in this chapter?

- We learned not to make it a sad day for everybody.
- We learned how drastically different life can be for the people you leave behind based on your decision to buy life insurance or not.
- Only buy life insurance from independent insurance agents who can shop it, in case you have health issues or a minor impairment.
- Wally's insurance company is not the best.
- Wally Street works at banks, insurance companies and Wall Street firms and they all sell life insurance that benefits those companies, not you.

Chapter Eleven

Wills: Why You Need One

"If we become increasingly humble about how little we know, we may be more eager to search."

~ Sir John Templeton

[This page intentionally left blank]

Wills: Why You Need One

Since we are talking about life insurance, then we might as well go right into talking about wills. I routinely talk to younger people who do not have a will. I tell them until I am blue in the face to get a will. Yet, for some reason, younger people don't want to spend the money on an attorney to draw up a will. Well let me give you a little story to spur you on a bit.

I had a client who was a young doctor who was married with a couple of young kids. As some doctors are prone to do, he traded his wife in on a trophy wife. He was making all the money and he just felt he deserved better, so he got a divorce. He was too busy with his new trophy wife to go get a will. Sadly, he realized the error of his ways by treating his first wife the way he did. It really bothered him, so he committed suicide.

This happened in Arkansas. At that particular time, in Arkansas when you died intestate (without a will) your estate had to go through the county probate court. This means anyone can see everything you own. It also means that things might not go according to plan. Since there wasn't a will, there wasn't a plan. The court had to decide what to do. In Arkansas, the intestate rules were that (2/3rd's) two-thirds go to the minor children and (1/3rd) one-third goes to the wife.

This doctor had the foresight to at least purchase a life insurance policy. However, he cut his first wife out as the beneficiary and named his two minor children as the sole beneficiaries. Unfortunately, minor children cannot decide for themselves, therefore the judge had to have guardianships setup. Equally unfortunate is the trophy wife got cut out of any life insurance money, too. She didn't like that too much, so she got herself an attorney. She wanted her cut and according to Arkansas statutes, she was entitled to one-third of the insurance policy, or so she thought. It is a tough life being a trophy wife, let me tell you. Her attorney knew all along that she didn't stand a snowball's chance in hell of getting one-third, but gladly took her money in order to help her out. He got 3% for filing the probate, plus I'm sure a little extra for filing the lawsuit for the one-third of the young doctor's life insurance death benefit.

The poor ex-wife had to also hire an attorney to try and get the money from the life insurance company for her kids. She wasn't getting anything from the life insurance herself, since she was not a beneficiary. Yet, here she was having to spring for an attorney. The problem was that she wasn't named as the kids guardians, because there was no will. Yes, they were her kids, but you see, the court has to setup guardianships when there are minor children involved, like it or not.

With these Arkansas guardianships, you have to invest in a very limited scope of investments. They had to be completely safe, like FDIC insured CD's or Arkansas Municipal bonds. You cannot risk any of the money. Further, every year whomever the court had appointed as guardians for the kids, they would have to do an annual accounting to the court with a court appointed attorney. I wonder what that cost every year?

Now, the trophy wife was getting the picture, so she had her attorney sue to be named the guardian for the kids that were not even her kids! The ex-wife had to hire an attorney to defend herself as the guardians for her own kids! The insurance company would not write the check, because there was no guardianship setup. They just let the court decide. They stayed out of it.

The trophy wife was trying desperately to get her hands on the life insurance money and get guardianships over two kids that were not her own. She wanted control and she wanted it bad. I'm sure she had the kid's best interests at heart, didn't she? No. Say it isn't so. You mean she

[150]

might be only interested in controlling the money? A trophy wife? No way.

Ladies and gentlemen. We had a good old fashioned cat fight on our hands, except it was all playing out in public.

After lots and lots of attorney fees, in the end it was all settled after about a year and a half. The ex-wife got nothing but a big legal bill. The trophy wife only got what she was entitled to and that was only one-third of the house she was living in. Also, she only got one-third of the money the poor doctor had left. That was the Arkansas statutes. Two thirds goes to the minor children. Thankfully, she did not get any of the kid's life insurance money, because that passed by contract, outside of probate. Although the court had to help it along a little.

In the end, there were two guardianships setup for the kids. These were in effect until they reached the age of eighteen (18). After that, they got the money. No strings attached. It was all theirs to spend as they wish at age 18. Their mother couldn't do anything about it. The two kids, well they got about $150,000 a piece from the life insurance, plus the other two-thirds of his estate. I moved away from Arkansas before they turned 18, so I don't know if they spent it or saved it. I suspect they spent a little of it. What do you think?

Further, how do you think the trophy wife felt after finding out she was only getting one-third of the poor doctor's estate, including the house she was living in and no life insurance to boot? A lien was placed on the doctor's house for the two-thirds share due to the minor children. The trophy wife ended up having to sell the house and move out.

All of these problems were a result of no will. The doctor didn't have to worry about any of it, but remember when I mentioned earlier that life insurance is for the people who live? So is a will. A will just makes it easier on your family to take care of things according to your wishes. If you do not have a will, then make the call right now to an Estate Planning attorney. If you have a more complicated situation, like maybe a trophy wife and kids by another marriage, then the Estate Planning attorney knows what to do.

It is just plain idiotic not to have a will. You know it and I know it.

Chapter Summary

What did we learn in this chapter?

- It is very important to have an updated will that corresponds to our wishes, especially if we have minor children.
- Leaving assets to minor beneficiaries can cause problems for heirs with guardianships that must be created involving attorneys and court costs.
- Dying without a will in some states may mean that your spouse only gets one third of your assets and your minor children get two-thirds.
- Trophy wives need to be better taken care of, or else they might cause legal problems.

Notes

Chapter Twelve

Trust Types and Benefits

"We can't help everyone, but everyone can help someone."

~ Ronald Reagan

[This page intentionally left blank]

Trusts Types and Benefits

Feeding off of wills is a little more sophisticated form of Estate Planning with the use of trusts. There are many types of trusts. Some of the more popular trusts are:

- Living or Revocable Trusts
- Irrevocable Trusts
- Asset Protection Trusts
- Testamentary Trusts
- Bypass & Q-TIP Trusts
- Dynasty Trusts
- Charitable Trusts & Donor Advised Funds
- Intentionally Defective Grantor Trusts
- Beneficiary's Trusts
- Qualified Personal Residence Trusts
- GRAT's (not GRIT's)

Each type of trust has its own goals. Some are for asset protection, or to save in estate taxes. Some are for fulfilling family wishes, or helping out charities. Other types of trusts are for "making sure my kids don't blow it all," or controlling the money after you are gone.

I will go over these more popular types of trusts one by one and add some relevant stories here and there as examples.

[This page intentionally left blank]

Living or Revocable Trusts

These trusts are fairly well known to a lot of people. However, when I see those man on the street interviews on television, I might have to reconsider. Some people don't even know who the Vice-President is, so I cannot assume they know what a living trust is either. This is a sad but true example of today's society. There are a lot of clueless people walking around out there, so I am here to help.

Living trusts are revocable by the grantor. These trusts are not just for the rich. Any middle class family with children, a house, cars and investments should have a living trust. In conjunction with the living trust, you normally also get a pour-over will, health care powers of attorney, durable powers of attorney and a living will. I will explain each below.

Married people have living trusts where everything passes to the surviving spouse. This is fine, but as older spouses tend to do, they remarry. When they do, the new spouse comes in and eventually expects their inheritance. This is another reason that you do not want to use those online legal document companies for living trusts. An attorney can make sure that there is language in the living trust, so that any new spouses are not entitled to your assets that are meant for your children. If you have an "I love you" living trust where everything passes to the surviving spouse, then this could be a major mistake. The following story will explain why.

Imagine being married for 40 plus years and then the wife passes away. Generally, in the neighborhood and at his church, it is known that the surviving husband has a little money. Along come the trophy wife candidates looking for an easier life. These are trophy wives except they are little older now, but they are still trophy wives nevertheless. A trophy wife at 30 years old is no different now that she is 60 years old. She is still after that easy life with money to spend. She is even thinking about getting the money for her kids.

The husband, you see, he is a little older. He is 70 years old and not thinking as good as he used to. The trophy wife sweet talks her 10 years older new husband into changing his living trust to leave out those adult children and put herself in their place. You see, living trusts are revocable while you are alive. Of course, the trophy wife will not tell the adult children what she has done. They will not find out about it until after their dad dies. It is then they will discover that they are not getting anything that their mom or dad had originally intended.

Oh by the way, the trophy wife likes those online legal document companies. That way she can keep everything she is doing private and away from the adult kids. They will never know until it is too late.

If only mom and dad had gone to a real attorney. Mom's passing would have meant that her assets did not pass to directly to dad, but rather to a bypass trust that is irrevocable and cannot be changed. Of course, dad could get the income from the trust while he was alive, but even he could not change the beneficiary to the trophy wife. The real attorney would have prevented that from happening.

Leaving all your assets to your surviving spouse without consideration of something like this happening is not a good idea. I am telling you ladies that you just might want to knock your cheap ass husband in the head, if he ever tries to go to one of those online legal document companies. Widowed men are pigs just like young men are pigs. You know it to be true. Hopefully, that story will make you straighten up.

Pour-over will

The pour-over will is simply where your will says that you leave everything in your estate to your living trust. After your death, the pour-over will is filed in the probate court if your estate is sizable enough. Each county is different, but generally, if your estate is not considered a small estate, then you have to file a will in the probate court.

The pour-over will keeps everything private and out of snooping eyes, because the only thing it says is that everything in your estate is poured over into your living trust. The living trust is private and does not have to be filed in probate court.

This paragraph pertains to regular wills, not pour-over wills. I wanted to put it in here as a comparison between a regular will and a pour-over will. Small estates for people with little or no assets are exempt from the probate filing requirement. Each state has their own small estates minimum. In Florida, it is estates under $75,000. This means that you do not have to go through probate and the assets can be immediately distributed.

Health Care Power of Attorney

The health care power of attorney with HIPPA features is a document that allows someone to make health care decisions on your behalf. For example, if you were in a car wreck and unconscious, but needed a blood transfusion, then the hospital would need someone with a health care power of attorney with HIPPA features to sign off on the blood transfusion. All hospitals have a standard HIPAA release form and generally make you sign it, before they do a thing. If you cannot sign it yourself, then someone else must sign it for you.

If you have a health care power of attorney that has been prepared and updated with HIPAA provisions, then you can bring that to the hospital to show that you have the legal authority to make decisions for that particular loved one or friend. The hospital will probably still want you to sign their form however.

Durable Power of Attorney

A durable power of attorney can be a very dangerous thing in the wrong hands. Most attorneys add a springing feature to them for protection. By springing feature I mean that it only goes into effect upon you being legally declared incompetent or disabled and unable to take care of your own affairs. Conversely, it springs back to being idle when you are no longer incapacitated. A court has to make a legal interpretation on you being either legally incompetent or disabled and unable to take care of your own affairs.

If you were just to hand over a durable power of attorney to someone without the springing feature, then you would in effect be giving them access to everything that you own. They could use the durable power of attorney to take over your bank accounts, your investments and everything else. That is why these can be dangerous. Without the springing feature, you could get wiped out by an unscrupulous relative or friend. Even with the springing feature, they can be abused.

Imagine if you are an elderly father and your spouse has already passed away, then you become incapacitated. Without a durable power of attorney to manage your financial affairs, then no bills can get paid. This could cause your house to get behind on mortgage payments, the light bill to get turned off and other bills to not get paid. Someone needs to be able to step in and take care of these type of issues, if you were to become incapacitated. The durable power of attorney will solve this problem. You just want to be real careful who you name in the document.

Living Will

The living will is basically a document that says what to do if you are near the end of your life. Generally, on the living will there are a bunch of items to initial or sign off on saying that you want this to happen or that to not happen. For example, perhaps you do not want a feeding tube inserted. Another example, would be that you do not want to be resuscitated, if you were to have cardiac arrest.

One of my best friends was murdered several years ago. Although he was taken to the hospital with life threatening injuries, he was already gone. However, they put him on a machine so his family could come and say goodbye. Once they unplugged the machine, he passed away. A living will gave his family the authority to pull the plug.

Imagine the opposite. What if there was no living will? Someone in the family would have to be the one that signs off on pulling the plug. I have seen the agony and desperation of family members when faced with this decision. They do not want to make this decision. To them, it feels like it is not supposed to be their decision. They are extremely hesitant about their decision, because it will riddle them with guilt for the rest of their lives. They will constantly wonder if it was the right decision. Should they have let the machines keep you alive longer? Perhaps, you will come out of it by a miracle of God. All of these thoughts go through their minds. My question to you is:

"Why would you put someone you love through that gut wrenching process when with proper planning you can remove that burden?"

Do not put your family members in this predicament. It is not fair to them. Quit thinking about yourself for a minute and think about doing the right thing. Get yourself a living trust with all the ancillary documents described above. It is the right thing to do.

By the way, if you already have a living will and all the ancillary documents, pull them out and look at them. Make sure that they still are exactly what you want. If not, then go see an Estate Planning attorney and update your legal documents.

Please do not go to one of those online legal document preparers. Let me tell you why. I look at legal documents a lot in my practice and although I am not an attorney, I can read. Imagine that. Someone who can read. I cannot tell you how many times I have seen mistakes in legal documents and powers of attorneys from those online legal document companies. It is not the online legal document company's fault. It is the tightwad's fault. The idiot who did not want to hire a real attorney to draft their documents.

Just so you understand, the risk of accepting a durable power of attorney from someone on your behalf is large. In fact, a lot of the major brokerage firms will not accept them. Instead, they will ask you to have the incapacitated person sign their form. Well, if they are incapacitated, then they cannot legally sign. This causes a problem. They do not feel comfortable accepting your poorly drafted durable power of attorney, so they refuse it. Then, they demand that the incapacitated person sign it, but they cannot. What are you to do? You will have to go hire an attorney, take the crappy durable power of attorney to a judge and attempt to get it legally authorized. However, the problem is in the wording. You see, when you were trying to save a buck, you inadvertently did not give the right powers to the document. It doesn't make a hill of beans what the judge says in this case, since you do not have the right words in the document. If the right words are not in there, then it is basically worthless.

I can tell you from experience that you are not putting a durable power of attorney that is poorly written on any account that I am an adviser on. It simply will not happen and it is not because of me. It is the brokerage firm that will deny it. In almost all cases, it is because of the wording of the document. An example would be when you try to open an account. Most of the time, the agent or the one acting on your behalf cannot open an account for you. This is because you didn't put the right powers in the document, or it is not allowed in your state. Did you know this?

Now I need you to think _critically_ again. Once you create the document using that online legal documents firm, then how do you know it will work? You do not know and you cannot know until it comes time to use it in a real situation. Don't you see? Just because you have (don't make me laugh) "created it" yourself, doesn't mean that it is worth a hill of beans. The odds are that you have failed to include the proper wording in the document as it relates to your state. Why? Because, you are not an attorney!

If you are not an attorney, then **_do you_** know the requirements for your state in regard to Durable Powers of Attorneys? That's what I thought. And you still think you can just go online and figure it out? How stupid is that? Let me clue you in. It is real stupid.

My advice is to go to an Estate Planning attorney, pay the attorney their customary fee and get your documents drafted correctly. These attorneys are indispensable, in my opinion.

[This page intentionally left blank]

Irrevocable Trusts

Irrevocable trusts are primarily used in asset protection. There are a myriad of irrevocable trusts designed by attorneys to accomplish specific needs of the grantor. By the way, the grantor is the one putting the assets or money in the trust.

People tend to be scared of irrevocable trusts, because of the word "irrevocable." The reality is that any irrevocable trust can be closed out anytime that you want to do so. They can be closed out just like a corporation.

For example, let's suppose you wanted to make annual contributions to an irrevocable trust as a gifting strategy to reduce your taxable estate. You make the first year gift to the trust for each trust beneficiary. When the second year comes around, you have changed your mind. You no longer wish to contribute to the irrevocable trust, because of changes in your family dynamics. In other words, one of your kids is a screw up. All you have to do is stop contributing and the irrevocable trust holds its value at whatever the prior year contributions were for the beneficiaries. It will only grow based on its investment earnings, not on future contributions.

Further, if each beneficiary is of legal age, then you may be able to distribute out to each the value in the trust at that point. Once the money is paid out, then for all practical purposes. The irrevocable trust is finished.

At this point, you can start a new irrevocable trust with new beneficiaries minus the screwed up kid, if that was your goal.

[This page intentionally left blank]

Asset Protection Trusts

You can get really creative with these irrevocable trusts. For example, I recommended to a guy an Estate Planning attorney who created a master irrevocable trust, then created separate sub-trusts for each of the client's real estate properties. The purpose of this strategy was to shelter each of his real estate properties from potential lawsuits.

The sub-trusts named the master irrevocable trust as the beneficiary. There were ten sub-trusts for the ten different real estate properties. No person was a beneficiary of each of the sub-trusts, instead the master irrevocable trust was the beneficiary of all the sub-trusts. The master irrevocable trust had the family members as its beneficiaries. However, the master trust was empty until the grantor died, or became incapacitated. There was one exception. The grantor had a life estate for all of the trusts which means he could enjoy the income from the trusts while living.

Here is an important thing to remember when you are doing Asset Protection Trusts. Do not name your trusts anything that another person could tell what is in the trust. In other words, if you named your trust the John Q. Public Jefferson Street Trust. All an opposing attorney would have to do is look for a property that was formerly owned by John Q. Public on Jefferson Street that was transferred into a trust.

If you named the trust, the Idaho Trust, then you would have a wild goose chase going on in the state of Idaho looking for your properties. Except, you have no property in Idaho and you have never even been to Idaho. You only used that name for asset protection purposes to throw people off who are looking for your assets.

In addition, real estate transfers are public records. If you own property as John Q. Public and then you have it re-titled to the Idaho Trust, then they can find it. If on the other hand, you had it re-titled to the Idaho Trust and then soon after re-titled again to the Cheyenne Trust, then what are they going to find? They will think that you moved the domicile of the trust from Idaho to Wyoming. Or, they may think that you sold the property. This is an added step which may provide enough confusion as to keep your assets protected a little bit longer. I might even have one trust created with a weird name for the sole purpose of using it to simply move other assets through and kill the public record trail. This is especially important when you are using irrevocable trusts. It is not as critical with living trusts or revocable trusts, so don't panic.

Nothing is ever fool-proof and if you are committing fraud, then this asset protection strategy with unique names will not work, because a judge can force you to hand over the fraudulently hidden assets.

Back to my story. Each sub-trust held a piece of real estate that was donated by the grantor. If a piece of property in a sub-trust was sold, then the proceeds stayed in the sub-trust and either was invested, or used to buy more real estate. The income from the real estate was paid to the master irrevocable trust for the grantor's income needs.

Picture the situation. The grantor donated all of his real estate to ten separate sub-trusts. Each sub-trust named the one master irrevocable trust as its beneficiaries. The grantor enjoyed the income from the sub-trusts which was paid to the master trust which was the beneficiary of the sub-trusts, then on to him. The income could be turned on or off by all of the trustees of each sub-trust, if needed in case of a creditor dispute or legal attack.

Each trust had a separate and distinct co-trustee. No two co-trustees were the same. Oh by the way, the co-trustees were all in a separate state from the grantor with the exception of one co-trustee who was on all the trusts and that person was local.

The trusts were also domiciled in another state. If a trust was sued in that state, the trustee could simply move to another state and make the attorney follow them to the new state. This ability to move the domicile that the trust is located in makes it more difficult for the attorney filing the suit. Not impossible, but rather more difficult. It means he has to split fees that he may not get with an attorney in another state if he is not licensed with the bar in that state. Those attorneys that he has to split with are not going to do the work unless they get paid. He will have to pay the new attorneys their fees upfront.

A manager was named for each real estate sub-trust. The manager of each trust took care of the real estate, paid the taxes, kept the properties up, hired real estate agents as needed and so on. So, everything was setup and in place.

I will admit that it seems a little complicated, but bear with me. This is a really good asset protection strategy.

One day, the grantor decides to get married. The irrevocable trusts did not let the grantor add his new wife as a beneficiary. For all practical purposes, he gave away all of his real estate assets when he setup all these trusts. Legally, he didn't own anything except the income that the trustee decided to pay him. The trustee had discretion to turn the income on or off and for good reason.

As luck would have it, the marriage turned sour. It is never a good idea to marry someone who won $8,000 a month in alimony for the rest of her life. This emboldens them and makes them believe that they can come out smelling like a rose in any divorce situation.

Back to my story. The wife filed for divorce saying, "I'm going to bust those trusts." She had gotten a hold of the trusts and made copies of every one of them for her attorney. She was really confident that she was going to get at least half of the real estate assets.

The grantor called me in a panic and was worried that she could bust the trusts like she threatened to do. I told the grantor not to worry. Her attorney would simply send out a threatening letter which he could ignore. When the attorney figured out that all of the trusts had co-trustees in another state and he would have to file eleven separate lawsuits in another state, then he would go away. From a legal standpoint, all eleven trusts had eleven different trustees and neither was responsible to the other trusts for anything.

The reason I told the grantor that the attorney would go away is because the wife would eventually quit paying the attorney his fees. The soon to be ex-wife had paid the attorney about $15,000 up to this point.

I don't know of any attorneys who would do this kind of work on a contingency basis. A contingency basis might work if, the attorney knows there are some assets to split. Where he can see them and eventually get his hands on them. In this case, there was nothing that the grantor legally owned. There were no assets that the attorney could see, like a joint checking account, investment accounts and so on. None of the real estate was owned by the grantor. Everything was in trusts and the real estate was put in the trusts _before_ the marriage which is a key point.

When the attorney said he needed to get paid _more money_ to file the eleven different lawsuits out of state, the wife didn't like that idea. The attorney and the now ex-wife went away. She went away pissed, too.

[172]

This asset protection strategy worked. The grantor was very happy. It was my recommendation to use the Estate Planning attorney and implement this strategy. I told him not to marry that women in the first place, but who am I? I am just a peon that people treat like every other Wally Street.

Full disclosure. I am not an attorney and I do not draft legal documents. We hired one who specialized in complex asset protection strategies. Imagine that. Hire an attorney that can save your stinking bacon.

Like I said before, I can read. I understand complex legal asset protection strategies involving irrevocable trusts. Please do not treat me like I am just another Wally Street.

[This page intentionally left blank]

Testamentary Trusts

Sometimes people have just a will and no trusts. However, in their will it says to create a trust or trusts upon their passing for the benefit of certain beneficiaries. Perhaps, a person doesn't want to leave a lump sum to their beneficiaries, but instead would prefer to leave it to them in trust. Or, perhaps they have a disabled person beneficiary that needs a trust created for them.

The will in this example is taken down to court and the probate attorney is directed by the court to create the trust. This type of trust is called a testamentary trust. It only is created after death.

Testamentary trusts are irrevocable and cannot be changed. If a person's will is not reviewed by any family members before death, then they could be in for a big surprise. Instead of getting a lump sum amount, they are going to find themselves as a beneficiary of a newly created testamentary trust. Most of these testamentary trusts are created to protect the beneficiaries from themselves. People who put the testamentary clause in their wills do it to control how their assets are paid out. In other words, they do not want their beneficiaries to blow all the money.

Another concern of these testamentary trusts are if a beneficiary predeceases the person with the will. This would cause the testamentary trust to be created, but the deceased beneficiary's share would pass according to their will or living trust. If the deceased beneficiary did not have a will of their own, then it would go to the probate court for a determination. More and more legal fees and costs would be unnecessarily created. You can avoid all this by just making sure that wills are periodically reviewed.

[This page intentionally left blank]

Bypass and Q-TIP Trusts

When you have your living trust created, in most cases, you probably have a clause in it to create a bypass trust with a Q-TIP provision. These trusts are for estate tax planning and avoidance. Generally, if you have a large estate subject to estate taxes, then you should certainly have this setup.

Here is how it works. Let's assume that your estate is valued at $15,000,000 for estate tax purposes. You go to your Estate Planning attorney and he sets up a living trust for you and one for your spouse. In each of the living trusts, there is a provision to put the exclusion amount into the bypass trust for the benefit of your children. The Q-TIP provision on the bypass trust allows your spouse the right to enjoy the income from the bypass trust for as long as she lives. Ladies, this is how you avoid that trophy wife situation that marries your husband and snatches the money meant for your kids that I described earlier under the Living Trusts section.

The exclusion amount for 2015 is $5,430,000. In our example with a $15,000,000 taxable estate, while still living, the $5,430,000 would drop into a newly created irrevocable bypass trust with a Q-TIP provision. At first death, the balance which is $9,570,000 would pass via the marital deduction to the surviving spouse estate tax free. The surviving spouse would then take $5,430,000 and drop it into their own bypass trust with a Q-TIP provision.

When the surviving spouse eventually passes away, then that is when any final estate taxes would be paid. If the surviving spouse died soon after the first spouse to die, then the $9,570,000 would go through a similar process. Except the money in the second bypass trust would go to the adult children. The residual estate would then be valued at $4,140,000 and estate taxes would be due on that amount. Once you put the money into the bypass trust, it is not yours any longer. Therefore, instead of paying taxes at second death on $9,570,000, you are only paying taxes on $4,140,000. That is, if you didn't have any second-to-die life insurance to pay those estate taxes. This is the best way to pay them, by the way. Did I mention that I could help you shop for second-to-die life insurance?

By utilizing the bypass trusts for both spouses, the pair were able to save estate taxes by utilizing both exclusions. If they just went with the unlimited marital deduction, then their estate tax bill would have been higher. For example, if the first spouse died and left the entire $15,000,000 estate to the surviving spouse, then when the surviving spouse died, she could only deduct out $5,430,000 of assets from estate taxes. The exclusion amount from her spouse that died first would be lost. This means that her estate taxes would be based on $15,000,000 minus her exclusion of $5,430,000 which equals $9,570,000.

If both spouses used the exclusion with the bypass trusts, then the estate taxes would be based on the $4,140,000 previously calculated. The moral of the story is to use the bypass trusts with the full exclusion amounts for each spouse in order to get the taxes down. Also, buy second-to-die life insurance to pay those estate taxes.

With a $10,860,000 estate, you could probably avoid any estate taxes altogether. While the first spouse is still living, he would put the full $5,430,000 in his bypass trust which the surviving spouse could derive income from because of the Q-TIP provision. There would be no estate taxes at first death, because he gave it all to the bypass trust. While the surviving spouse is living, then she would put her full $5,430,000 in her bypass trust and there would likely be minimal if any estate taxes due. The only estate taxes due would be for the portion of the estate that was outside of the bypass trust.

Here is another important point to remember in regard to the Unlimited Marital Deduction. Suppose you had a simple will _without_ a bypass trust provision. In the will, it says everything goes to the surviving spouse. How can you take advantage of the $5,430,000 exclusion on the first spouse to die? Believe it or not, the IRS will allow you to file an estate tax form to take advantage of this missed opportunity. So, if the estate was $10,860,000 and all you had was a will, then you could still eliminate estate taxes later by utilizing the exclusion of $5,430,000 of the first spouse to die. Of course, you have to file the form though. If you do not file it on a timely basis, then you lose it. This is another reason to not go online and buy a will. You need an Estate Planning attorney who knows this stuff.

I have actually seen estates where they lost their exclusion amount, because they did not know that the IRS would have allowed them credit. Just so you know, this is at least a two million dollar plus mistake and in reality a lot more. The estate tax is based on the full amount of the estate. It works like this. If the estate's total value is $15,000,000, then the taxes owed is based on the $15,000,000. You do not deduct out the $5,430,000 and figure taxes on $9,570,000. No, no, no. It is based on the full $15,000,000. You figure the total taxes due on that larger amount first, then you take off a tentative credit at the end. So, you see, the estate taxes due is based on the higher amount, or the true valuation of the estate. Some people mistakenly believe that it would be based on the net after exclusion figure, but they would be wrong.

If your estate is valued at $15,000,000 or more, then congratulations. You must be doing something right. However, you need an Estate Planning attorney and probably should consider some 2nd to die life insurance to pay estate taxes at the surviving spouse's death. By the way, I can help you with getting an Estate Planning attorney and also with shopping for a 2nd to die life insurance policy. Sorry, for the shameless self-promotion, but it is what I do.

[This page intentionally left blank]

Dynasty Trusts

These trusts are to pass family assets down from generation to generation. Unfortunately, family assets rarely survive past one generation, because assets are left outright and the heirs blow it all. The Dynasty Trust is a way to avoid this from happening. Think Rockefeller family when you think about Dynasty Trusts. We rednecks from Arkansas have always called them "The Rockerfellas."

The Rockefeller family created a Dynasty Trust in 1934 and another trust in 1952. The details of their trusts are private and few know how much money is in them, but let's assume it is a sizable amount. After all, the Rockefellers owned Standard Oil and all of its successors. Can you say Exxon Mobil? Plus the Rockefellers were big in the railroads and owned all the land associated with the train tracks. Not to mention all of the other real estate that they own. They used to own the Rockefeller Center in New York, a very popular tourist attraction, but have recently sold it.

Their trust is run by a committee of trust officers who handle the affairs for the family. The trust is supposed to end after the fourth generation passes away. In other words, this Dynasty Trust will still be going strong long after you and I have passed away. I think there are still some second generation Rockefellers still alive, so that means probably another couple of hundred years to go.

The Rockefeller Trusts, according to Wikipedia has five main divisions. These are a money management division, a venture capital division, a trust company that manages other family trusts, an insurance company and an insurance brokerage firm. All of these are as a result of the Dynasty Trust created back in 1934. It is simply amazing.

The Rockefeller Family Dynasty Trust is probably the best example that I know of to showcase how to properly setup and establish such a trust. This family did it the right way. They have given countless amounts to charities over the years. They have created thousands upon thousands of jobs. They have left a family legacy that will survive for generations. They have taught financial stewardship to their own family and now they are teaching other wealthy families those same values via their Rockefeller Trust Co. arm.

If you have significant family wealth that you would like to leave for generations to come, then I would look no further than the Rockefeller Trust Co. as your example of how to do it right. By the way, there is nothing in it for me by pointing you in their direction.

See their web site at: http://www.rockefellerfinancial.com.

Charitable Trusts

Since we are talking about wealthier people, then we might as well talk a little bit about philanthropy. Specifically, I wanted to talk about a few different ways to give to charities. There are two main types of Charitable Trusts. These are:

1. Charitable Remainder Annuity Trusts
2. Charitable Lead Trusts

The difference between the two is fairly straightforward. With the Charitable Lead Trust, you make a donation to your favorite charity and they get the income and your family gets the principal when you die. The other one is a Charitable Remainder Annuity Trust where the charity gets the principal when you die and you get the income while living. You get an income tax deduction with both from your adjusted gross income, too. It depends on what your adjusted gross income is in the year of the gift.

The charity that you choose can help set these up for you, but be advised that they will refer you to their favorite Wally Street. As an alternative, you can control it to some degree yourself by doing it in conjunction with an insurance company and an independent insurance agent or with a donor advised fund.

There is a risk to allowing the charity to take your money and pay you an income, not to mention the Wally Street risk. If the charity makes some bad investment decisions, or runs their charity in a poor manner, then this could put your income at risk for not being paid. For this reason, I am not a big fan of letting the charity control it. Plus, Wally Street is getting all the referrals from the charity because of pure unadulterated cronyism. Wally networked his way into the charity and he is getting all their referrals. Wally has it made, doesn't he?

With an insurance company, you are basically buying an annuity and naming the charity as the beneficiary, or the annuitant depending on how you want to do it. The owner is the charitable trust with a trustee. The charity will want to be the trustee, but that is not necessary. Again, I like to be in control, so I would control who the trustee is if I am the one donating the money. What if you wanted to change charities? You can do it if you control the trustee.

If you named the charity the beneficiary, then you would be the annuitant and receive the income. The reverse would be where the charity was the annuitant and they received the income while you were alive, then when you passed away, your family members would get the principal balance.

You have to think of the trust as a separate entity that just owns the annuity. That is all it is, a trust that owns the annuity.

There are basically three types of annuities to use for the Charitable Annuity Trust. It does not matter whether you choose a Charitable Remainder Annuity Trust or a Charitable Lead Trust. The following three options are the same.

1. Fixed annuity
2. Fixed indexed annuity
3. Variable Annuity

I'm not crazy about Variable Annuities as I have discussed earlier in this book for a host of reasons. Therefore, I am more inclined to go with choice number one or two.

The first choice is going to pay a low rate of return in today's low interest rate environment. Since you get a tax deduction based on what you give the charity, if you give them 2% in income, then it is not much to deduct. This is what fixed annuities are paying these days. Plus, your principal that you leave to your family members is not going to grow, because you are giving the charity whatever the insurance company is paying on the fixed annuity. If you pay out all the income, then our principal just sits there stagnant. This would be a better choice if interest rates were higher down the road, but at 2%, it is not a good choice today.

If on the other hand, you use choice number two, the fixed indexed annuity, then you have the potential to grow your principal for your heirs. You could use the fixed indexed annuity to schedule an income stream to the charity each year, like 3%, but keep everything else over and above that for your family. The downside is that you have to pay the agreed upon 3% out every year no matter what. In some years with a fixed indexed annuity, you may only make the 1% guarantee, so you would lose 2% in that year. However, in good years, you might make 6% and add three of that percent to your principal for your family.

The fixed indexed annuity has a little more opportunity for growth, plus when you put it in a charitable trust with a charitable income beneficiary, you get the annual tax deduction against your income taxes. In addition, it is a simple way to do it. We need things to be simpler these days, don't we?

If you want to leave the principal to a charity, then you would get a bigger tax deduction of course. You would get the income for as long as you live, then the principal goes to the charity when you die.

By the way, I am proud of you for thinking about someone other than yourself and giving to your favorite charities.

[This page intentionally left blank]

Donor Advised Funds

You can actually make your own Charitable Trust utilizing regular investments like stocks, ETF's, mutual funds, bonds and other investments, but you need a registered investment adviser. Instead of using the insurance company, you just use a donor advised fund to pay the charity. These are generally offered by most major brokerage firms. The nice thing about these is you can defer payments to a charity until you need the tax deduction. Things can get a little complicated when you use donor advised funds and there is the risk of bad investing, principal risk and all the other risks that are involved in investing.

Donor advised funds with most brokerage firms have pre-defined model portfolio choices. Personally, I'm not crazy about these robotic models.

These donor advised funds will have a conservative, moderate and growth type group of portfolios that you choose from depending on the size of your gift. If you want more control, (which is what I prefer) then you have to go through a registered investment adviser who can manage pretty much anything you want inside the donor advised fund. If you put a lot of money into a donor advised fund, you can even buy hedge funds, make investments in venture capital and real estate. Of course, all the risk that goes with those investments applies.

A donor advised fund might work for some, generally wealthier people, but I think it would be a whole lot less headache just going with a Charitable Trust with a fixed indexed annuity for the average Joe. Especially, if you are only talking about giving the charity a couple of hundred thousand or less. The fixed indexed annuity is one investment without any investment management headaches and it is guaranteed not to lose money by the insurance company. If on the other hand, you are talking about giving millions, then setting up your own charitable trusts with an attorney and hiring a registered investment advisor (not Wally) might be a better alternative.

The thing to keep in mind is that charitable trusts are irrevocable and they are set in stone. Also, if you can maintain some kind of control, like the ability to change charities, then this is a good thing. Further, be careful what you commit to as far as a charity is concerned. A lot of them want you to commit to a firm amount so they can start spending the money on their new project. You do not want to find yourself in a situation where you cannot meet a previously agreed upon commitment. That would be a little embarrassing. You know how people talk.

If you can afford it, then being a philanthropist might be a good thing. Be smart about it and use an Estate Planning attorney to help you plan a charitable gifting strategy. Wally, on the other hand, will tell you that you do not need an Estate Planning attorney and instead, he will tell you to buy his Variable Annuity.

Intentionally Defective Grantor Trust

That is a mouthful to say. This is another use for an irrevocable trust. Okay, we know from my earlier chapter that a grantor is the one donating to the trust. That part is easy to understand. However, the intentionally defective part is a little more of a challenge. The abbreviation for this type of irrevocable trust is IDGT, so I will refer to it in this manner going forward.

The IDGT is where a grantor has some assets that they want to leave to family members. These assets are generally growing pretty steadily. The grantor usually has a significant estate tax problem. If the grantor were to wait until he died to give away the assets, then these assets would just continue to grow and compound their estate tax problem. By utilizing the IDGT, the grantor can effectively freeze a portion of his assets from growing. The grantor sets up the IDGT and gifts the assets for each of the beneficiaries into this IDGT. Assuming the grantor has three adult children and eight grandchildren, the grantor could gift up to $5,430,000 and use up all of their exclusion in one lick. Instead of using their lifetime exclusion amount when they die, they use it while they are living. They just have to file a gift tax return to let the IRS know that they are using it and have gifted it to an IDGT. Did you know about this? That's what I thought.

In addition, this effectively removes from the grantor's estate $5,430,000, thus saving them from future taxes on the growth. Further, because the IDGT is a grantor trust, the grantor would pay the income taxes due on any interest, dividends or capital gains on the investments in the IDGT. This acts as another gift in that the IDGT does not have to sell anything to pay taxes. The grantor pays all the taxes.

On top of the $5,430,000 one-time gift, the husband and wife can each give $14,000 per beneficiary to the IDGT. That is another $28,000 per year for all eleven beneficiaries which is $308,000 total each year. As a result, the grantor can get their estate downsized fairly quickly, thus saving substantial estate taxes in the process.

The IDGT accomplishes the main goal of reducing the grantor's estate for estate tax purposes. In addition, it allows the assets to continue to grow for the benefit of the family beneficiaries without any taxation to the IDGT. This is a pretty sweet trust for the benefit of both the grantor and their trust beneficiaries. The thing is however that you cannot use one of those online legal document companies to set this up. You actually need to hire an Estate Planning attorney. Imagine that.

Once again, here is another example of how an Estate Planning attorney can literally save you hundreds of thousands, if not millions in estate taxes. Trust me. These Estate Planning attorneys are worth every penny.

Not So Fast Kemosabe

An important point to remember with trusts in general is that trusts are the only entity that allows either the trust to pay the taxes, or the beneficiary to pay the taxes. Typically, if the trust generates income, then it is subject to trust tax rates. In case you do not know, trust tax rates get up to 39.6% fairly quickly. Once you exceed $12,300 in income, then everything over and above that is taxed at 39.6%. Yikes! This is why in most cases the trust distributes the income generated by the trust to the beneficiary, so the beneficiary can pay the taxes at their presumably lower tax bracket.

Normally, when someone is a beneficiary of a trust and the grantor has passed away, then the beneficiary takes the money out of the trust. After all, they just inherited it, so they feel the need to get the money in their hands as quickly as possible. The question becomes however, is this the best strategy? Maybe. Maybe not.

Normally, it depends on the terms of the trust that was drafted by the Estate Planning attorney. If there is a clause in the trust document that allows the beneficiary to leave their share in the trust, then it might be a very smart thing to do.

There are a few reasons why this could be a smart thing to do. One reason is if there are any issues such as a potential divorce. Another reason is for protection against potential lawsuits. A third is business succession.

Let's look at an example where the grantor (a father) passed away, but left his beneficiary (his son) $1,000,000. Suppose the beneficiary was recently in a car wreck and is being sued by the other driver for damages over and above their insurance policy limits. Well, if that was the case, then if the beneficiary takes the money out of the trust he just inherited, he would lose any creditor protections. If he lost the lawsuit, then those inherited assets could get taken away as a result. Therefore, it might be foolish to be in a hurry to yank the money out of the trust.

Another reason why it might be a good idea to leave the assets in the trust is in case of marital problems. If the beneficiary is currently going through a divorce or contemplating a divorce and they took the assets out of the trust, then those assets would have to be split with the divorced spouse. However, if he left them in trust, then they are protected. The spouse has no rights to them.

The grantor is the one who created the trust in the first place and chose the beneficiary, the contingent beneficiaries, future beneficiaries and the trustee. The trust is irrevocable and cannot be changed. The beneficiary didn't put the money into the trust. The grantor did. The beneficiary did not choose the trustee and has no control over the trustee. In a creditor attack, the beneficiary cannot order the trustee to do anything, much less pay out any money assuming it was properly drafted.

If the irrevocable trust _was not_ drafted with the proper language and instead orders the trustee to pay out the proceeds of the trust at the grantors death, then that would be where the divorcing spouse could get their hands on the money. However, a smart Estate Planning attorney knows how to properly draft the irrevocable trust to protect against such a scenario from happening. I am telling you these guys are worth every penny.

Estate Planning attorneys know how to protect the beneficiary at all costs. They put language in the trust document that allows the trustee to refuse to distribute any income or principal to the beneficiary in the case of a creditor attack. In addition, some Estate Planning attorneys build into their irrevocable trust documents language for a _trust protector_. The trust protector is the one who protects the beneficiary from fiduciary breaches by the trustee. Let's face it. When you are talking about millions of dollars in a trust, trustees, especially the Wally Streets who work for a bank, may bill the crap out of a trust in order to generate fees. The trust protector keeps on eye on Wally Street, the trustee or trust officer and makes sure there is no hanky-panky going on. The trust protector can fire or replace the trustee. You may trust Wally, but I don't.

You also need to watch out for the proper language in the irrevocable trust document in regard to the trust protector. You do not want the trust protector to be allowed to fire the trustee, then substitute themselves as the new trustee. Estate Planning attorneys know how to protect against this issue. However, having a trust protector is a good thing in general. I know an attorney here in town who acts as an independent trust protector for grantors of irrevocable trusts. He keeps an eye on things for the grantors and their beneficiaries. Granted there is an added fee, but in my mind it is worth every penny. Especially when you are dealing with Wally Street, the trust officer.

Here is another interesting point. Once the trust is created and funded, then the beneficiary can actually sell his business assets to it for further creditor protections and for business succession purposes. The business succession opportunity can be very appealing to a beneficiary of an irrevocable trust properly drafted.

For example, suppose the beneficiary owns a business and they want to help their children to buy the business. Ordinarily, they might do some type of outright sale where the business borrows the money. As an alternative, perhaps they use a Limited Liability Company where they gift a certain number of LLC units each year to their children. With this strategy, they may take a discount on the value of the business, because of the lack of marketability of those LLC units. The IRS routinely challenges this arrangement, because people are advised to take large discounts. Perhaps, this might not be the way to go as far as business succession planning is concerned.

This gifting of LLC units and taking valuation discounts due to a lack of marketability is a typical way of transferring a family business to adult children. However, although there is some protection against a creditor attack due to the use of the LLC itself, it is not totally foolproof. The LLC protects other assets owned by the business owner personally, but not the LLC itself from a creditor attack.

What if you could protect the business, too?

If the business owner was also the one who inherited the $1,000,000 that I described earlier, then the irrevocable trust can be used by the business owner for business succession purposes. The business owner (beneficiary) can sell his business to the irrevocable trust for fair market value and not have to pay any income taxes in doing so. It is only if the business was sold to the irrevocable trust for less than fair market value, then that is when income taxes would become due.

So, imagine the scenario where you have an irrevocable trust created by a grantor who leaves $1,000,000 to the son, his only beneficiary and his two grandchildren as contingent beneficiaries. The son owns a business worth $2,000,000 that he wants his children (the contingent beneficiaries) to own. The son does a sale at fair market value to the irrevocable trust for the benefit of the contingent beneficiaries (his two children.) The irrevocable trust in turns pays the son via an installment sale for a term of years which in effect is his retirement income stream.

The irrevocable trust now owns the business which the contingent beneficiaries will inherit when the son passes away. The major point being that there was no discounting of LLC units or gifting of LLC units necessary when the irrevocable trust was used in this scenario. As

[194]

contingent beneficiaries, they will inherit their trust share when their dad, the grantor's beneficiary passes away. In the meantime, the business runs as usual. Discounting LLC units becomes totally unnecessary, because the business was sold at fair market value to the trust.

It depends on how you structure the sale, but you could structure the sale of the business to be a self-canceling installment note where when the son passes away, then the payment for the business ceases. At that point, the contingent beneficiaries would inherit the business and owe nothing more. If the son lives the full term of the installment note, then the son would receive the full payment for their business plus interest. If the contingent beneficiaries leave the business in the irrevocable trust, then they too would have the similar creditor protections that were afforded their dad, the beneficiary and son of the grantor. With proper drafting by the Estate Planning attorney, the trust language would allow the addition of future beneficiaries which would be the children of the contingent beneficiaries.

In effect, what you are doing is creating your own version of a dynasty trust. However, the major points are that you have creditor protection from future divorces or lawsuits for all the beneficiaries and contingent beneficiaries built right into the original irrevocable trust document.

Now there are some other issues involved with this scenario and I have only scratched the surface, believe me. The points that I wanted to make in this chapter are that the grantor makes a gift to the irrevocable trust to reduce their estate taxes. The beneficiary can keep the assets in the trust for creditor protection, plus estate tax protection. You see, if the beneficiary were to yank out the money, then the size of their estate would go up by $1,000,000, in my example. However, if they left the money in the irrevocable trust, then it is outside of their estate, because it was never actually paid to the beneficiary. Therefore, they do not own those assets. The trust proceeds are now intended for the contingent beneficiaries. Do you follow me Kemosabe?

In addition, the contingent beneficiaries have found a solution for how to buy the business from dad. The $1,000,000 that dad inherited originally in the trust can be used to pay dad his installments for the sale of the business. No cash flow has to be taken out of the business itself to pay dad until the $1,000,000 is depleted. By the way, isn't that better for the business from a cash flow perspective?

How are the contingent beneficiaries going to be able to pay dad for the business outside of the trust? It would have to be a loan, cash flow from the business or by discounting and gifting LLC units annually. I would suspect that it would not be near as easy if the business was sold by dad to the irrevocable trust instead.

Every situation is different and has its own complexities, but I would venture to say that if you own a business, that you had no idea about this strategy. When you add the cherry on top with the creditor protections, estate tax savings, business succession opportunity and retirement income stream generation for the sale of the business, then this makes for a smart Estate Planning idea. All you need is a grantor to fund an irrevocable trust with as little as $5,000 and name beneficiaries and contingent beneficiaries who may have business succession issues. Of course, a good Estate Planning attorney would help, too.

Did Wally tell you about this? Forgive me. For a second there I actually thought that Wally Street might actually know how to do something that benefits you and not him. Sorry, my mistake. What was I thinking?

Alas, I am just a peon that everyone thinks is just like every other Wally Street. Hopefully, I am making some headway proving otherwise. Stay with me. I will turn your train around eventually.

Qualified Personal Residence Trust

Now that you understand what an Intentionally Defective Grantor Trust is, then you will easily understand what a Qualified Personal Residence Trust (QPRT) is also. They both are a little bit similar with the exception that the QPRT uses a primary residence instead of cash and securities like the IDGT.

Enter the life estate. What on earth does that mean? Well, it means that you have the right to enjoy and live in your primary residence rent free for the life expectancy term of your life. You contribute the principal to the QPRT, which in this case is the primary residence. When you contribute the primary residence, you have made a gift of the fair market value of the house. In addition, the grantor retains an interest in the house, the life estate value of the life expectancy.

How do you value the life estate? Well, it is based on your age, your life expectancy, IRC Section 7520 and some weird factors that the IRS makes you use. You might be thinking, "Oh, no. I have to know about Internal Revenue Code 7520!" Do not panic. You will not have to figure it out. Your CPA will do it for you.

In a nutshell, if you had a 10 year life expectancy and the house you put in the QPRT was valued at $425,000, then based on an estimated calculation, the value of the retained interest would be roughly $176,000. You file a gift tax return for a completed gift in this case which is $249,000 ($425,000 - $176,000). This in effect removes $425,000 from your estate for estate tax purposes plus the future appreciation of the property, _if you live more than 10 years_. At 5% real estate growth on this $425,000, then this would grow to roughly $692,000 at the end of 10 years. That real estate growth would be removed from your estate entirely.

Keep in mind however that you are probably not going to make 5% growth on that house. It might be closer to 1 – 2%. There is always hope I suppose.

By the way, you can use part of your gift tax exemption and not pay the gift tax on that $249,000 gift to the QPRT. Also, you are removing $425,000 from your estate at a cost of using $249,000 of your gift tax exemption which means it costs you nothing in effect.

You live rent free during the term of the QPRT which is 10 years in my example. However, if you outlive the QPRT, then you have to pay fair market value rent. That may seem like a bad thing, but whatever you pay in rent reduces your estate tax problem further.

If you are married, then you can have your spouse also have a right to live in the house for the term of the QPRT, or setup two QPRT's. If they predecease you (the grantor), then the house passes directly to the surviving spouse at that point. The survivor may have to pay 50% of the fair market value rent if one spouse dies early.

If you are single and die before the 10 years is up, then the residence reverts to your estate as if the transaction never happened. As a consequence, you do not want to have a QPRT for a 10 year period if your health is not good. It is all kind of a waste of time if you die before you reach your normal IRS life expectancy. Also, if the house is not expected to grow in value, then it might not make any sense. Generally, this is used when you have a highly appreciating personal residence and a big estate tax problem, too.

Once the grantor gives the property to the QPRT, then you can kiss it goodbye. You cannot buy it back. However, you can pay rent at the end of the term and continue living in it.

If the beneficiaries sell the property before your death, then they lose any stepped up basis in the property. This is generally not a good idea. Once the 10 years passes, then they own it.

If there is a mortgage on the property, then it kind of complicates things. It is better if there is not any mortgage.

Some Estate Planning attorneys recommend one QPRT be setup for married couples with partial interests in the personal residence. Other attorneys recommend a separate QPRT for each spouse for their share where they leave the personal residence to each other, if one were to die. There are a myriad of ways to structure a QPRT or multiple QPRT's. Estate Planning attorneys are the ones that know best how to figure it all out. You cannot do this strategy on your own.

QPRT's are not something that I can tell you whether it is appropriate for you unless I know your exact situation. Even then, I would defer to the experts. An Estate Planning attorney can tell you for sure whether it is appropriate in your situation.

The online legal documents place cannot help you with this one. Sorry.

[This page intentionally left blank]

GRAT's

My thanks to Alliance Bernstein for this information. Remember how I described the Charitable Remainder Annuity Trusts previously? Well the GRAT's work exactly the same way, except there is no charity.

The GRAT is a grantor retained annuity trust, similar to the charitable remainder annuity trust. The exception is the grantor receives the income and the beneficiaries get the principal, instead of the charity. Also, with GRAT's you have to have all those pesky IRS calculations, too. In this case, you have to figure the present value of those grantor income payments for the term of the GRAT. Yikes! Again, that is what CPA's are trained to do.

With a GRAT, you can use an annuity as the funding vehicle, or you can use stocks or ETF's that invest in stocks. What you are trying to do is grow your assets. If you use a fixed annuity paying 2%, then you have no opportunity to grow your assets. However, if you use stocks or ETF's that invest in stocks, then you do have a much greater opportunity to grow your assets. When you grow the assets inside the GRAT, then you have effectively removed that growth from your estate. "I see" said the blind man.

If you did not have the GRAT and you were invested in stocks and ETF's that invested in stocks, then your estate tax problem is just going to compound. Do you really want to grow your assets so you can give Uncle Sam more money? I hope not. With the GRAT technique, you may be able to shelter significant future asset growth from estate taxes.

Like I mentioned above, advanced estate planners, recommend two year rolling GRAT's. By the way, that would not mean your online legal documents firm.

If you will recall that if the grantor does not survive the length of the term, then it is all kind of a waste of time. However, advanced estate planners, that would be smart attorneys by the way, use rolling 2 year GRAT's to remove assets from your estate. The thinking here is that most people can survive a 2 year term. If you do survive the term, then you start a new 2 year GRAT and do it again with another pool of assets.

Instead of doing a 10 year GRAT that you may not outlive, you do a series of two year GRAT's with mainly stocks and shelter estate assets from estate taxes that way. You do not know in advance which stocks will perform the best, so you split them up into separate GRAT's.

Depending on if you clear the IRS Section 7520 rate when you reach the end of the 2 year term, then you are home free with the growth of the stocks that cleared that hurdle. You roll it again with another pool of stocks for another 2 years, or if you didn't clear the Section 7520 rate, then you can use the same stocks that were in the first 2 year GRAT. What happens is you are being paid the money from the GRAT over two years and the amount that exceeds the Section 7520 hurdle is removed from your estate.

If you do not clear the Section 7520 hurdle rate, then you are no worse off. If you have investment success, then you are growing the assets that clear the Section 7520 rate outside of your taxable estate and leaving more money for your family. Isn't that what you wanted to do in the first place? Or, were you growing your estate to give it to those idiots in Washington, D.C. to spend? I hope not.

GRAT's are of course more appropriate for people who have a big estate tax problem. In other words, these are people who do not want to make more money just to give it to the government. Those people in government are not very good with other taxpayer's money. They spend it like they just won the lottery. The bastards.

[202]

GRIT's

A GRIT is a grantor retained income trust. It works just like a GRAT with one major exception. The family members of the grantor cannot be the beneficiaries of it. What? That's right. The family members cannot be the beneficiaries of it.

Well, who in the heck would want to do that? Pretty much nobody, except maybe someone who has no family members, but still has an estate tax problem and doesn't want to make more money just to give it to the government. Maybe they have a girlfriend or boyfriend, but do not want to get married and are okay with leaving them some money while at the same time reducing their taxable estate. If that is the case, then perhaps a GRIT might work for them.

I wanted you to know what a GRIT was in comparison to a GRAT and tell you why you probably may never need a GRIT. Now you know.

I could actually go crazy with these trust initials. There are CRUT's, NIMCRUT's, GRUT's and a whole lot more that I could tell you about. However, I do not want to bore you. These types of trusts generally do not apply to most people, unless you are richer than Jed Clampett. Therefore, I am leaving them out of this book. Nevertheless, if you just have to know, then feel free to contact me.

Chapter Summary

What did we learn in this chapter?

- We learned about Living or Revocable Trusts, pour-over-wills, health care powers of attorneys and durable powers of attorney.
- We learned not to be fearful of the word "irrevocable" in Irrevocable Trusts.
- We found out how to protect assets using multiple Irrevocable Trusts from lawsuits.
- We found out that Wills create Testamentary Trusts generally for spendthrift or disabled beneficiaries.
- We found out a simple way of reducing potential estate taxes at the surviving spouse's death is by utilizing Bypass & Q-TIP Trusts.
- We saw how second-to-die life insurance can help solve a potential estate tax problem down the road.
- When we think of Dynasty Trusts, then we will think of the Rockefeller family.
- We learned the differences between a Charitable Lead Trust and Charitable Remainder Annuity Trust.
- We learned about Donor Advised Funds.
- We learned how an Intentionally Defective Grantor Trust can be utilized to remove assets intended for beneficiaries from the grantor's estate and effectively freeze those assets from further growth in the grantor's estate.
- We found out if we inherit money via an irrevocable trust, then we might be able to use it for creditor protection, estate tax reduction and business succession by leaving the money in the trust.
- We learned about a Life Estate and how it relates to a Qualified Personal Residence Trust.

- We learned about rolling 2 year short-term GRAT's and how we might be able to freeze estate assets and let them grow outside our estate.
- We decided we only like grits when they are on our plate, not when they are an acronym for a Grantor Retained Income Trust which is not good for our family beneficiaries.

Notes

Chapter Thirteen

Beneficiary Designations

"There is nothing more difficult to take in hand, more perilous to conduct, or more uncertain in its success, than to take the lead in the introduction of a new order of things."

~ Niccolo Machiavelli

[This page intentionally left blank]

Beneficiary Designations

While we are on the subject of Estate Planning, I thought it would be a good idea to tell a story about why periodically reviewing beneficiary designations is important.

When I was the Branch Manager II for Charles Schwab & Co. Inc., I had a lady who came in to the branch office because her husband had passed away. The lady wanted to complete the required paperwork to treat her husband's IRA as her own, so she could stretch it out over her life expectancy. This is a common strategy among husbands and wives when one passes away with an IRA.

Upon further review, I went to the video replay and pulled up a copy of the original form that had the beneficiaries on it. I cannot let her have the money, you know, if she was not the beneficiary. What I discovered was that the beneficiary was actually a living trust. It was not her at all.

She had to go home and get her trust, then make another appointment to come back and see me. When she came back, I read over the trust. Again, some people may find this hard to believe, but I can read trusts and interpret what they mean, too. I've seen a million of these things. More importantly, I can spot the mistakes in drafting the trust. On a side note, most of the mistakes are made because the trust documents are never reviewed periodically, or bought online without an attorney.

Anyway, in this living trust, it said she got a third and her two kids got a third each. By the way, her two kids were minors. My avid pupil should be thinking to themselves, "Uh-oh. That means guardianships have to be set up." That's right. You are getting so smart by reading my book!

The IRS says that in order for the spouse to treat an IRA as her own, then the trust must be a "see-through" trust. This means that it must be like the trust did not even exist. More precisely, it means that if you use a living trust as a beneficiary of an IRA, then the living trust should name your spouse as _the only primary beneficiary_. Unfortunately, if it is not a "see-through" trust, then it all has to be liquidated within five years.

So, here was this poor lady who just lost her husband. She thought she could treat the IRA as her own. Come to find out, she could not. In addition, she had minor children, so my astute pupil would know that guardianship accounts had to be setup for her two minor children. She had to go hire an attorney and get herself named as guardians for her own kids, mind you. They could not roll their share into an IRA either. Who knows what setting up those guardianships cost? Plus, add in the fact that she was going to have to pay taxes on the entire IRA within the next five years.

Everything that comes out of an IRA is taxed as ordinary income rates. This mean 100% of her husband's IRA was going to be taxed by the end of five years, like it or not. The only thing she could do was spread it out over five years to minimize the damage.

Yes, my friends. This was all the result of a husband who went online to a legal document company to save money by creating his own living trust, without an Estate Planning attorney, I might add. Do you think his wife was initially okay with him creating his own living trust? Probably so, because he justified it by saying, "I am not paying no stinking attorney fifteen hundred dollars when I can do it online for less." She went along with him without giving it a second thought. She had no idea that all of this mess could happen to her.

Ladies, this is why you do not want to let your idiot and cheap ass husband prepare his own legal documents. My dad had a saying for guys like this, "He is so tight you can't drive a nail up his ass with a ballpein hammer." Sorry for the crude quip, but my dad could be a little edgy sometimes with his quips.

This "smart" guy made a very costly mistake. He wanted to save a few hundred dollars, but in the end, it cost his wife and kids thousands of dollars in unnecessary taxes, legal fees (with real attorneys) and court costs. It all could have been avoided by going to see an Estate Planning attorney.

My fine lady friends, please pay attention to me. If you see or hear your idiot and tightwad for a husband talking about doing his own will or trust online, then knock him in the stinking head with a fly swatter or something. I do not care how old you are either. Make him go see an Estate Planning attorney instead and you had better go with him. Okay? Thank you very much. No telling how much money and headaches that I just saved you by telling you this. You can thank me later.

Chapter Summary

What did we learn in this chapter?

- Beneficiary designations are very important especially when it comes to trusts as beneficiaries of IRA's.
- We learned what a "see-through trust" is and why it is important anytime that a trust is the primary or contingent beneficiary of an IRA, Roth IRA or any other retirement account.
- We learned how using an online legal document preparer can be a very stupid thing to do. Very stupid indeed.
- We learned that paying for an estate plan with an Estate Planning attorney can be worth its weight in gold.

Chapter Fourteen

RMD's & Inherited IRA's

"Nobody who ever gave his best regretted it."

~ George Halas

[This page intentionally left blank]

RMD's

RMD's stand for required minimum distributions. At age 70 ½, if you have a balance in any type of IRA or 401(k), then you have to start pulling money out of it. There is a standard table that says you have to divide your account by a specific number each year. The account balance is the December 31st balance from the prior year.

This is very, very important, so please pay attention. The first time that you have to pull money out of your IRA after you turn 70 ½, you must do so by _April 1st_ of the following year in which you turned 70 ½. It is not April 15th. It is April 1st. This causes a lot of confusion. The penalty for not pulling out the money on time is 50% of what should have been pulled out. Fifty-percent! So, do not make this easy little mistake.

Once you get past this first year, then you have until December 31st of the following year to pull out your RMD's. Just so you are not confused, here is how it would work. You are turning 72 this year and you calculate the December 31st balance from the prior year. After you know that amount and take the RMD factor to it, then you must take that RMD by December 31st of the year in which you turned 72. So, there are two December 31st's in the mix. One is to determine the prior year's value. The other is the deadline for taking the RMD. You see? Good.

What if you get to age 70 ½ and you do not really need the money from the RMD's? Assuming you are healthy, you can take the RMD's and buy a life insurance policy to leave to your family. You simply take the RMD's and pay the life insurance premiums each year. Whatever your RMD's amount to, then you just buy a cash value life insurance policy with those funds. The software from the insurance company will calculate the death benefit based on your RMD withdrawal schedule.

You are going to have to pull out these RMD's every year anyway and you said you didn't need the money, right? Well then, by purchasing cash value life insurance with the RMD's, then you can leverage up the amount of money that you leave to your heirs. Life insurance death benefits are tax-free to your beneficiaries.

This is a good strategy that is not used enough, believe me. Oh, by the way, I can help you with this strategy, too.

Inherited IRA's

Now that we are discussing RMD's and taking money out, I wanted to shift gears a little bit and talk about Inherited IRA's. There are a bunch of IRS rules around Inherited IRA's that are important to know about. I think this is best told with a story.

When I was the Branch Manager II for Charles Schwab & Co., Inc., I had a couple of brothers come in to talk about their dad's IRA account. They were both the named beneficiaries at 50% each. They wanted to setup a couple of Inherited IRA's. The only problem was that their dad had died eight years ago.

Why is this a problem? Well, for one thing, they had to setup Inherited IRA's for their share of their dad's IRA by December 31st of the year following their dad's death. That was eight years ago, so they missed that boat.

The second thing was the fact that if you do not comply with that December 31st date in the year following death, then you are mandated to take the entire account out within 5 years. Uh oh, it has been eight years already, so they missed that boat, too.

I had to ask them why they had not come in before today. They said, "We are doing well financially and we didn't really need the money all that bad." That is a good thing I thought to myself, because they were not going to get much of their dad's IRA now. Wally must have been too busy to help.

Their penalty for missing the boat, or shall I say boats, was 50% of the entire IRA account. Good thing they were well off financially, because they were not getting much of their dad's IRA. Plus, they had to pay taxes on the whole thing. By the way, their account was not with Schwab. It was with Wally's firm.

If something like this happens to you, you may be able to request a waiver from the IRS on form 5329 which is attached to your 1040 tax return. Notice that I didn't say 1040-A or 1040 EZ? You have to file a 1040 and attach the 5329 form along with it.

The problem for these two brothers was that the five year window had already passed. They did not get a waiver from the IRS in their case. They lost 50% of their dad's IRA to penalties and they had to pay the full tax on the whole IRA. That would be immediately for those of you who are unsure.

Generally, you use the 5329 form when you let that first year go by and you want the IRS to give you a waiver so you can treat the Inherited IRA as your own and pull out RMD's each year based on your age. The IRS will generally be nice about it in these situations, but not if you wait eight years.

There is a tricky little calculation when it comes to Inherited IRA's that you need to know about. The amount you pull out depends on whether your parent died before age 70 ½ or after age 70 ½. I know what you are thinking. "Why does everything have to be so damn complicated?"

If your parent was under 70 ½, then you have three choices. You can take a lump sum. You can setup an Inherited IRA and take the money out over five years. Or, you can setup an Inherited IRA and spread the distributions over your lifetime. The tricky little calculation that I am talking about only applies to this last option.

Here is another factor to make it more complicated. If there were two brothers that were beneficiaries of their dad's IRA, then they would have to setup two separate Inherited IRA's by December 31st of the year following death. If they do not, then the tricky little calculation is based on the oldest beneficiary.

Where that tricky little calculation would be a problem is when mom and an adult child are named as primary beneficiaries of dad's IRA. If mom and the adult child do not know that they have to setup separate Inherited IRA's by the end of the calendar year following dad's death, or fail to do it on time, then the RMD is calculated based on the oldest beneficiary. In this example, that would be mom. As a result, the adult child would have to pull out a lot higher RMD amount than they should have. If only they knew this tricky little rule. I wonder why Wally didn't tell them. Oh, I forgot. Wally does not like to talk about details that get in the way of his sales.

The other tricky part of the calculation is that it is not like a regular RMD. For example, with mom and an adult child as the primary beneficiary, if you miss the December 31st boat after the year of death, then you have to use mom's factor number. We will gloss over the fact that we are going to have to apply for a waiver now to be able to use the life expectancy option. We will also gloss over the fact that your friend Wally Street didn't help you out.

Assume mom is 65 years old. Her factor number is 21. Sadly, the adult child's factor number is also 21, if they failed to setup separate Inherited IRA's by the end of the calendar year following dad's death. Somehow, good old Wally Street let this slip through the cracks.

Consequentially, you figure the value of the IRA on December 31st of the year that dad died. Let's say dad had $200,000 on that day. Mom and her adult child split dad's IRA 50/50. So, you take $200,000 and split it in two for calculation purposes. Then, you take the remaining $100,000 and divide it by 21. The end result is the RMD amount which is $4,761.91. So, each of them has to pull that amount out of the Inherited IRA.

Assume the adult child was 48 years old. Ordinarily, if this was done properly and separate Inherited IRA's were indeed established on time, then the adult child's RMD would be based on the factor 36. The correct RMD should have been $100,000 divided by 36 which equals $2,777.78. This smaller RMD is about half of what he had to take out as opposed to Wally dropping the ball on everything. This would have allowed his share of dad's IRA to last a lot longer.

Oh, don't think for a minute that I am finished with the tricky little calculation. When you inherit an IRA, that factor is reduced by one each year thereafter for non-spouse beneficiaries. In other words, if the adult child's factor was 36 in the first year, then in the second year it is 35. The third year it will be 34 and so on. You reduce it by one each year from that initial first year factor. This is for non-spouse beneficiaries.

If your parent was already taking his RMD's when they died, then you have to make sure that you pull out the RMD in the year of death. Not the year after death, but the year of death.

If your parent was in fact older than 70 ½ when they died and only named their spouse as the primary beneficiary and no one else, then the surviving spouse can treat the IRA as her own and open a Spousal IRA or transfer it into their own IRA, or transfer it into an Inherited IRA. However, if anyone else is a beneficiary with the spouse, then you cannot do this at all. Don't blame me. I didn't make this stinking rule.

Of course, you can always take a lump sum. Further, the spouse only beneficiary can open an Inherited IRA instead of rolling it over into her own IRA. Why would you want to do this? In case the surviving spouse is several years older than the deceased spouse, then they could use the deceased spouse's life expectancy factor for her RMD's. In other words, if mom survives dad and mom is 80 years old and dad was only 75 when he died, then mom can use dad's longer life expectancy factor and spread out the taxes due over dad's life expectancy by setting up an Inherited IRA. I doubt Wally told you about this either.

If dad died and there are multiple beneficiaries, then you need to do the Inherited IRA thing for sure. Keep in mind that they need to be setup and opened by December 31st of the year following dad's death. If you do not open separate Inherited IRA accounts for the multiple beneficiaries, then you have that oldest beneficiary thing kick in again.

What you might want to consider is, instead of having one IRA with two beneficiaries, as an alternative, you may want two IRA accounts. Put mom's share in one and the adult child's share in the other one. This way you eliminate that oldest beneficiary issue altogether.

Another thing that you may want to be somewhat prepared for is our fine Senators are up to no good. They have a bill that has already passed the Senate to make anyone who inherits an IRA take all of the money out within five (5) years. You see how this idiots in Washington, D.C. think? They are always after your money. They know that spreading out Inherited IRA money over a lifetime delays them the possibility of getting their greedy little hands on it. So, these bandits are hard at work trying to sneak one by the voters. Hopefully, the House of Representatives will not let it go any further. We will see how this all works out one way or another. Let's hope it works in our favor, but I have my doubts.

The thing to remember in regard to inheriting IRA money is that that are lot of tricky little rules and calculations involved. Leaving it to Wally Street to figure out might not be a good idea.

[This page intentionally left blank]

Disclaiming an IRA Share

Sometimes, for whatever reason, a beneficiary may want to disclaim their share of an IRA. This can be done, but it must be done by September 30th of the year following death. I know what you are thinking. "This is all very confusing." Don't blame me. I did not make these stupid rules. This September 30th date is the date the IRS looks and asks, "Who are the beneficiaries entitled to this IRA?"

Whoever the beneficiaries are on September 30th, then that is what the IRS bases its Inherited IRA rules on. If you want to disclaim your share of an IRA, then you must do so before this date. This does not mean that any distributions have to occur by this date. It only means that the beneficiaries have to be established by this date.

In order to accomplish a qualified disclaimer for the beneficiary, that beneficiary needs to send a letter to the custodian of the deceased person's IRA and inform them that they are disclaiming their rights to it. I wonder if Wally knows about this disclaimer letter requirement date. Just for fun, ask the next Wally Street that you see or meet. It will be fun watching them squirm trying to come up with an answer.

After September 30th, then the Inherited IRA's must be setup for the beneficiaries by December 31st of the year following death and their RMD's taken, if that is their choice to spread it out over their life expectancy. If they fail to take their RMD's from the Inherited IRA by December 31st of the year following death, then they miss out on any further opportunity to do so as described in my two brother's story above.

If you want to disclaim your IRA share, then you need to get the letter to the IRA custodian of the deceased person's IRA well before September

30th of the year following death. This will give the custodian time to process your request. If you send it on September 30th, then who knows what will happen. Don't leave it to Wally to take care of either.

However, you do not want to disclaim an IRA and let it go to the estate. This would be a very, very bad idea. It only makes sense to disclaim an IRA if there are real life contingent beneficiaries on the IRA account of the deceased person. Further, for the same reason, you do not want to disclaim an IRA and let it go to a trust unless the trust document has been fully reviewed for its "see-through" ability. Come again? Move to the next page and I will explain.

Trust as Beneficiary

What a minute. You mean it can get more complicated? Sad, but true.

Remember when I talked about those "see-through" trusts? Well, that factor is kind of critical when you name a trust as the beneficiary of an IRA.

Here is the easy part. If your trust *is not* a "see-through" trust, then you only have two choices. You have to take a lump sum from the IRA, or you can spread it out over five years. There is no option to spread it out over anybody's life expectancy. Period. There now. That was easy, wasn't it?

Oh, no! You mean we have to figure out that dying before 70 ½ and dying after 70 ½ thing again? Sad, but true.

Okay. Assuming that the trust *is* a "see-through" trust, and the IRA account holder died *before* turning 70 ½, then here are the options. You can take a lump sum. You can spread it out over five years. Or, you can spread it out over the life expectancy of the oldest individual beneficiary. Interesting.

If there are multiple beneficiaries in the trust, then all beneficiaries must take the distribution based on the oldest beneficiary's life expectancy. But wait there is more. Not so fast Kemosabe. I can say that because I am part Cherokee Indian. So, it is not racist for me to say it. Get off my back, will you?

Back to my story. The trust must take distributions depending on whether each of the multiple beneficiaries are a spouse or a non-spouse. Just when you think there are not any more twists and turns, damn it man. In pops another one. A spouse as beneficiary can take the distribution based on their recalculated or non-recalculated single life expectancy. Say what? What the heck does that mean?

A recalculated single life expectancy is where the spouse can look up their factor for each year as they age and recalculate their RMD. So, if a spouse was 65, then her RMD would be based on the factor 21.0. When she turned 66, then her RMD would be recalculated on the factor for a 66 year old which is 20.2. At age 67, it would go down to 19.4. You got the picture? Good.

A non-recalculated single life expectancy is where the spouse looks up their factor and just reduces it by one each year. Assuming the spouse was 65 again, then her RMD factor number is 21. At age 66, it would be reduced by one to 20. At age 67, it would be 19 and so on.

Now we arrive at the non-spouse beneficiary's calculation. They can only use a non-recalculated factor. Damn it man. Another curve ball. So, if our non-spouse beneficiary was 48, then their factor would be 36. When they turned 49, it would be reduced by one to 35. It would do the same for each year thereafter. Reduce the factor by one each year. Keep in mind this is for when you name a trust as the beneficiary of an IRA, it is a "see-through" trust and you have a non-spouse as the beneficiary.

Yes, my friend. It gets even more complicated. What if the person who had the IRA and passed away was _older_ than 70 ½ and had already taken their first RMD and named a trust as the beneficiary?

Well, we have that stinking "see-through" trust issue again and the lump sum option remains in place. However, there is no five year option. Huh? Don't ask me. I don't know what happened to it. All I know it is not around anymore.

If the spouse is the only beneficiary of the trust, then her distributions are based on her recalculated life expectancy. What about the non-recalculated option? Don't ask me what happened to the non-recalculated option. All I know is that it is not around if you have a "see-through" trust as the beneficiary, the spouse is the only beneficiary and the account holder was older than 70 ½.

Here is another stinking curve ball. What if the trust names a non-individual as a beneficiary, like a charity? You just had to do it didn't you? You just had to make things more complicated. If one of the beneficiaries is a non-individual like a charity, or a company, then the distributions are based on the single life expectancy of the original IRA account holder. But wait. There is more. It is calculated based on reducing the factor by one each year.

And, you thought that I was just another financial advisor didn't you? Trust me. You need a guy like me more than you will ever know.

[This page intentionally left blank]

Estate as Beneficiary

Yes my friend. There is even more to discuss when it comes to Inherited IRA's. Let's take a look at what happens when someone puts down as the beneficiary of their IRA, their estate. They literally write in "estate" or they leave the beneficiary form blank altogether.

You have to open an Inherited IRA that would say something like this:

Inherited IRA FBO: John Q. Public **Estate**.

At least we can dispense with all those rules revolving around trusts. However, we cannot dispense with the under 70 ½ and over 70 ½ date of death rules.

If the IRA account holder dies *before* age 70 ½ and the estate is the beneficiary, then you have two choices. The first is the lump sum and the second is the five year choice. That's it. Now, that wasn't too tough.

Okay, what about the estate as the beneficiary and the IRA account holder died *after* he turned 70 ½? You have the lump sum option, but not the five year option. Huh? I told you not to ask me these silly questions. I have no idea why these idiots and Washington, D.C. do this kind of thing. You will have to ask them. Sorry. I'm digressing again.

Now get this other option for IRA's with the estate named as beneficiary and the IRA account holder was *over* 70 ½ at the time of death. Are you ready for this one? Here you go. The distributions can be based on the IRA account holder's single life expectancy and it must be reduced by one each year. The estate is taxed on each distribution. Oh, by the way, estates are taxed at very high rates. Anything over the laughing low figure of $12,300 is taxed at $3,179.50 plus 39.6%. There is a distinct possibility that everything coming out of the IRA is going to be taxed at 39.6% pretty much. This is the stupid penalty for not naming a beneficiary of your IRA, or worse actually writing in as the beneficiary the words "estate." And you mean to tell me that Wally Street told you this was okay? That Wally guy can be kind of an idiot sometimes.

Sorry, my friend. Since you didn't name a real person as a beneficiary, then there is no option to treat the Inherited IRA distribution based on your beneficiary's life expectancy, because you did not name a beneficiary! You blew it. Or, perhaps your friend Wally blew it.

Here is some really good advice. Never sign an IRA, Roth IRA, SEP-IRA, 403(b), 401(k) or any other retirement plan application without making 100% sure that you have named your beneficiaries on the form. Whatever you do, please do not leave it blank or write in "estate" as your beneficiary. Okay? Thank you.

Now, tell me why you are so lackadaisical about our Internal Revenue Code. After reading all the above regarding the rules involving Inherited IRA's, can you stand there and tell me that you are okay with our tax code? You cannot be serious. We need a simple plan. A nice flat tax would be better, don't you think?

Chapter Summary

What did we learn in this chapter?

- We found out that when we turn 70 ½, that we have to pull out money by April 1st of the year following, not April 15th.
- We found out that our RMD's can be recalculated every year while we are alive.
- We realized that if we do not need our RMD's, then we can leverage up the money we leave to our heirs by buying a life insurance policy with those annual RMD's.
- We learned that the IRS has some very complicated rules when it comes to inheriting IRA accounts.
- We now understand that it matters whether we inherit an IRA from someone who died before age 70 ½ or after age 70 ½.
- We found out that decisions involving inheriting IRA funds have to be made fairly soon after death.
- We learned that there is a difference in spousal beneficiaries and non-spousal beneficiaries.
- We learned that we reduce our factor by one every year for non-spouse beneficiaries.
- We learned that if we have both a spousal beneficiary and a non-spousal beneficiary of an IRA and we do not setup separate Inherited IRA's by December 31st of the year following the date of death, then the RMD's will be based on the oldest beneficiary.
- We learned that if we want to disclaim our share of an IRA, then this must be done by September 30th of the year following death.
- We reiterated the importance of making sure if a trust is the beneficiary of an IRA, then it must be a "see-through trust".
- We learned that naming the estate as the beneficiary of an IRA is not smart, nor is not naming a beneficiary at all.

Notes

Chapter Fifteen

Roth IRA Strategies

"Truth is by nature self-evident. As soon as you remove the cobwebs of ignorance that surround it, it shines clear."

~ Mahatma Gandhi

[This page intentionally left blank]

Roth IRA's

I guess I better start with explaining what a Roth IRA is first. You cannot assume anything these days. Especially, with me. Every time that I assume something, then that is when I mess up. I always tell myself to never assume anything. This helps me stay out of trouble.

A Roth IRA is a tax-free, tax-deferred account that is funded with after-tax dollars. The *cost basis* is always able to be pulled out without any tax consequences and at any time.

After five years, all of the *earnings* can be pulled out without any tax consequences, with one exception. If you pull out any earnings within the first five years, and you are under 59 ½, then you are subject to a 10% early withdrawal penalty. That is a 10% early withdrawal penalty on the earnings portion. In addition, you would have to pay taxes on that earnings portion, too. Also, it doesn't matter if you have held the Roth IRA for more than five years, if you are under 59 ½ when you make this distribution. The 10% penalty and taxes due still applies.

Even if you are over 59 ½, you still have to wait the five years to take money out of the Roth IRA penalty free. The five year clock starts when you open and make the first contribution. You still would owe taxes on the earnings and the 10% penalty if you pull money out in the first five years.

There are a couple of things to consider in regard to Roth IRA's. One is that you probably want to open a Roth at the very latest by age 54 ½ if you have not done so already. This way, when your five years is up, you will already be 59 ½.

The other thing to consider is to just open the account with a hundred dollars if nothing else. Get the five year, first contribution requirement out of the way. You can add all you want to this Roth IRA later. You will have satisfied the funding requirement with that one hundred dollar initial contribution. This five year clock thing only works for Contributory Roth IRA's, not Roth Conversion accounts. More on this in a bit.

For 2015, if you are under age 50, then you can contribute $5,500 to a Roth IRA. If you are over age 50, then you can contribute up to $6,500 into a Roth IRA. However, you must have earned income of at least of $5,500 or $6,500 in order to make those maximum contributions.

In order to make the Roth IRA contributions, your adjusted gross income must be under $183,000 for 2015, if married and filing jointly, or $116,000 if you are single, married filing separately or head of household. If your adjusted gross income is over these amounts, then it depends on how much over it is. If it is just a little bit over, then you still may be able to do a partial contribution. If it is a lot over, then you cannot do a contribution at all.

Here is an important point regarding Traditional IRA's and being covered by a retirement plan at work. If you are covered by a retirement plan at work at any time during the year, and you are the one making the contribution to an IRA, then you are further restricted. If you are married filing jointly, then your AGI limits drop down to $98,000. If single, it dips down to $61,000. This is for when you or a spouse has a retirement plan at work (i.e., 401(k)) and are the one contributing to an IRA, too.

If you are married to a spouse with a retirement plan at work, but you do not have a retirement plan at your job and you want to contribute to an IRA or Roth IRA for that matter, then your AGI limits are the normal

AGI limits. That is they are $183,000 if married filing jointly and $116,000 if single.

The bottom line on contributions is that you are more limited in how much you can contribute to *an IRA*, (not a Roth IRA) if you have a retirement plan at your job and you are the one contributing to the IRA.

However, if you personally do not have a retirement plan at work, then you can contribute to *an IRA* up to the higher AGI limit maximums. Got it? Good.

Important difference in regard to Roth IRA's. <u>It does not matter if you have a retirement plan at work for either you or your spouse</u>. You can contribute up to the $183,000 AGI limit, if married filing jointly or $116,000 AGI limit, if single.

We will discuss Roth Conversions next.

[This page intentionally left blank]

Roth Conversions

Now, a Roth Conversion is a little bit different. This is where you take money out of your Traditional IRA account and "convert" it to a Roth IRA Conversion Account. This is very important:

Do not do a Roth Conversion and add the money to an existing Roth IRA account that you already own.

The reason you do not want to commingle a Roth Conversion with a regular Roth IRA account is because, *you may want to* recharacterize the conversion amount later and put the money back into to your Traditional IRA. More on this later.

The rules around Roth Conversions say that the converted amount must stay in the Roth Conversion account for at least five years, before you can take any tax-free withdrawals. However, if you take a withdrawal from a Roth Conversion account within the five year period, then the *whole account* is subject to a 10% penalty. Luckily, there is an exception to this rule. If you are 59 ½ or older, then you would not be subject to the whole account 10% penalty. Leave it to the government to penalize the people who need the money the most. The younger people.

The government recently removed the income limitation on Roth Conversions. Anyone can do a Roth Conversion. After all, the IRS is getting the taxes for 100% of the amount converted, so why should they object? You see how these people in Washington, D.C. think? They are always trying to get more money out of you.

An important point to remember is that since you are paying taxes on the IRA and turning it into a Roth Conversion, then that amount is considered *all cost basis*. However, you have to wait those five years for each amount converted to get to the earnings portion of a Roth Conversion. Otherwise, you might be subject to a penalty of 10%, if you are under age 59 ½, unless, you use the money for one of the withdrawal exceptions (see next section) allowed by the IRS. If you are older than 59 ½, then there is no 10% penalty.

Another little used technique to get money into a Roth Conversion account is by making non-deductible IRA contributions each year and then converting that amount into the Roth Conversion account. By golly, here is a loophole for people who make too much money to contribute to an IRA or Roth IRA. Any earnings while in the non-deductible IRA converted would be taxed, but the contributions would not be taxed since it is considered cost basis. However, there is one big caveat that you have to watch out for with this strategy. _It is best if you do not have any IRA accounts at all._ Otherwise, you will be taxed on the non-deductible contribution based on the ratio of your IRA accounts to non-deductible IRA accounts. For example, if you have $100,000 in an IRA and you make a $5,000 non-deductible contribution, then your ratio is 95% taxable and 5% non-taxable, or 19 to 1. So, 95% of the $5,000 would be taxed. The thing to keep in mind is if you have an IRA rollover account and you have a 401(k) at your employer, then re-roll that IRA rollover into your 401(k). Then, you would not have any existing IRA that would subject your non-deductible contribution to taxes.

When you make a non-deductible IRA contribution, there is no requirement to tell your custodian. However, you do have to tell the IRS with Form 8606. With this loophole idea, you make the non-deductible IRA contribution, then turn right around and convert it to a Roth Conversion account. You can repeat this process each year, but _each yearly conversion has its own five year clock_. You only have to pay taxes on the earnings, but since you are basically converting it right away, then there is likely to be no earnings to pay tax on (_unless you have an existing_

IRA, then you have that ratio to figure out.) Also, you can make the maximum non-deductible IRA contribution each year ($5,500 or $6,500) and back door it into a Roth Conversion account. Sweet! You're liking that loophole aren't you? Oh by the way, did Wally tell you about this? That's what I thought.

While I am on the subject, if you have after-tax money in a retirement plan with your employer, then those *after-tax* funds can also be converted to a Roth Conversion account, **if you are older than 59 ½.** *Don't forget a new five year clock starts when you do this.* It doesn't matter if you are still working. You *cannot* do it, however, if you are under 59 ½, unless you are terminated from that employer.

The after-tax money is broken down into contributions and earnings. The after-tax contributions can be converted tax-free to the Roth Conversion account, while, the earnings would be taxed. A lot of people have these after-tax accounts with their employers. This is a sweet little idea to turn that money into tax-free Roth Conversion dollars for those over 59 ½. Did Wally tell you this? That's what I thought.

By the way, you can also take money out of your *pre-tax* 401(k) and roll it over to an IRA Rollover account once you reach 59 ½, even if you are still working. So, if you want to get your money out of that crappy 401(k), then you can with this strategy. By the way, I can help you with that process, too. Personally, I recommend anyone over 59 ½ do this strategy. More often than not, you have better investment choices outside of a crappy 401(k).

Lastly, if any of your after-tax money in your retirement plan was deposited before 1987, then *all of that* can be converted to a Roth Conversion account without any taxes whatsoever. Nice, but you probably have to be an old dude to take advantage of this, because 1987 was 28 years ago. Plus, only those contributions before 1987 would be totally tax-free to convert. I know Wally didn't tell you about this.

Early Withdrawal Exceptions

There are several exceptions to the IRA, Roth IRA and Roth Conversion accounts early withdrawal penalties. It is important to know these if you are younger than 59 ½. These early withdrawal exceptions are:

1. Disability.
2. Death.
3. Substantially Equal Periodic Payments. (72t rule)
4. Paying for unreimbursed medical expenses that exceed the 10% AGI threshold.
5. Paying for medical insurance premiums if you have received unemployment compensation for at least 12 weeks.
6. First time home purchase. (limited to $10,000)
7. Qualified education expenses for self or family members.
8. Paying back taxes to the IRS.

If you meet one of the criteria on this list, then it means that you do not have to pay the 10% early withdrawal penalty, if you are under age 59 ½. You still have to pay the taxes however. It does not matter that it is a Roth IRA withdrawal and you are past the five year requirement. Taxes would still be due on the amount over and above your contributions (cost basis) if you are under 59 ½.

[This page intentionally left blank]

Roth Recharacterization

Most people may choose to recharacterize a Roth Conversion when they converted their IRA to a Roth and the value of the account declined precipitously. For example, perhaps you converted an IRA with $100,000 and your friend Wally invested it in a Variable Annuity for you. Later that year, the Roth Conversion account dropped by 10% to $90,000. However, with surrender charges, it dips down to $80,000 with Wally's brilliant expertise of putting you in that Variable Annuity in the first place. Tough luck on the surrender charges. If you need to recharacterize it, then those surrender charges will kill you, which is another reason not to let Wally put your Roth Conversion money into a Variable Annuity!

Without a recharacterization, you would owe taxes on the $100,000, not the $80,000. So, people would be smart to put the money back into their IRA. It would not do anything for the loss in value, or those surrender charges on the Variable Annuity that Wally stuck you in, but it would save taxes on the lost amount, which in this example would be the $20,000 difference.

In a 25% tax bracket, Wally has cost you $5,000 in taxes by putting your Roth Conversion in a Variable Annuity, plus helped you to lose $10,000 in surrender charges. Whatever you do, do not let Wally sell you an IRA that is a Variable Annuity when you recharacterize the $80,000 back to the IRA. Although he would love it since he would be making nearly double the commissions off of you. Once for the Roth Conversion and then on the recharacterization back to the Variable Annuity IRA. This is great for Wally, but not for you.

The recharacterization can be done as late as six months after your regular tax deadline. This means that you have until October 15th of the year following the conversion year to recharacterize it.

Another reason that you might want to recharacterize a Roth Conversion is because, you thought you could afford to pay the taxes on it, but found out later that it would be difficult to do it. In this case, a recharacterization would be a good idea.

Also, you may just want to do a partial recharacterization. Perhaps you thought you could pay the taxes on the entire conversion, but realized that maybe you should spread it out over a couple of years instead. You can then do a partial recharacterization and pay the taxes on the smaller amount converted. You can then do the re-conversion in the next and following tax year. By then, you have a whole new choice as to how much to convert in the second and following tax year.

The IRS has a worksheet with a handful of questions to help you calculate a Roth recharacterization. It is not very tough to complete, but I recommend using a CPA.

Some people like to convert positions instead of cash. They do this in case they need to recharacterize a losing position. In other words, for simplistic sakes, let's assume that you convert two stocks in your IRA to a Roth Conversion account. One stock goes up and the other goes down. You may want to take the one that went down and do a partial recharacterization on it. _However_, the IRS calculation makes you figure the overall profit on the whole conversion, not just the one losing stock. This is where that IRS worksheet comes into play. You have to run the numbers to see the potential benefit and tax savings. Whatever you do, don't just take Wally's word for it. Further, you don't want to be preparing your own tax return when you have a Roth recharacterization, either. You want a qualified CPA involved before you do this strategy.

A Roth recharacterization is a good thing to know, especially when dealing with the likes of Wally Street.

Roth Conversion using a HELOC

When you are looking at doing a Roth Conversion, you have to calculate how much the conversion is going to cost you in taxes. If it kicks you up to the top tax bracket, then most people will shy away from doing it. There is a way to do a Roth Conversion and leverage money from your Home Equity Line of Credit (HELOC).

This strategy is where you take an interest only loan for the taxes due from your HELOC. You pay the interest for five years. The principal of the loan remains the same, because it is an interest only loan. After five years and one day, you take a withdrawal from your new Roth Conversion account and pay off the HELOC.

Let's look at this a little closer. Assume you wanted to convert a $200,000 IRA and you realized that the taxes on it would be about $66,000. Ordinarily, you would probably never do this Roth Conversion, because of the taxes.

With this neat idea, what you do is take an interest only HELOC out for the $66,000 and pay the taxes. Let's assume that the interest rate charged is 6%, or $3,960 per year. You pay that $3,960 for five years. Your HELOC principal, because it is interest only, remains flat at the $66,000 figure. During that five years, as long as you do not let Wally invest it, your Roth IRA may grow at a 6% average annual rate. If it does, then it will grow to a value of $267,645.12 at the end of that five years.

Well look at that will you? The Roth IRA has grown enough to pull out the $66,000 and pay off the HELOC. Remember, you can always pull out your cost basis without penalty at any age.

What is your cost basis in this example? It is $200,000 which is the amount that you converted on day one. So, even if your Roth IRA didn't make a penny, you always have access to the money to pay off the HELOC. There is never any risk that you will not be able to pay off the HELOC, because you can always pull out that $200,000 cost basis at any point. You only need $66,000 to pay off the HELOC.

Ordinarily, if you did not use the HELOC, then it would have cost you the same $66,000 in taxes. Remember when I talked earlier about lost opportunity costs? Well, by paying the $66,000 yourself, then you would have also lost the opportunity costs on those funds. However, by using the HELOC for five years and paying the $3,960 per year, then it only cost you the $19,800. You do not have any lost opportunity costs on the $66,000, because you are using the bank's money, not yours. You see?

Let's evaluate this outcome. Two hundred thousand dollars converted without a HELOC costs you $66,000 in taxes, plus lost opportunity costs. However, $200,000 with a HELOC costs you $19,800 which is a smidge less than 10%. Nine point nine percent to be exact. The last time I checked 9.9% was better than 33%. Don't you agree Kemosabe?

By the way, old Wally might be keen on this idea, but what Wally will try to tell you is that you can also deduct the interest on that HELOC loan. That would be totally wrong and I would not do that if I were you. The IRS doesn't allow it. Or as my dad would say, "You can't dance in them tight drawers." Wally sure is a piece of work. He will say anything and I do mean anything to make a sale.

This use of a HELOC makes a lot of sense to do a Roth Conversion, but remember, it never makes sense to use a HELOC to pay whole life insurance premiums to be your own private bank.

Chapter Summary

What did we learn in this chapter?

- We learned the pertinent rules involving Roth IRA's.
- We found out that what a Roth Conversion is and how we do not ever want to commingle a Roth Conversion account with a regular Roth IRA account.
- We found out all the exceptions to the 10% early withdrawal penalties.
- We learned that there is a five year clock that starts on the first contribution with a Roth IRA account.
- We understand there is a different five year clock for each amount converted when we are talking about a Roth Conversion Account.
- We learned about a Roth recharacterization and when it might be beneficial to do one.
- We learned how to do a Roth Conversion using a home equity line of credit and only pay about 10% in taxes instead 33% or more.
- We learned not to believe Wally when it comes to deducting our HELOC interest on our tax return.

[This page intentionally left blank]

Chapter Sixteen

401(k)'s: Don't Dive in Head First

"Opportunity is missed by most people because it is dressed in overalls and looks like work."

~ Thomas A. Edison

[This page intentionally left blank]

401(k)'s: Don't Dive in Head First

Aw yes. The 401(k). The end all to be all. The answer to all your retirement dreams. Fat chance.

There is a time to invest in a 401(k) and there is a time not to invest in a 401(k). I will discuss when it is not a good time to invest in a 401(k) in more detail a little bit later. For now however, we will discuss the venerable and much ballyhooed 401(k) account.

If you have a 401(k), then you probably work for a company that offers one. Typically, they usually have some type of matching contribution like a match on the first 5% contributed by you. This is like free money to you, so you contribute 5% in order to get their 5% matching contribution.

Here is one of the major problems with a lot of 401(k)'s out there today. Fees, fees and more fees. Good old Wally Street works as a benefits broker, too. Typically, he has been promoting 401(k)'s from life insurance companies. These life insurance companies have deals with the major mutual fund families that allows them to offer the top funds in their 401(k) that they sell. The trouble is that there is a lot of fees involved in this scenario. It doesn't take a smart fellow to figure out that if you use an insurance company with mutual funds, as opposed to just mutual funds alone, then you are probably paying double the fees. Why is the insurance company in the mix anyway? They do not have the mutual funds. They have just made a deal with the mutual fund companies so they can offer the top funds in their version of a 401(k). Yes and our friend Wally Street is getting his cut, too. That can be a big cut, by the way.

The Department of Labor (DOL) is the government agency in charge of enforcing ERISA which is the act that regulates 401(k)'s. Well the DOL wised up to these high fees being charged to 401(k) plan participants and said, "Let there be light!" Now, all the roaches are scattering. In other words, you now have to disclose the fees and that means all the hidden fees, too. Uh oh! The insurance companies are worried big time, because they know they have the highest fee structure there is for 401(k)'s.

Insurance companies utilize a product called a group annuity for their 401(k)'s. You see there is a loophole in the law that allows them to offer mutual funds, inside of a group annuity and not have to register the group annuity as a security. Why is this important? It is important because it means Wally Street does not have to get his securities license to sell you a 401(k)! Isn't that great for Wally? You know, we have to take care of Wally Street. He is the engine of the train that creates the revenue for the insurance company. Wally doesn't have to worry about passing that nasty old securities test or being regulated by FINRA. All he has to do is get an insurance license to sell life and annuities, then he is all set to cash in on the 401(k) business. It sure is great being Wally Street.

Picture this scenario. You have a guy, named Wally Street, advising you on your 401(k) from an insurance company with double the fees and who is not licensed to give securities advice. Yet he is selling your employer on a group annuity contract for your 401(k) and then telling you how to invest it. Remember, every time an employee contributes to that insurance company group annuity 401(k), then Wally gets his cut.

Well, the DOL has said, "Okay Mr. Wally Street and conniving insurance company, if you are going to sell people a 401(k) like that, then you have to put in writing all the fees that you are charging." Yikes!

The insurance companies are panicking over this full fee disclosure. What most of them will do is not change a thing and just disclose it. They know that most people do not read legalese looking documents regarding their 401(k). After all, when was the last time you read the Summary Plan Description from your 401(k)? That's what I thought. You truly believe your employer is going to read that thing? They know you are not going to read it, so all they have to worry about is the employer reading it. The way I figure it, the insurance companies will skate by for a few years until more and more employers wake up.

ERISA attorneys have to make sure that companies comply with the rules. In addition, there is a bevy of lawyers out there who cannot wait to sue employers for failure to control 401(k) plan fees. It is going to take a few high profile lawsuits, before most employers will take their fiduciary responsibility seriously.

With new regulations come new opportunities. An employer can never fully absolve itself of fiduciary liability. This is because they could technically abscond with all the money, so they always maintain some fiduciary responsibility. However, the employer can remove a lot of their fiduciary responsibility, especially when it comes to the investment selection, portfolio management, third party administrators and plan fee scrutiny. There are now firms that will step in and accept responsibility in these areas by putting forth a menu of investment choices, design pre-defined model portfolios and shop for reasonable fees on behalf of the 401(k) plan participants. Further, they also will shop for a third party administrator who charges less in fees.

Every employer out there needs to take this seriously and <u>take it seriously now</u>. Not tomorrow, but now! Lawsuits are waiting in the wings, believe you me. The next time you read about a lawsuit being brought against an employer over their 401(k), then I want you to remember this little peon who told you so in this book. The odds are that the employer getting sued will have fallen for Wally's BS and bought a group annuity 401(k).

I said this in my last book, but it is worth repeating. The advice people get for their 401(k) is awful. Typically, Wally Street shows up with his projector and a brochure. Wally then goes on to tell you what a wonderful opportunity you have to invest in this 401(k) that your employer was so gracious enough to implement, just for you! Wally will focus a lot on the employer matching contribution in order to get you to sign up.

Wally doesn't like to get too complicated or spend a lot of time at your work place, so he typically has some model portfolios that his insurance company told him to promote. Wally simply tells you to invest in one of those models and tells you to go to their web site for more info on those models. Oh, don't get me wrong, he will take out his investment questionnaire and ask you a few questions. (Remember what I wrote about investment questionnaires in a prior chapter?) Wally will then recommend those model portfolios on their web site, then that will probably be the last time you see Mr. Wally Street. Oh, you might see him again, but he will be talking to a new employee, advising them on a model portfolio and telling them to go to that web site. He will not be there to talk to you about how your 401(k) model portfolio is doing, or whether it needs to be adjusted. Wally doesn't have time for that. Remember, he has to hit that revenue quota.

So, here you are, a full-fledged 401(k) plan participant with a model portfolio. Everything is just great. Except when the market goes down a bunch and the model portfolio doesn't hold up worth a flip. The sad part is that you are busy with other things and you only get a statement once a quarter and rarely ever log on to your 401(k) account to see how it is doing. Once you do log on and look at your 401(k) account, it is then that you realize that you are not doing so well. Perhaps, you garner up a little courage and talk to your HR department about it. Of course, you know that HR cannot give you any advice on your 401(k). However, they tell you not to worry, because all you have to do is call Wally Street and he will help you out. At this point, you hesitate as to whether to call Wally Street, because you do not even know the guy. Suppose you did call him. This is what he will tell you:

"Markets go up and markets go down. You are dollar cost averaging into your 401(k) and you have a long term time horizon. Hold on and don't worry. The market will come back."

That's Wally's famous words of advice to all. He repeats that to everyone. Grudgingly, you feel sheepish about it and hang up. Boy, doesn't investing in a 401(k) make you feel good? I'm being facetious of course. You just cannot get good 401(k) advice from Wally Street, no matter what line of BS you hear.

I know what you are thinking. "Okay, Mr. Smarty Pants. What do you suggest I do?"

Unfortunately, if your employer is doing business with Wally Street and your company has a group annuity for a 401(k), then you are completely out of luck. Your employer is an idiot. You will get high fees and no real 401(k) advice. Well, you will have that web site to look at. That web site will solve everything for you. Yes, I am being a smart aleck again.

If however, on the other hand, you choose to do business with an *independent* (with independent being the key word) registered investment adviser who has a plan and a process, then you will be immensely better off. This plan and process will include a selection of low cost index funds. It will include a group of model portfolios that are efficiently designed to provide broad diversification. It will include an automatic strategy for investing your contributions into specific asset classes. It will include an automatic rebalancing of your 401(k) account on a quarterly basis. It will include a due diligence process to remove poor performing funds and replace them with better funds. It will include ongoing investment advice from real people who are available to answer the phone, review your account and make recommendations as needed. And, for your employer, these independent registered investment advisers will relieve your boss from most of their fiduciary responsibilities as the plan trustee.

Now, doesn't that make a little more sense? I hope so whether you are a plan participant or an employer for that matter.

My advice to you if you are an employer, is to find out if you have a group annuity and if so, then find out what you are paying in fees. That fact alone should make you get the hell away from Wally. I promise you that you do not under any circumstances want to continue to use a group annuity as the 401(k) choice for your company. A lawsuit will happen before you know it. Don't doubt me on this, either. I know what I am talking about regarding this issue.

My advice to plan participants is, if your employer is an idiot and keeps doing business with Wally Street and his group annuity, then call your own independent registered investment adviser and agree to pay him to help you manage your crappy insurance company group annuity 401(k). Any fee that you pay would be well worth it. Since you are stuck in it, then you might as well make the best of it. The alternative is Wally Street's advice solution that includes his famous words, "Hold on. Don't worry. The market will come back."

Individual 401(k)'s

If you are self-employed, then you may want to consider an individual 401(k) or as it is sometimes called, a solo 401(k). These plans allow you to sock away a lot of money. In 2015, if you are under 50, you can salary deduct $18,000 directly into your individual 401(k). On top of that amount, at the end of the year, you can make a profit sharing contribution of $35,000. That is a total of up to $53,000. The actual choice is $53,000 or 100% of compensation whichever is less. Theoretically, you can put the first $53,000 of your income in your individual 401(k).

Small business people like attorneys, real estate agents and consultants who work primarily on their own can take advantage of the individual 401(k). Even husband and wife real estate teams can take advantage of the individual 401(k). You just need a company where you pay yourself a salary. If one spouse makes a good enough income, then you might consider using the other spouse to make the full $53,000 contribution. After all, as a married couple, it is half yours anyway, so it really doesn't matter whose account it is in. In a divorce, it has to be split 50/50 like it or not, unless one spouse waives their share of it.

If you are age 50 or older, then the 100% of compensation or $53,000 limitation still applies, but with one exception. If you are age 50 or older, you can salary deduct an extra $6,000 per year. This means you can salary deduct $24,000 per year and the balance of $29,000 would be considered your employer profit sharing contribution portion to meet the $53,000 limitation.

Leave it to Congress to come up with a rule that ends up at the same place, yet with different ways to get there in the end. If a young person can sock away $53,000 total and a person age 50 and over can do the same, then why have two different rules on the salary deduction amount? It doesn't make any sense. Do you see why our stinking tax code needs to be chunked out a ten story window? It has these kind of stupid rules all over the place.

A key point to understand with your Individual 401(k) is something that is going to upset poor Wally Street. You see, Wally wants all of your money. However, with an Individual 401(k), once established, you can take your IRA Rollover account and also your old 401(k) from your prior employer and re-roll it into your new Individual 401(k). This will probably make Wally cry, if you do this, but it allows you to have one account instead of two, or three.

This is a key point to know, because later I will be discussing how to buy real estate in your IRA, Roth IRA and Individual 401(k)'s.

Roth 401(k)'s or Roth 403(b)'s

These are called Designated Roth accounts. The retirement plan that has your 401(k) or 403(b) must amend or adopt their plan documents to allow for these Designated Roth accounts and contributions.

If your company allows Designated Roth accounts, then you can split your contributions between the regular 401(k) and Roth 401(k) buckets in any amount that you choose up to allowable limits. In addition, as long as your AGI is under the limits discussed previously, then you can also contribute to a regular Roth too. This would allow someone to max out both their Roth 401(k) and their Roth IRA. However, the AGI limit is kind of low to do this, but if you fall under that $98,000 married filing jointly or $61,000 single limit, then you can do it.

If you are making the money, then you can salary deduct up to $18,000 if you are under 50, or $24,000 if you are over 50 years old.

In addition, if you have an Individual 401(k), then you can also have an Individual Roth 401(k). You just have to have it written in your plan documents and find a custodian that allows it. By the way, I know how to do it as long as your plan documents allow it on your Individual 401(k).

Not many custodians are actively pursuing this Roth 401(k) area right now. I have no idea why, except I think it is because there is a cost to get an IRS determination letter for retirement plans when it used to be free. Sorry, I am digressing again.

If you rolled over a Designated Roth account to a Roth IRA Rollover account, then you can re-roll that back into your new employer's retirement plan, if it has a Designated Roth account, too. Wally would not want you to do that however, because there is nothing in it for him. You might make him cry.

When you make a distribution from your Designated Roth account, it is subject to the same 5 year rule on earnings. The cost basis is tax-free, but the earnings would be taxable if withdrawn in the first five years. In addition, if you are under the age of 59 ½, then you would be hit with the 10% early withdrawal penalty, too.

Here is another one of those quirky rules to watch out for in regard to Designated Roth accounts. If you had the account at your employer for more than 5 years, and you rolled it over to a Roth IRA Rollover account, then you have to start a whole new 5 year clock. What? I know that does not seem fair. However, if you happened to have taken my advice and opened up a regular Roth IRA with at least $100 and that was more than 5 years ago, then you would be exempt from the whole new 5 year clock requirement. You see, it pays to read this book.

Get a Roth IRA open will you? Even if it only has $100 in it. You can get rid of that stupid 5 year clock requirement. Plus, you might need it someday to accept your Designated Roth contributions rollover. But, whatever you do, do not open it with Wally, because he wants to sell you a Variable Annuity.

Debt and the 401(k)

Okay class. Here is a quiz for you. If you have $25,000 in debt and $25,000 in your 401(k), then what is your net worth? Most people would say, "Zero." Wrong!

From a liquidity standpoint, it is less than zero. What if you lost your job and had to cash in that pre-tax 401(k) not only to live on, but to pay on the debt? If you are under age 59 ½, then you are going to be subject to a 10% penalty for early withdrawal and you will also have to pay taxes on the whole $25,000 401(k) withdrawal. So, it is not a zero net worth. It is a negative net worth. In a 25% tax bracket with a 10% early withdrawal penalty, you are looking at a net worth of $-8,750.00.

This begs the question: "Should you contribute to a pre-tax 401(k) when you have $25,000 in debt?" My answer would be an emphatic not no, but hell no, especially if you do not have an emergency fund either.

Here is the correct way to do this:

Pay off the debt first, build the emergency fund, establish savings accounts for things like vacations, home improvement projects, or new cars, then after all that is setup, then you can contribute to a 401(k).

I don't care about the free money employer match. You have no emergency money when you have money in a 401(k). You cannot get that employer contribution out anyway until you are fully vested which might be six years later, depending on the vesting schedule of your 401(k).

I know some 401(k)'s have loans, but that can be very risky especially in today's job environment. You have to consider the fact, especially if you work for Corporate America, the very distinct possibility that you might get laid off someday. You know that I am stinking right about this fact. Look around. I guarantee that you know people who have been laid off. If that is a possibility, then why on earth on are you going to put yourself in a position where you may have to pay a 10% penalty and taxes to boot on a loan, because you lost your job? That is stupid with a capital "S". Your loan would become a deemed distribution if you got laid off and you would owe taxes and penalties on that loaned amount. For this reason, 401(k) loans can be risky. If you want to gamble, then go to Vegas. Don't gamble with a 401(k) loan.

In order to prove my point, consider this fact. If you do have debt, no emergency fund and you contributed to your 401(k) and later borrowed from your 401(k) and got laid off, then you have proved the fact that I am right. Specifically, I am right about it being a dumb way to do things.

If you followed my studious advice, you would have no debt and an emergency fund that you could access without a penalty. If you paid off your debt, you could build that $25,000 in an emergency fund next, and then you would have a positive net worth with full liquidity. I go into greater detail on how to handle debt later in the Gaining Control Debt Plan® section near the end of the book. This plan will make you the smartest person in the neighborhood. I will get to it soon enough. Don't jump ahead just yet, however.

Which is smarter, a less than zero net worth with $25,000 in debt and no liquidity, or a positive net worth with no debt and a $25,000 emergency fund? It shouldn't take a rocket scientist to figure this out. Yet, I cannot tell you how many young people I see just blindly throw money in a 401(k) with lots of credit card debt and no emergency funds. Working for Corporate America these days is like being on a game of "Survivor." The layoffs are coming. Are you safe? Prepare for the possibility, please.

Chapter Summary

What did we learn in this chapter?

- Employers make dumb decisions when it comes to 401(k)'s.
- Wally Street and his insurance company are adding double the fees to our 401(k) with their group annuity.
- Wally Street may not even be securities licensed to properly give us advice on our 401(k).
- The Department of Labor is trying to shed some light on the fees in 401(k)'s which is a good thing, because it makes all the roaches scatter.
- Employers have much clearer choices now in choosing 401(k)'s because of the fee disclosures.
- We have to fend for ourselves with our 401(k).
- Employers had better take this fiduciary responsibility thing seriously, or get sued.
- Independent registered investment advisers with a plan and a process are better choices than Wally Street for a 401(k).
- We learned about Individual or Solo 401(k)'s for the self-employed.
- We learned about Designated Roth 401(k) and 403(b) accounts and if we have not already started the five year clock on a Roth IRA, then we must start a new five year clock when we roll it over.
- We wised up and realized that it is stupid to have debt and no emergency fund and contribute to a 401(k) at the same time.

Notes

Chapter Seventeen

403(b)'s and Payroll Slots

"There is no comparison between that which is lost by not succeeding and that which is lost by not trying."

~ Francis Bacon

[This page intentionally left blank]

403(b)'s and Payroll Slots

Just because you are a teacher, don't think you are getting off scot-free from me. You, my dear friend, are one of Wally Street's favorite clients. Wally loves teachers, because he sells all teachers Variable Annuities! Remember what I said about Variable Annuities in a prior chapter? If you don't, then go back and read it again.

If you are a school superintendent or a school board member, then you have the same new DOL fee disclosure and fiduciary responsibilities as our employer friends with the 401(k). The same DOL ERISA rules on full fee disclosure and being a fiduciary applies to school districts and their employees.

School districts have long made deals with insurance companies to sell Variable Annuities and group annuities that look the same as Variable Annuities to teachers and school employees. Double the fees and double the risks in fiduciary responsibilities. Yes, my friends on the school board, you have a fiduciary responsibility to all of your teachers and employees as a result of the DOL's latest ruling.

The question then becomes, "Are you going to just go with the flow, or make a change?" Please do not be complacent enough to believe that your school district will not be sued. You signed off on a 403(b) plan that put in place a group annuity. Can you say fiduciary responsibility? You certainly have a fiduciary responsibility whether you like it or not. The insurance company isn't taking the risk. That I can guarantee you.

I have a question for you teachers. Is your school district making a matching contribution on your behalf? In a lot of school districts around the country, there has never been a matching contribution for teachers. That is unheard of for teachers.

If there is no matching contribution, then you are investing your own money directly with Wally Street. Remember, you are one of his favorite clients. You see, Wally's insurance company has negotiated a payroll slot at your school. These payroll slots are very lucrative and only certain insurance companies can get these slots. Yes, I know you have a choice between the different insurance companies and their version of Wally Street, but it doesn't hide the fact that you are getting the shaft.

As I discussed earlier, VA's have expenses easily of 3% or more. Wally gets paid 6 to 10% in commissions on everything you put in and I know you don't mind. Most of these Wally Streets are not securities licensed. Remember they have that loophole where they only need a life and annuity license to sell you that 403(b) from their insurance company.

Typical Wally Streets give advice like this:

Put 25% in Large Cap, 25% in Mid-Cap, 25% in Small Cap and 25% in International.

That is Wally Street's typical advice. He seems to always recommend 100% stocks and divide it by four into 25% increments. Wally is not even securities licensed, remember? How do you expect Wally to know how to diversify a portfolio of investments? He is not trained to do that, nor even licensed to do so. How silly of you to even think Wally could give you good advice. Seriously, you would not believe how often I see this 25%/25%/25%/25% advice from Wally. It is incredible how often it happens. Did it happen to you? Oops!

I had this wonderful lady and her daughter that used to be a couple of my securities reps. This lady was a former Wally Street for an insurance company that called on teachers. She was the state rep for this insurance company, so the whole state was hers. This was all before she retired and came to work with me. This lady wanted to get her daughter in the securities business and she could work for me without worrying about any revenue quotas. However, whatever they produced, helped me with my revenue quota. Yes, I had a revenue quota back in the day when I was in Wally World. Back in the 1980's, if you wanted to be in the securities business, then you pretty much had to be in Wally World. It's different now.

This lady wanted to help her daughter call on all her old teacher contacts and basically re-sell them all VA's. At the time, I was working on the dark side. This was in the late 1980's, before I realized what bad investments VA's were for teachers and everyone else for that matter.

Anyway, as a result of working with this lady and her daughter, I sat in on a lot of meetings with teachers. What I discovered was that teachers are really wonderful at doing what they do every day. However, they were absolutely awful at taking care of their finances. Most teachers just go with the flow. Whenever old Wally Street pops in the door to sell them a 403(b) VA, they just go along and buy right in. They never give it another thought.

However, one thing that I will give them is that they are simply fantastic at saving money in their 403(b). I have to give them props for that. In fact, they are probably some of the best savers in the country.

Going forward, things are going to be different in the 403(b) world, or is it Wally World? It might take a little longer than our 401(k) employer friends to right the ship though.

Insurance companies have those lucrative payroll slots at the school districts. They have even less incentive to worry about their high VA fees. No competitor can even get their foot in the door without a payroll slot and they take awfully good care of the school board and

[271]

superintendents to make sure that those payroll slots stay limited. Therefore, there is not as pressing a need to change the 403(b) plan. Besides, you know how teachers are, in that they just go with the flow. They are not going to even notice the fees.

Oh my dear friends, you have forgotten about those lawyers who know ERISA DOL regulations inside and out. They need to get paid, you know and how they do that is to sue school districts who are not paying attention to high fees. So, if you are a teacher, then take heart. There will be a lawsuit that slaps your school board and superintendent into making the required improvement in your 403(b) plan. It just might take a while because of those crony deals with insurance companies and those payroll slots.

If you are a teacher and you do not want to wait to improve your 403(b) account, then get the hell away from those insurance company VA's and group annuities. Those things are awful. Instead seek out an independent (again, independent being the key word here) registered investment adviser for help. Pay them for advice on your 403(b). It will be way better for you in the long run.

If you are going to be stuck in a 403(b) VA, then first of all, I would stop contributing to it. Start contributing to an IRA or Roth IRA instead. If there is no matching contribution, then why do you really need Wally? For the money that you already have in the 403(b) VA, I would get some advice from somebody who knows a thing or two about how to invest it. I guarantee you that an independent registered investment adviser can choose the lower cost options in the VA and probably offset their fee until the surrender charge goes away. In addition, the independent registered investment adviser would give you a better opportunity to grow your account. Unfortunately, as long as you work at that school, then you will have to keep that crappy 403(b) VA in place. By the way, did I mention that I was an independent registered investment adviser?

Chapter Summary

What did we learn in this chapter?

- We learned that fiduciary responsibility also applies to 403(b) plans.
- We found out that Wally Street has a loophole to give us advice without any need for a securities license.
- We discovered that insurance companies have lucrative payroll slots that limit the choices teachers have for 403(b) plans.
- We realize that it may be best to get your 403(b) plan account advice from an independent registered investment adviser as opposed to Wally Street.
- We learned that we do not really have to have a 403(b) from Wally, especially if there is no employer matching contribution. We could just open an IRA or Roth IRA instead.

Notes

Chapter Eighteen

College Education Ideas

"Every man's life ends the same way. It is only the details of how he lived and how he died that distinguish one man from another."

~ Ernest Hemingway

[This page intentionally left blank]

529 Plans

I have to admit that when it comes to giving investment advice, I am a control freak. I like to decide how to invest the money on behalf of a client. With 529 plans, this is not possible, therefore I am not a fan.

Here is another place where mutual fund companies, brokerage firms and state governments are all "in cahoots." Everyone has their hands in the proverbial pie. The mutual fund companies strike exclusive deals with a state to be the only 529 plan in that particular state. Right there, you know without a doubt that any time that you have a monopoly like that, there is less tendency to have to be competitive on fees. In my opinion, 529 plans are cronyism at their finest hour. I just do not like them, because of the monopolistic factor and the added fees which to me seem unwarranted. Nevertheless, I will put you in one, if that is what you want.

Here is my thoughts on the 529 plan fees:

Isn't a college education expensive enough as it is? Why do you want to take money from poor struggling parents?

Suppose you already have a 529 plan. Here is what I would want you to know. The money that you put in it is tax-deferred and if you use it for qualified education expenses, then you can make tax-free withdrawals. In addition, you can use a 529 plan for any qualified educational expenses which means it doesn't have to be a college. It can be a vocational or technical school, too. Further, if your child decides not to go to college, then you can change the beneficiary of the 529 to someone different, including yourself. Also, with a 529 plan, you can choose age based plans which change their allocations from aggressive at younger ages to more conservative at college age. This is done automatically as your child gets older. A 529 plan has a lot of good qualities to it, even if hard headed me doesn't like the cronyism part of them.

Every now and then, I will see a study that says this particular 529 plan is better than another particular 529 plan. While probably true, I wish things were more like an IRA or Roth IRA account. By that I mean that anyone in any state should be able to open up a 529 plan and buy whatever they want to buy in it. To me, it is totally unnecessary to have the mutual fund companies, the brokerage firms and the states all "in cahoots." The parents need to be in control, so they can hire an independent registered investment adviser to help them invest for their kids' education. By the way, I know some other options that might be better than a monopolistic 529 plan. More on this in a bit.

Alas, I am just a little peon. A small speck on an elephant's rear end. My words will have no impact on making any changes in the 529 plan world. Wally Street has got this 529 plan thing all sewed up. There is no way that this book is going to make any difference. You see, Wally Street is very, very good at keeping things *status quo*. Nobody cares what I think about it.

A Roth IRA as a College Education Fund

Here is another option that is underutilized for college education funding. That is a Roth IRA. A Roth IRA? Yep. You heard me right. A Roth IRA.

If you will recall from my earlier writings about Roth IRA's, then you will remember what I said about that first $100 contribution. You want to get that five year clock going. In addition, you will recall that you can always pull out the cost basis at any time from a Roth IRA. Hey, what do you know? A Roth IRA is tax-deferred and tax free too, just like a 529 plan. In addition, you can pull money out of a Roth IRA to pay for qualified education expenses even if you are under 59 ½ without the 10% early withdrawal penalty. Interesting.

Yes, my dear friends and avid student, you can almost make your Roth IRA into a 529 that you can control. If you are under 50 and married, then you can sock away $5,500 per spouse, per year. If you are over 50, you can sock away $6,500 per spouse, per year. That ought to cover what you were putting in your 529 plan in the first place.

If you have a Roth Conversion account, then you can use that for a college education fund, too, but keep in mind, that you have a five year clock on each conversion amount.

However, do not forget about the loophole if you make too much money. You can still do the non-deductible IRA thing _if you do not have an IRA already_, then immediately convert it the next day to a Roth Conversion account and there you go with your college education funds. Keep in mind the rolling five year clock thing with the Roth Conversion. More on this in a bit.

The difference between saving for college education expenses in a 529 plan and saving for college education expenses in a Roth IRA are miniscule. The 529 plan allows you to pre-fund 5 years of gifts, currently $14,000 per year, per beneficiary into it. You cannot do that with a Roth IRA, so there. You can only put the $5,500 or $6,500 per year into it based on your age. That is one of the differences.

The thing I like about the Roth IRA over the 529 plan is the control. Remember, I am a control freak when it comes to investing. I do not like robotic investment plans too much. There is no flexibility, or let me rephrase that. There is no quick, trading flexibility if market conditions warrant a quick change. With 529 plans, you have to call someone, or sign a form and ask them to make a change which will happen at the end of the next business day. This could delay movement of funds for up to two days. With a Roth IRA, I can place a trade within seconds. This is why I like the Roth IRA option better for college education savings. Plus if your kid doesn't end up going to college, then you have just grown your own Roth IRA without the restrictions involved in liquidating a 529 plan. There is a 10% penalty with 529 plans if you do not use the money for qualified education expenses. In addition, you have to pay taxes on the earnings. With the Roth IRA, you do not have that issue.

It is also very important to keep in mind that there is no 10% penalty on withdrawals for those under age 59 ½, if you use the money for qualified education expenses. Yippee, a loophole!

With the Roth IRA account, you can make contributions, let it grow tax-deferred and if you have had it for more than five years, then you can pull the _contributions_ out tax and penalty free even if you are under age 59 ½. Gee whiz. That seems to work just like a 529 plan, except the difference is the 529 plan has a 10% penalty if the funds are not used for qualified education expenses. If you do not use or need the money from the Roth IRA account for qualified education expenses, then you have just built up your Roth account without any penalties whatsoever. Get it?

Remember, however, that it gets a little trickier when you are using a Roth Conversion account, instead of a regular Roth IRA account. The Roth Conversion account has that five year clock for each conversion amount. So, if you converted $5,000 a year via a non-deductible IRA for five years in a row, then you would have a laddered amount available to you. For example, you would be able to get to the $5,000 conversion amounts only starting in years six through ten, for example.

In other words, if you did the non-deductible IRA to Roth Conversion and each year you converted $5,000 for five years in a row, then $5,000 of cost basis would be available in year six, then another $5,000 in year seven, another $5,000 in year eight, nine and ten, then you would be home free after that. The difference is that the Roth IRA only has one five year clock. The Roth Conversion has a five year clock for each amount converted. You see? This takes a little management, but you are probably not paying for four years of college all at once anyway. Therefore, a backdoor non-deductible IRA to Roth Conversion can also work for you. And you thought that I was just another Wally Street.

You need to compare whether or not a regular 529 plan or a Roth IRA is the better option. There is also another choice besides these two. The use of cash value life insurance.

[This page intentionally left blank]

Life Insurance for College Education Funding

Another alternative is to use cash value life insurance as a source for college education funding. However, you have to know how to do this, because most life insurance guys don't have a clue. Typically Wally will gladly sell you a life insurance policy for college education purposes. However, Wally will most likely underfund the premium based on what you tell him. Remember, Wally is all about sales, not details.

Almost all life insurance policies are underfunded, because Wally wants the sale so bad that he figures he has to make it cheap for you to buy it. Wally tends to way underfund life insurance illustrations when he really should be showing a good premium that will sustain the policy at guaranteed rates until age 95, age 100 or longer. By the way, Guaranteed Universal Life which is a hot seller right now, will not work with this idea because they do not have much of any cash value.

Typically, most Wally Streets will show you current costs of insurance and mortality rates. These are not guaranteed, so to me, it is all make believe or funny money. Insurance companies are great at making their illustrations look really favorable. They do this by having really low *current* cost of insurance and mortality charges. What really matters are the *guaranteed* costs of insurance and mortality charges. This is how you can tell the difference in life insurance illustrations. Listen up. This is important. If a company guarantees 4% interest, then get the independent insurance agent, not Wally, to run the *current* projection at 4% also. What this will do is allow you to see the difference between the guaranteed mortality costs and the current costs in an apples to apples comparison. You will be amazed at the difference when you do this. Wally will not do this for you, because he knows the outcome and he will not want you to see this outcome. When you are buying life insurance, this will help you to understand the differences between current and guaranteed mortality rates shown by insurance companies.

The Wally Streets who sell whole life are saying to themselves, "Rick, don't you know that whole life is guaranteed?" Yes, Einstein, I know that the premiums are guaranteed, but I also know that those dividend rates of 7.5% to 8% that you are showing is a bunch of bunk. So, don't talk to me about how great whole life is compared to Indexed Life or Universal Life. All insurance companies do hocus pocus with their illustrations including whole life companies. Every dad gum one of them. You can put that in your pipe and smoke it.

The way to do this is to ask for a cash value illustration for $100,000 which is the amount needed to cover your kid's college education, in case you were to die unexpectedly. After you know the premium for that, then add on top of that, the amount that you were going to save for college education. A whole life policy with a cash rider (paid up additions rider) will work, as will an Indexed Life insurance policy, or even a Universal Life insurance policy.

The main thing to keep in mind with this idea is that you must have 10 to 12 years to go before you need the money, because of the surrender charges. If you pull money out after a year or two via a withdrawal, then you will get hit with those pesky surrender charges. Thus my reason to wait 10 to 12 years.

Down the road, however, when it comes time to pull money out, you can take a withdrawal without any surrender penalties. Plus, even though the death benefit will drop incrementally based on the amount you pull out, this will not be that big of an issue, because you did this for college education reasons, not for the death benefit. You only needed the death benefit until you build up the funds needed for college education. Keep in mind that you have no death benefit protection of making sure that

[284]

you kids can go to college with a regular 529 plan. With the life insurance, you can make sure that your kids can still go to college, if you were to die unexpectantly.

There is one caveat to watch out for on the cash value life insurance policy. You want one that has a minimum death benefit of like $25,000 or $50,000, because when you take those withdrawals, the death benefit incrementally reduces. If the minimum death benefit on the policy is $100,000, then it cannot reduce, so it creates a problem. Thus my reason for getting a policy with a lower death benefit minimum even though you may be buying it initially at $100,000. You want room to drop it down to $50,000 which will happen if you pull $50,000 out for college education via a withdrawal. Got it? Good.

Wally will tell you to take a loan, but this will eat up your cash value. You want to take a withdrawal instead of a loan. Here is why. If you paid $300 a month extra into the cash value policy, then when you pull out the funds to pay for college, theoretically, you should have pulled out all the extra money you put into the policy without taxes or any costs. If you were to take a loan, then you would have an outstanding loan of tens of thousands of dollars with running interest charges. You have to pay interest on that loan. Over time, it will cause your policy to crash, unless you pay back the loan. Why do you want to put your own money into something, then borrow your own money back out and then pay interest on your own money? It doesn't make any sense. That Wally guy can be kind of an idiot sometimes.

This is why a withdrawal to your cost basis is the way to go. If you pulled out some money for college education, then that is all there is to it. The life insurance policy will continue to function, because you paid the normal premium for the $100,000 in the first place.

Remember, you added the extra college savings money, in my example that was $300 per month, on top of the normal life insurance premium. Therefore, it will not be a problem taking a withdrawal. It will not create any problems down the road, either unless you underfund it. By this I mean pay $300 a month, then stop and start it. Further, you never want to pull out so much of the cash value to put the policy in jeopardy.

You kind of need to manage this a little bit by keeping a copy of the illustration, _without_ the $300 a month added to it. In other words, you want a plain old life illustration for the $100,000 death benefit showing the regular premium and cash value. Make sure it lasts to age 95 or 100 with the guaranteed premium. After you know those figures, then get another illustration showing the $300 a month added on top of that. Down the road, when you are ready to make a withdrawal for college expenses, then you revert back to the plain illustration and see what the cash value was supposed to be for that particular year. Compare the cash value to how the policy has performed to that original illustration.

If in year 10, it showed a cash value of $25,000 on the original illustration, then you do not want to go below that figure. If you did, then you would be putting the life policy in jeopardy. Also, I want you to compare that $25,000 to what was shown on the original illustration to what you actually have in cash value at this point. This will prove my point about illustration hocus pocus and life insurance companies.

The only negatives to the life insurance policy college education option is the timing of withdrawals. Insurance companies tend to drag their feet and it may take 2 to 4 weeks to get a check from your policy. As a result, you have to plan ahead a little bit. Other than that issue, the cash value life insurance policy with an additional college education savings component will work fine if you have 10 to 12 years or more to save.

There are no tax issues on the life policy as long as you do not take out more than your cost basis, which would be that college savings amount of $300 a month in my example, plus the regular policy premiums. So, the money grows tax-deferred and you can take it out without taxes up to your cost basis. Theoretically, there could be some taxes due on any amount you pull out over and above your cost basis. In addition, if you put too much money into your policy and it becomes a Modified Endowment Contract, then the first dollar pulled out would be taxable. This is why you need an independent life insurance agent who knows these rules.

Life insurance policies do have loan features, but again, I am not crazy about taking out a loan and never paying it back. This would cause problems for the policy to stay in force down the road. Another thing to watch out for with cash value life insurance are the policy's guaranteed expenses. Most policies have some type of monthly premium fee like $5 per month. Other policies may charge 8.5% of every premium. Well obviously, it would not make any sense to put $300 a month into one of those policies, because $25.50 (8.5%) comes out in a policy load right off the bat. This is why you need an independent agent, like me! Your one company agent is going to sell you his one company life insurance policy and it probably has that 8.5% premium load, too. If you are not aware of the premium loads, then this makes for you making a dumb mistake. Personally, there is never any reason to go to a one company agent. Those guys are named Wally Street!

By the way, after you have taken out all the withdrawals that you need to help pay for your kid's college education, then I want you to do me a favor. Keep paying the life insurance premiums. You need it for those who survive whether you think you do or not.

There you have it. Three different ways to save for college. Pick one that you like and roll with it.

[287]

Rick's Rant on College Tuition:

I'm sorry but I cannot help myself when it comes to ever rising college tuition. Again, I can never assume anything, so I am going to explain it. Here is why this is happening:

> When the government provides free money to colleges, then colleges have no incentive to lower their tuition. As long as the government provides student loans, then colleges can continue to raise their tuition prices. They have no free market incentive to lower their tuition. If you were to restrict student loans, then you will see the tuitions decline.

Personally, I believe that colleges better get ready for bad days ahead. I suspect that when college tuition gets to be so high that parents can no longer afford it, then colleges are going to be up a creek. It is a simple supply and demand issue. If parents quit paying those ultra-high tuition payments, which I think they are beginning to do right now, then Katy bar the door. Further, if the government starts restricting the availability of money for student loans, then this is going to be a double whammy.

Keep in mind, the people at colleges are teachers. You know the kind of teachers who just go with the flow and agree to payroll slots and think it is okay to do crony deals with insurance companies. Yes, these same people are going to be the ones who will be thrust into dealing with a declining pool of college students, plus having to pay all those tenured professors and their retirement benefits. That means less money to run the college, by the way. I wonder how they will adjust. I suspect Wally will run and hide when this happens.

Chapter Summary

What did we learn in this chapter?

- We learned more detailed information about a 529 plan.
- We found out how states and mutual fund companies are "in cahoots" to control your 529 plan options.
- We learned that a Roth IRA can also be used for qualified education expenses with no 10% early withdrawal penalties.
- We learned that cash value life insurance, properly structured, can be used for qualified education expenses.
- We learned that we need to take withdrawals up to cost basis in a life insurance policy, not loans.
- We found out that it was important to understand the policy loads in a cash value life insurance policy.
- We learned that colleges are fixing to be in a heap of trouble if enrollment declines and the government restricts student loans.

[This page intentionally left blank]

Chapter Nineteen

Real Estate IRA's

"I think it is important to be gregarious, and that friendships are not just a leisure pursuit, that they are an integral part of what it is to be human, and one does better work if one has a circle of friends that is active."

~ Niall Ferguson

[This page intentionally left blank]

Real Estate IRA's

Here is a neat idea for your IRA money. Buy some real estate in your IRA, Roth IRA and or Individual 401(k). In this chapter, when I say Real Estate IRA, I also mean Real Estate Roth IRA or Real Estate Individual 401(k), too. It is just easier for me to write Real Estate IRA, then having to write out all that other stuff, too. Got it? Good.

You can purchase any type of real estate for your IRA. Such as:

- Residential
- Commercial
- Farm Land
- Apartments
- Condominiums
- Raw Land
- Tax Liens

It doesn't matter what type of real estate it is, but you want to be smart about how you go about it.

Let's lay some ground rules down first. There are several IRS rules in regard to buying real estate in your IRA. One is that you have to treat the real estate just like it was a security. By this I mean, you have to look at the real estate as if it were a stock or a mutual fund in your account. When you own shares of Apple, you certainly don't go running out to Cupertino, California barking commands on how they should run their company. Well maybe some idiots do, but most of us just hold the stock in the account and hope it goes up. This is how you have to think of the real estate in your IRA. You buy it, hold it and at some point hopefully sell it at a profit.

Another factor in regard to the rules is that you cannot manage the real estate yourself. You have to hire out all the work. For example, if you bought a rehab property and did all the work yourself, then the IRS would say that is a business and not a security in your IRA. Therefore, your _whole IRA_ is subject to taxes and penalties and you would get hit with a full lump sum distribution. There is a way to flip houses with your IRA money, but you have to be smart about it and I will get to that in a little bit.

Another rule is that you cannot buy property from yourself and put it in your own IRA. That is known as self-dealing and against the rules.

In addition, you cannot buy properties from any disqualified person or related person and put their property in your IRA. For example, you cannot buy your business partner's property and put it in your IRA. Neither can you buy your parent's house and put it in your IRA. Nor can you buy your spouse's or children's properties. These would all be considered disqualified persons by the IRS.

You want any transaction to purchase real estate for your IRA to be a new arm's length transactions. There must be normal risk to the transaction. In other words, you cannot do a real estate transaction where you have a simultaneous closing where you buy and sell at the same time, knowing in advance of your profit. That would not constitute an arm's length transaction. That would constitute a rigged deal and would be a no-no for your IRA.

The logistics of buying real estate in your IRA is that you have to go with a custodian who allows it. There are only a few custodians that allow it. You have to be really careful in who you deal with for a custodian, because some of them are not regulated in the way that you might think. In some states, you can setup a trust company with no public disclosure of balance sheet and net worth required. You cannot go to that trust company and get any financial information. How do you know if they are sound and trustworthy? Just because it says "trust company" in their name doesn't mean they are financially sound. If a South Dakota trust company, for example, goes belly up, then your real estate will sit there floundering in legal limbo, until some judge decides how to handle it. The point is that you want to go with proven names in the custodian business for alternative investments.

After you select a custodian, then you simply open an IRA account with them and fund it with a trustee to trustee transfer, just like you would from Fidelity to Schwab, for example.

Some alternative custodians will allow the use of an LLC with your IRA to make things easier to manage the real estate. If you do not use an LLC with your Real Estate IRA, then you will have to get every check request sent to the custodian, then sent out to the vendor. With the additional LLC, you can appoint a manager (that would be you) and you can then write checks to pay the taxes, do the landscaping, paint the house and so on.

The LLC is not a regular LLC. It is a Real Estate LLC security. You have to look at this LLC just like it was a stock or mutual fund, too. Further, you can never, under any circumstances make a deposit in this LLC. You have to have all money from the real estate owned made payable to the custodian in this manner:

ABC Trust Co. FBO: John Q. Public IRA

Even if your LLC has as two LLC members, such as:

*ABC Trust Co. FBO: John Q. Public **IRA***
*ABC Trust Co. FBO: John Q. Public **Roth IRA***

Did you see that? You can actually combine your IRA and your Roth IRA and buy real estate with the proceeds of each. In addition, with an LLC in the mix, you could also use your spouse's IRA and Roth IRA accounts, too. When you add them all up, then you may have plenty of funds to buy real estate. Although, you will probably make Wally cry again, because this means he is not getting your account.

With the LLC and multiple members, you would each just get a percentage of ownership units in the LLC based on your percentage contributions. For example, if your IRA contributed 75% and your Roth contributed 25%, then each would own that proportionate share of the LLC. All income, dividends, capital gains and losses would flow through in those same percentages. However, keep in mind, the LLC is only needed for ancillary expenses. All closing of real estate is handled through the custodian IRA account, not the LLC.

Personally, if you cannot buy real estate with your IRA, your Roth IRA, your spouse's IRA and Roth IRA, then you probably should not be buying the real estate. I like all cash purchases. No loans!

If you do not have enough funds with all your IRA accounts, then you may want to bring in family members and their IRA's. After combining all of your IRA's plus your family member's IRA accounts, and then you still only have $19,000 total, then forget about it buddy rub.

By the way, it is best if you use all IRA type accounts and leave the taxable investment accounts out of it. If not, then you have UBTI to deal with. Yikes!!

UBTI and UDFI

Loans and non-IRA partners are not good when you want to use them with Real Estate IRA's. Other idiots will tell you that it is okay, but I'm not an idiot. I'm looking out for you. Do you know what UBTI or UDFI is? If you do not, then you do not want any part of a loan or non-IRA partner to help you buy real estate for your IRA, unless you fully understand the ramifications.

Unrelated Business Taxable Income, or UBTI is when you have a non-IRA partner like a taxable investment account. If you have a non-IRA partner, then they cannot be considered a security within the LLC owned by your IRA. It is an outsider. Therefore, it has a different business objective than the IRA.

UBTI is where you have an IRA that contributes 50% to the LLC and another entity contributes the other 50% who is a non-IRA partner. All UBTI says is that any income, dividends, or capital gains from the investment must be taxed to the non-IRA partner at their rate of contribution. For example, if a rental property paid $1,000 a month in income to the LLC held in the IRA, then $500 of it would be considered UBTI and taxable to that non-IRA partner. The other $500 would be tax-deferred within the IRA. That is easy enough to understand.

With UDFI, or Unrelated Debt Financed Income, this is where instead of using a non-IRA partner, you would borrow the money to help you buy the real estate along with your IRA. Again, using my 50/50 example, we would have the IRA own 50% and borrow the other 50%. This is where things get really muddy. The IRA only put up 50%. Do they get all the income? Who pays the loan interest? What happens when the loan is paid off? What is deductible and what is not deductible? What about depreciation? Bring on a team of real estate CPA's with valuation

[297]

experience and the corresponding fees to go with them. You are going to need them when you involve a loan with your IRA to purchase real estate. Why go through all this rigmarole? Beats me. Personally, I believe that if you cannot do an all cash deal, then do not do it at all.

When you are thinking of buying a piece of real estate for your IRA's, then you should think in this manner. About 75% or so of your IRA's should go to pay for the property itself. The other 25% of your IRA's would be used for ancillary expenses and what if's. You do not want to get into a situation where you spend your whole IRA on the property and have to use outside funds to pay for upkeep on the property, real estate taxes, etc. If you do that, then this UBTI kicks in and causes all the headaches that goes with it, too. My advice would be to avoid UBTI altogether.

Special Allocations

Normally, without anything to the contrary in the LLC Operating Agreement, all income, dividends, capital gains and losses must flow out based on the initial contributions. By this I mean, if the IRA contributes 75% and the Roth IRA contributes 25%, then that is how all income, dividends, capital gains and losses must be split.

There is a neat exception however. Now pay close attention to this, because this can really benefit you. Using my same 75% IRA and 25% Roth IRA split, with something written into the LLC Operating Agreement called Special Allocations, you can make some different splits. There is an IRS table of rates that are published monthly called the Applicable Federal Rates, or AFR for short. In a nutshell, this table is used to pay a minimum rate of interest for investors. As long as you pay the AFR rate from the Revenue Ruling 2015-8 Table I rates, then you are fine. Those Table I figures are what is allowed by the IRS to use.

In addition, in the AFR table, there are three terms. One is a short-term time period (3 years or less), another is a mid-term time period (3 years to 9 years) and the last is a long-term time period (more than 9 years). Basically, if you own an investment which in our case is real estate and you sold it later, then you would look up the time period in the AFR table. If it was 4 years, then you would use the AFR mid-term rate table. This is how AFR works. It depends on the holding period of the real estate.

For our Real Estate LLC IRA purposes, let's evaluate this in more detail using our newly discovered Special Allocations. What if you wanted to leverage your Roth IRA contribution to potentially make more money with it? This is possible with Special Allocations.

Here is how it works:

Special Allocations Split

- *75% IRA contribution.*
- *25% Roth IRA contribution.*
- *IRA gets the AFR rate, plus all income & dividends.*
- *Roth IRA gets all of the capital gains.*

With Special Allocations, you are compensating the IRA for the larger contribution by giving them the AFR rate for the time period the real estate ends up being held, plus all the income and dividends from the real estate during that time period. The Roth IRA only gets the capital gains and nothing else. This is potentially great for the Roth IRA with a successful real estate purchase. Of course, if there is no profit, then the Roth IRA can end up with nothing.

Think about it for a minute. What you are doing is shifting some profits to the Roth IRA at the expense of the IRA. The IRA will get the AFR mid-term rate which today is 1.99% for the 4 years in our example. In addition, if it is an income producing property, it will get the income and dividends for those 4 years in our example. The Roth IRA has to wait until the property is sold, four years later in our example, to see if there was a profit or not. If there was a profit, then it all goes to the Roth IRA minus the required 1.99% AFR for each of the four years which goes to the IRA.

Here are the numbers not taking into account any income from the income producing property. We are just looking at the capital gains below:

- *$200,000 property bought.*
- *$150,000 contributed by the IRA.*

[300]

- *$50,000 contributed by the Roth IRA.*
- *Property sold 4 years later for $300,000.*
- *IRA gets 1.99% on the original investment of $150,000 per year held. (4 years)*
- *Roth IRA gets the capital gains minus the AFR payment to the IRA.*

The <u>ending</u> capital gains split result:

- *The IRA gets $162,301.16 which is the 1.99% AFR annual interest plus its original contribution.*
- *Roth IRA gets $137,698.84 which includes its original contribution plus the capital gains minus the 1.99% AFR interest to the IRA.*

Did you see that? The Roth IRA contributed 25%, or $50,000. The Roth IRA had to risk the fact that the property was going to make a profit, so nothing was guaranteed as far as the outcome was concerned. The IRS says that it has to be an arm's length transaction and everything has to be "at risk." There is never a guarantee when you buy real estate that there is ever going to be a profit, so this meets the "at risk" requirement. Your Special Allocations clause has to be spelled out in the LLC Operating Agreement. No ticket. No laundry. If you do not have it spelled out, or worse yet, there is no Operating Agreement, then you cannot do this kind of a strategy.

Looking at my example again, the Roth put in $50,000 and ended up with $137,698.84. A pretty nice way to boost your tax-free Roth IRA wouldn't you agree? I know that I was being a little extreme with a $200,000 property growing to $300,000 in four years, but I wanted you to see the potential in shifting money to your Roth IRA with Special Allocations. Savvy real estate purchasers can take advantage of this strategy as long as they don't use Wally. Besides he will be crying in his beer if you buy real estate with your IRA, because it leaves him out.

With Special Allocations, you can do other splits, also. For example, you can pay the IRA the AFR rate, plus split the income, dividends and capital gains 50/50, or 60/40. This would still leverage money into the Roth IRA as opposed to no Special Allocations. You just need someone with knowledge of Special Allocations and the partnership rules to implement this strategy. It would not hurt to use an independent registered investment adviser who knows the rules and who is also a real estate agent. Oh, silly me. That would be me. I think the price of this book was a small price to pay to find out about this idea.

Flipping Houses Inside an IRA

Let's now talk about flipping houses with your IRA. You can do it, but you just have to be a little more careful in how you do it. The biggest thing to keep in mind is that you have to be hands off. You cannot do any and I mean any of the work yourself. You have to hire out the work. If you do not, then your _whole IRA_ could be considered distributed by the IRS. This means you have to pay taxes on the whole thing, plus 10% penalties if you are under 59 ½.

There is a better way to flip houses. I want to discuss flipping houses in general. In or out of an IRA.

Do you ever watch those reality shows on television about people who flip houses for a living? There are a lot of people who believe that it is easy to flip a house and make a lot of money. Here are their main mistakes. They believe that they can do it:

On budget, on time and with no surprises.

What a joke! Here is what you have to understand.

- _The contractor is in it for _their_ profit._
- _The lender is in it for _their_ profit._
- _The buyer is in it to _get a bargain,_ i.e., buy at below comparative values._

All of these people are against you. The contractor quotes you a price and you accept it. However, the first thing he does is find problems. Why does he find problems? So, he can make more money off of you dummy! He has you over a barrel now. You have a problem. You have hired him and he can fix the problem. However, it is going to cost you more. This is the way this game is played my friend.

If you try and squeeze the contractor, then he will just put more priority on his other jobs. Your project will take a lot longer. You think you are being fair with the contractor, but he doesn't care about you. He knows that you will wise up and pay him, or be stupid and try and find another contractor. Either way, he wins. He will just slap a lien on your flip property until you pay him.

By the way, that short-term rehab loan that you took out for a 5% origination fee and 12% interest is going to grow a lot more than you think when you piss off your contractor. You can forget about flipping this house in a few weeks. That only works on television and generally all those guys and gals are contractors! They control their own costs.

Take heart my friends. I have a solution for your problem. Here are my rules:

- *Use a real estate agent.*
- *Do not rehab yourself.*
- *Do minor (and I mean minor) upgrades.*
- *After minor upgrades, take new photos and re-list on MLS.*
- *Sell to other real estate investors and contractor buyers.*

You are probably thinking, "What are minor upgrades?" Well, I am glad you asked. Minor upgrades are things that you can control. You cannot control the contractor! Remember, I am a control freak. Do not let anyone else reach in your pocket and control your expenses! Contractors know how to do this all day long.

Here are some minor upgrade examples:

- *Pressure wash.*
- *Remove trash.*
- *Remove overgrown, bushy shrubs.*
- *Re-sod the yard.*
- *Take new pictures after your minor upgrades.*
- *Re-list it on MLS.*

Instead of trying to make $50,000 on a flip, be happy with netting out $10,000. Real estate agents and their buyers know what you paid for the house. It is public information you big house flipping wanna-be dummy!

If you did a full rehab and you are trying to make $50,000 on a flip, they will laugh at you. A contractor buyer or sophisticated real estate investor is not going to pay you that. Are you serious? I cannot even believe you thought that was possible.

They will however see that you made some minor upgrades to the curb appeal and are not trying to rake them over the coals on your re-listing price. They will pay that price and when they do, then you can repeat the process. You may be able to do four or five flips with minor upgrades per year and still make that $50,000. However, if you think you can do four or five full rehabs in a year on time, on budget and with no surprises, then you are sorely mistaken.

Don't be greedy. Do minor upgrades where you have complete control over the work. How much does it cost to hire someone to do a pressure washing? How much does a few palettes of sod cost? How much would it cost to remove a few bushes? How much does it cost to take a few pictures? You should have no problem controlling these expenses. Control is the key word to remember. Keep it simple, stupid. That is the way to go.

Now, that you know about flipping houses the right way with minor upgrades, then you can think of your profits going into your Real Estate IRA. When you do the minor upgrades, you have to hire out all the work and keep good records. Just in case of an IRS audit, you want to be able to easily pull out where you hired someone to do the minor upgrades. Hire someone to do the pressure washing and a sod company to lay the sod. I would hire someone else to remove the bushy overgrowth and I would even pay someone to take the pictures. Keep receipts of all of it, just in case of an IRS audit and you need to prove your LLC in your IRA is a security and not a business.

Those minor upgrade expenses could be paid for with your IRA LLC. However, when you sell, everything is paid to the custodian trust company for the benefit of your IRA. Got it? Good.

Also, you want to do all cash purchases. No stinking short-term loans on a flip. I do not care if it allows you to do it with no money down. Once you use a loan, then you have that UDFI tax mess kick in and you will need to hire a CPA. Don't be stupid. If the project takes longer than expected, you will be paying through the nose.

The main thing to remember about buying real estate in general is that you can lose more than your original investment. You have to calculate and consider your worst case scenario. Think about all the things that can go wrong.

- *Condo assessments.*
- *County assessments.*
- *Rezoning.*
- *Sink holes.*
- *Crime infestation.*
- *Theft.*
- *Extended time on the market.*

All of those items cost money over and above what you paid for the property. This is not an all-inclusive list either. There are plenty more items that I could add to the things that could go wrong. Like doing the rehab yourself with contractor overruns, short-term loan costs, foundation problems, mold removal, termites, and other similar nightmares.

You need to be smart in your real estate decision making. Hire a real estate agent who knows how to help you buy real estate in your IRA. (I'm one of those!) You will be glad that you did.

Chapter Summary

What did we learn in this chapter?

- Follow the rules.
- We learned how to incorporate LLC's to pay for ancillary expenses with a Real Estate IRA.
- We learned that loans bring in UBTI and UDFI and muddy the waters.
- We learned why LLC Operating Agreements are important, specifically in regard to Special Allocations.
- We learned we can potentially leverage up our Roth IRA's even though they are a minor contributor to the real estate purchase with Special Allocations.
- We learned different ways to use Special Allocations and what AFR stands for.
- We learned how flipping houses with minor upgrades might be a good way to buy real estate in our IRA's and Roth IRA's.
- We were reminded that we can lose more than we invested in real estate.
- We learned that a good real estate agent who knows full well how to buy real estate in an IRA, Roth IRA or Individual 401(k) is worth every penny.

Chapter Twenty

Investor Expectations

"Many people take no care of their money till they come nearly to the end of it, and others do just the same with their time."

~ Johann Wolfgang von Goethe

[This page intentionally left blank]

Investor Expectations

Investors' expectations for investment performance makes no sense. Yes, I am talking to you. In today's world of instant news via television, emails, the internet and text alerts, we are all bombarded with information. The thing that you have to keep in mind is that television financial news channels have to sensationalize things to get you to watch. If they didn't do that, then you would not watch. It is bad enough that we have to watch those, "My name is Doug. I am not an actor. I am the face of Mesothelioma" commercials. Sorry Doug, but I am sick of seeing your mug on TV. I probably should blame the attorneys who run that stinking ad four thousand times a day instead of poor old Doug. Sorry, I digressed again.

It is even worse when we have some financial guru who is trying to make a name for himself by scaring the crap out of people with his view of where the stock market is headed. I have always been curious as to why the financial reporters always asks these people the same stupid question. "Which way is the stock market headed?" Brutish. Freaking brutish.

Generally, when the market goes way down, these same financial gurus call it a "great buying opportunity." These idiots act like everyone is sitting around glued to the TV with a boatload of cash ready to buy stocks. These guys have been saying the exact same thing for as long as I can remember. Perhaps, they are just winging it. Did you ever think of that?

All of the major financial channels focus on issues that have no bearing on your life. For example, "The Dow Jones Industrial Average lost 122 points today as investors were disappointed in the latest jobs report." Yet, investor after investor will hear this "news" and think that they have to do something. Yes, you have to do something alright. Quit watching the financial news television!

People are inherently emotional beings. We make a lot of our decisions out of emotion. Think back when somebody ticked you off. This made your stress levels go up and you made a quick decision to either tell them off, ignore them, or do something to get even. These are all emotional decisions. A few hours later when we calmed down, we were probably saying we were sorry. When we were no longer emotional, then we could see things more clearly. Which was the better time to make that decision? When you were mad as a hornet, or when you calmed down?

Television news has a tendency to raise your stress levels. However, you cannot make investment decisions based on what you see and hear on television. Really now, tell me how the DJIA dropping 122 points is going to ruin your life. The truth is that it is not going to have any impact whatsoever on your life. Unless, *you allow it to happen*. By allowing it to happen, you will be living a hectic and chaotic life. If you make an emotional decision to get out of the market at every piece of bad news, then you will be making a stupid mistake, not to mention a helluva lot of trades.

Pull yourself together! You cannot go on living like this! Step back and take a deep breath. Do some Yoga or something and calm down.

I have to admit that after twenty seven plus years of answering the occasional frantic call from a client, I am getting a little tired of it. Notice that I said, occasional. Most of my clients are trained well and they know better than to call me with concerns about the stupid Dow Jones Industrial Average dropping 122 points. Every now and then however, I am reminded of how I did not do a good enough job explaining myself to some people. I promise to do better in the future. It will save us both a lot of stress.

Chapter Summary

What did we learn in this chapter?

- Investing decisions based on stress and emotions are not a good idea.
- Constantly staying tuned to financial television shows skews our rational and logical thinking.
- The so-called experts on the financial television shows are winging it and have been for a very long time.
- Rick will do better in the future explaining about financial television shows.

Notes

Chapter Twenty-One

The Accident

"I love those who can smile in trouble, who can gather strength from distress, and grow brave by reflection. 'Tis the business of little minds to shrink, but they whose heart is firm, and whose conscience approves their conduct, will pursue their principles unto death."

~ Leonardo da Vinci

[This page intentionally left blank]

The Accident

This brings me to the point where I need to fill in the gaps on what happened since my last book. No need to buy the old book, by the way. For those who have purchased this book, I moved all of our clients to cash on October 6, 2008. However, only our clients at the time know what happened after that date. Here is what happened. I stayed in cash until May 8, 2009. That is about six months, in case you are counting.

I want you to know that the things that you are about to learn are coming from someone who is open and honest and has nothing to hide. Wally Street would never be this open or honest with you, so give me a little credit, will you?

The stock market hit a low in late November of 2008, then again in late March of 2009 where it re-tested that low and reached its lowest point.

At the time, I didn't own the company like I do now with my partner Stan Rosenthal. Back then, my friend Bryan was the owner. When May 8th of 2009 came around, I had a conversation with my friend to get back into the market. I felt it was time. My friend, however was still a little skittish about it. Who could blame him with all the crazy things going on back then?

My position was to get back in whole hog. However, my friend wanted me to get back in at 50%, then get the other 50% in a few months. Since he was the President and I did not have the control on this decision, then this is exactly how we got back into the market.

On May 8th of 2009, I put our clients back into the market with 50% of their cash. The other 50% of their cash was invested in September of 2009.

As the Portfolio Manager, I was able to look at the situation without emotion and make a decision to get back in whole hog. However, my friend wanted to err on the side of conservatism, so that is what we did. If we would have gotten back in whole hog, then we would have performed just a little bit better. However, even with what we did, we were in the top 5% of financial advisors in the country who made the move to protect client assets. Did your Wally Street do that? That's what I thought. And you thought I was just another financial advisor. While your account with Wally was going down more than 30 or 40%, our client accounts were holding at their current levels.

When I joined my friend's firm, I was pretty much starting from ground zero. I had no clients when I started, because of a non-compete agreement with my prior firm. However, I was up to the challenge. Since my first day on the job, we have grown our client assets under management almost 500% with one major change along the way.

It could have been even better, except for one thing. One day in July of 2009, I was out riding my bicycle near my house. The Tour de France had just ended and I was feeling like Lance Armstrong, so I went for a bike ride around 6:30 p.m. There wasn't a cloud in the sky and it was an absolutely beautiful day. As I was going down Race Track Road, the street that my office is now on, I was hit from behind by a lady in her car. Witnesses later told me that they thought she was texting on her phone. Her car crunched the back wheel of my bike and made me fly over the handle bars and land on the pavement. Luckily, I had a helmet on and I survived the accident.

My collar bone was broken. I had a fractured clavicle, my neck had herniated disks, I pretty much ripped my right shoulder to shreds and I had a road rash that covered about half of my back. The accident knocked me completely out. I woke up, thankfully, on a back board in

[318]

the emergency room with a neck brace on. I was one sore dude. My clavicle would not heal for over 6 months. I had concussion symptoms for about a year along with balance problems. I ended up having two right shoulder surgeries. I have since recovered from the accident, but still have everyday pain. In my mind, I am blessed to be here, so you will not hear me complaining.

I knew that I was the portfolio manager and I had to get back to work. I missed one week of work after the date of the accident. That's it. I gutted it out, even though I was in a lot of pain. If my dad were alive today, he would tell you that I am "tough as nickel steak."

Soon after my accident, while I was in Indianapolis, we were in negotiations to bring Stan Rosenthal on to the team. Stan agreed to come on board with his clients. So, at that time, we were pretty much going to double our assets overnight. My friend's assets had grown to about $14,000,000. While Wally Street was telling you to hold on, my friend and I had more than doubled our assets. Stan had about $10,000,000 in client assets at the time. By Stan coming on board, we were looking at about $24,000,000 in assets now.

Soon after Stan came on board, my friend called me up and said he wanted to go in a different direction. I believe that my bike accident scared him into going with a big firm with multiple money managers. Even though we also had Stan on board now as another portfolio manager, it wasn't enough for him. He said that he would sell me the company, but he was taking his $14,000,000 of client assets with him. His company wasn't worth a nickel to me without Stan. I had known Stan for a while, before I went to work for my friend.

In my mind, Stan deserved to be a part owner of the company, too. Stan had just moved to our firm a couple of months earlier. I wasn't about to be the sole owner without giving Stan an equal or better opportunity

[319]

than me. In the end, my friend sold me and Stan the company and he took his client's assets out. My friend Bryan and I are still good friends and I still help him as an outside compliance consultant for his firm.

Stan and I were left to rebuild from there and we have done just that. Stan and I have grown from the original $10,000,000 to almost $30,000,000 today. Most of that growth is from Stan's efforts as he takes care of clients and I take care of the portfolios, although I have my own clients, too. However, my client list is nowhere near the size of Stan's client list because of my introverted nature. Nevertheless, it works well for both of us. He is the extrovert with his own radio show and I am the introverted money manager.

Stan has an engineering background and in case you do not know, a lot of engineers end up in the financial services business. Stan is no exception. He is an astute investor and is extraordinarily skilled at portfolio management, just like me. Today, instead of one portfolio manager, we have two that make decisions for our clients. Further, through our custodian, we have access to some of the country's top money managers, just in case our clients want to look at other billion dollar plus money management options.

In addition, we are constantly on the lookout for other sharp people who want to bring their client assets with them and join our firm. We plan to add more people as we grow closer to $50,000,000. So, if you are in Wally World and are thinking of leaving, then give us a call.

Just so you know, I have not gotten back on a road bicycle since my accident. I just ride a stationary bike instead at LA Fitness® a few times per week in addition to hitting the weights.

Chapter Summary

What did we learn in this chapter?

- We learned that Rick was one of the very few financial advisors in the country who got out of the market on October 6, 2008 and did not get back in until May 8th, 2009 which filled in the gaps from his last book.
- We learned about the career trip Rick took to get to this point in his career and how his bicycle accident was a factor.
- We learned that Rick bounces off cars and is as tough as nickel steak.
- Rick and Stan are both talented money managers and they have other billion dollar money managers at their disposal.
- We learned not to text and drive.

Notes

Chapter Twenty-Two

An Introverted Athlete

"Shallow men believe in luck. Strong men believe in cause and effect."

~ Ralph Waldo Emerson

[This page intentionally left blank]

An Introverted Athlete

My wife thinks I should have named this chapter, "Eat some humble pie." Perhaps she is right. However, introverts need to brag a little bit, so here goes.

Yes, I am an introverted athlete, too. I let my ability do the talking. This chapter is going to sound egotistical, I know. However, I already told you that you can be an introvert and also egotistical at the same time. That's how I am made, good or bad.

I have always been athletic in my life. I like to run and my favorite thing to do is play baseball. I have played baseball for the last 26 years in the Men's Senior Baseball League World Series and Fall Classic tournaments. In addition, I play in regional baseball tournaments.

I am a beisbol jugador. Yo soy un diestro bateador que los bates de plomo libre.

In Spanish, that means:

I am a baseball player. I am a right handed batter who bats leadoff.

Or at least I think it does. I am still studying Spanish, so I have much more to learn.

In the fall of 2012, I played in the MSBL World Series and the MSBL Fall Classic as I have done since 1989. I hit an inside-the-park home run in each tournament that fall. I stole over 15 bases in eight games at the World Series and hit about .295 batting 9th, which is low for me. A week later at the Fall Classic, I batted leadoff and hit .625. This is at age 56 mind you. I guess I needed a week to warm up.

Now how many guys do you know that still play baseball at age 56, bat leadoff no less, can steal 15 bases and hit two inside-the-park home runs to boot? That's what I thought.

I try to stay on top of my health. I work out like a fiend at LA Fitness, and I try to do it 2 or 3 times per week. Plus, I stay in shape playing baseball at every opportunity.

I am an ex-track runner. I used to run short distances like 100's, 220's and 440's and relays. I am not a marathon type guy. I would rather run full out short distances. When I run, I go up to the local football field and run 100 yard dashes, then walk back, then run another 100 yards, then walk back. Usually, I do about 6 – 8 one hundred yard dashes running. Let me tell you, I can still get with it when I run. Every time that I go up to the football field, I do this type of running.

One day, I was out there running and a coach had his football team working out. He had them running about ten yards, touching the ground, then running back. Then, he would stretch it out to 20 yards. You coaches know what I am talking about. These kids were all high school kids. They were huffing and puffing, let me tell you.

The coach saw what I was doing and told those kids to go down to where I was and line up beside me and race me for a hundred yards. I knew this was unfair to the kids, because they didn't stand a chance at beating me. I could tell how lazily they were running. They didn't want to run 20 yards. The last thing they wanted to do was run a hundred yards. Anyway, we all lined up on the goal line. I let them take off first. After about 40 yards, I looked to my right and I had passed them all. I blew them away in the 100 yard dash. The coach just started laughing his head off. He got on his kids for letting "that old man" beat them. I loved it, too. I don't think those kids liked me too much after that episode though.

Here is another example of me being an introverted athlete. We have a batting cage where you can go hit baseballs nearby. They have a slow, medium and fast cage. The fast cage throws 90 miles an hour, easily. I went up there one weekend and this high school kid was there with his mom. He was in the fast cage. He was trying hard, bless his heart, but he was just barely tipping the ball with his bat. He was way over his head, but his ego would not stop him from giving it a whirl. After a few rounds, he came out of the cage not satisfied with how he hit. All he did was tip the ball a few times.

I went in there after him while he waited to give it another go. Poor guy. He had no idea how I can hit a baseball. I stood in that fast cage and effortlessly hit several baseballs right on the nose. After I left the cage, I took a look at the kid and his mom. They stood there in disbelief. I could see it in their eyes. They couldn't believe that an "old guy" like me could hit a baseball like that. I should have offered the kid some pointers on hitting, but my introverted nature got the best of me. It is awful being introverted sometimes. I really should be coaching kids. Maybe one day.

These are my secrets to playing baseball and being able to do the things that I do. I know that most of the other guys that I play with do not do what I do from a preparation stand point. In fact, two of my close friends I talked to recently gave me this as their preparation routine. One has quit drinking for the last three weeks and the other is on a no carb diet and has lost 15 pounds. I just laughed my ass off at that. I guess it never occurred to them to, oh I don't know, maybe to actually do physical exercise and work out!

While my two friends are into their "routine," I am killing myself running hundred yard dashes like I was still in high school. My wife thinks I am crazy, because of how extreme my workout is for these baseball tournaments. I can do 1,000 abdomen crunches on my Bowflex while holding 50 lbs. rods on each arm. My friends think I am full of you know what, but I promise you I can do it. My six pack abs are hidden behind my gut. I know they are in there somewhere, but you just can't see them. Perhaps, my dad was right about me. He said that I didn't like to miss too many meals.

In my mind, you have to put forth the effort way before you ever play the game, in order to be successful. That is my secret.

I carry that same secret over to being a portfolio manager. I put forth the effort in studying my industry and doing the research necessary to get better and better. I can say it unequivocally, I know how to invest money successfully. My problem is that I am introverted and I am not very good at marketing myself face-to-face. The truth is that I am humbled when a client wants to do business with me. I always understand that it is their money and I must make the sacrifices necessary to do the best job that I can for their benefit. Although I have no control over those idiots in Washington, D.C., I do have control for making a plan, having a process and being a professional.

You cannot be successful investing each and every year. Some years you will have winners and some years you will have losers. You have to make changes and adjust along the way to improve. In order to be successful investing, the best strategy is to minimize your losses by reducing your risk. Most people mistakenly believe that they should focus on the upside returns, but the numbers prove otherwise. All aggressive portfolios eventually fall. When they do fall, they fall at a must faster pace than a more conservatively diversified portfolio. At that point, the hole is deeper than you expect. It takes a lot more to dig out of it, too.

Did you know that I could hit a baseball like that? You probably did not know either, the amount of time and effort that I have devoted to the financial services industry. It is not that I am the smartest guy in the world, but I have made the sacrifices necessary to excel in my profession. I do the preparatory work required.

I never forget that all of my abilities are a gift from God and I do my best not to take things for granted. There are times that you have great success and there are times when you are humbled. It is all part of life. How you deal with it all is what matters most. Recently, I was in the finals of the MSBL World Series and we were behind by two runs. There were two runners on base with two outs. One was on first and the other runner was on second base. A single, or a bunt would do us no good. I knew that I had to hit a double, triple or home run to give those two runners a chance to score. The pitcher had me with two strikes, then threw it right down the middle. I swung as hard as I could and somehow I missed it and struck out. We lost 10 – 8. I still do not know how on earth I missed that pitch, but I did.

Although I have done it before, this time I did not produce a walk off hit in a critical situation. Our manager left our pitcher in the game until the very last out. This was not smart at all. Although, he is a great athlete, he was not the right pitcher for the team we faced.

I did not lose the game by striking out. The opposing pitcher was good and he beat me in that moment. He earned the win. We lost the game earlier by leaving our pitcher in the whole game. He gave up 17 hits, our fielders made 6 errors and we left numerous runners on base. I would have yanked the pitcher out in the third inning, but once again, I wasn't in charge. I hate not being in control, especially when you can make a difference, but you were not the one chosen to manage. You cannot be afraid to hurt people's feelings when you are the team manager. You have to be cold blooded to manage and put egos aside for the team.

It is the same with managing money. You have to make decisions without consideration of emotions. In other words, you should make well thought out decisions based on your knowledge and expertise.

Baseball mirrors life sometimes. Both baseball and life can humble you and leave you frustrated, too. You just have to put it behind you and move forward.

My thoughts turned to God's lesson for me. He wanted me to have a big helping of humble pie. I believe that his message was to give it your best effort and be strong even if you fail sometimes. After all, most baseball players fail 70% of the time or more. The players who can overcome that kind of adversity are the ones that succeed.

Chapter Summary

What did we learn in this chapter?

- We learned about Rick's abilities to run and play baseball.
- We learned that Rick knows what it means to be humble and he had some of his wife's humble pie.
- We found out about Rick's dedication to learning about his profession.
- We learned that Rick doesn't like to lose or strike out.

Notes

Chapter Twenty-Three

Investing is Boring

"Good leadership consists of showing average people how to do the work of superior people."

~ John D. Rockefeller

[This page intentionally left blank]

Investing is Boring

The nitty-gritty of investing is boring. People want it to be exciting, but it is not. It is very boring.

People think when they see something on TV that they have to do something with their investments. Okay, go ahead. Go on with your bad self. Every time you see something on TV, then do something with your investment portfolio. What are you going to do? You do not know what to do, because you are not trained for it.

Every now and then, I will meet with people who think they are smart investors. Usually, they will bring with them a chart, an article from the internet, a magazine or the newspaper. I spent several years in a technical analysis study group, so I can hang with the best of them when it comes to this subject. Technical analysis is the study of using charts to make investment decisions. I use technical analysis to help me make decisions. However, it is a safe bet to say that I am probably a little more knowledgeable about technical analysis than someone with a chart they printed off from www.yahoo.com. No slam on Yahoo® mind you as they are a fine company.

I use a program for financial advisors from a firm called Morningstar®. You ever heard of them? On one of the screens that I customized with their program, I have a watch list of all of our firm's recommended ETF's. In this watch list, it is made up of a box for each security. Each box turns dark green when the market is going gangbusters, green when it is up, pink when it is down a little and red when it is down a lot.

In addition, I have the Bond Market yield curve that shows me 3 months to 30 years what bond yields are doing. Further, I have a style box that shows me whether Core, Value, or Growth is doing better. This style box shows me Large, Mid and Small Company assets classes. Plus it shows me the respective Core, Value, and Growth asset classes and how they are doing today, 1 week ago, 1 month ago, 3 months ago, 1 year ago and 3 years ago.

I also have another section of my screen that shows me how cyclical, sensitive and defensive sectors of the economy are doing versus the overall market. This also ranges from today through the last 3 years.

Finally, I have three technical charts where I can see what is going on minute by minute for any one particular security, then the 5 day look at it, plus the 15 day look at it. This gives me a trend. I can also modify the time frame on my charts for any security with just a click of the mouse.

Also, I can get a quote, except my quotes are a little fancier than you can get. In addition, I have up to the minute market news delivered right into my screen. Got the picture?

So, one day, here comes this guy with his Yahoo® charts. Again, nothing against Yahoo®, mind you. They are a fine company and I use them sometimes myself for their ease of finding historical quotes. Back to my story. This guy comes in to "test me" on my technical analysis knowledge. He had no clue about my technical analysis background.

When I meet someone like this, I can see under the surface as to what is really going on. He is really involved in his own investment decision making, but he is a little unsure of himself. He thought that he could come to a professional like me and either validate that he is doing the right thing, or perhaps if he wanted to admit his ineptness as a money manager, then he could hire someone like me. He wasn't fully committed either way. You see, if he was absolutely confident in his technical analysis and investment acumen, then he would have never come to see me. Apparently, he was unsure of himself, even if he didn't want to admit it. His charts told him to be 100% in cash and his portfolio was 100% in cash as a result. We had a nice chat about technical analysis and he told me that based on his charts, the market was headed for a major crash. I disagreed. Even looking at his charts, I could not see where he was getting his interpretation. Remember, I know technical analysis fairly well.

This was a smart guy now, don't get me wrong, but he didn't know technical analysis as well as he thought. He knew enough to be dangerous, that's all. In the end, we agreed to disagree. He probably thought to himself that I was inept, because I could not see what he saw on his charts. I sent him a follow up letter advising him to invest on his own, because he seemed like that is what he really wanted to do anyway. He did not become my client. Wally on the other hand would have taken him on as a client no problem, but not me. He didn't meet my ideal client profile.

After he left, about a month later, the market went up like a rocket. I thought about him and his charts. You know, the ones that were telling him we were headed for a crash. He was 100% in cash, because his charts told him to do that.

I was in a technical analysis group a while back with a really smart and talented CPA. He spent several years trying to develop a buy and sell strategy of getting in and out of the market. He would have successes and failures all along the way. Even this smart guy realized that there is no fool proof way to beat the markets with technical analysis. In the end, he gave up and hired a professional money manager.

Hopefully, that guy that came to see me with his charts learned something from his experience. Of course, there is no way he could let himself come back and see me to help him with his investments. He had already embarrassed himself. I think rather he probably found a turn in the charts to justify to himself his _new_ technical analysis interpretation and still considered me to be inept. I saw him recently and he turned and scurried the other way. I would say with that action he was really, really embarrassed. To this day, I can never understand why people act that way. You meet people, then they act like they don't see you. It's ridiculous. He is not the invisible man. I hope you don't do that.

This is the thing that people do not understand with me. They think that I am just like every other financial advisor out there which is totally wrong. Every other financial advisor is not as dedicated as I am, nor is as knowledgeable as me when it comes to technical analysis. I have spent years studying technical analysis and being in technical analysis study groups. In addition, I am very intuitive. I can read between the lines.

I had another guy come to me who was real skittish about the stock market. He was in 100% cash and had been for a few years no less. He came by to tell me that he was finally ready to get in the market. This always _scares the living daylights_ out of me as an advisor. I know that if they were originally scared enough to be totally out of the market, then the likelihood of them panicking and going back to 100% cash is very, very high. Yet, they picked me to be their guinea pig financial advisor. Lucky me.

Most of the time, I say no to people like this, but I kind of liked this guy and felt that I could control his emotions and keep him invested with my plan, process and professionalism. Either that or maybe I bumped into a wall that week and hit my head which knocked the sense right out of me!

A scant two weeks after we had invested his money, he called me up and wanted to get out of the market. My gut instinct told me to not accept him as a client in the first place. I knew it. I knew it and I knew it, but I felt sorry for him and did it anyway. My mistake.

I talked to him about a year later and told him that he missed out on a double digit return. If he had only stayed invested, then he would have done well with me at the helm. Of course, he was totally embarrassed and ashamed that he had acted this way and wish that he wasn't so foolish. His investment decisions were based on emotions. That was his mistake, but I made a mistake too. I will not take on clients who are in 100% cash when they come to see me. I will listen to my gut instinct instead.

Investing with emotions can cause you to lose money. You are much better off having a professional advisor with lots of dedication and experience who knows how to navigate tough markets. You have to know and understand this main fact:

It never feels good to be in a bull market. If it ever does, then that probably means we are at the top. The 1999 technology boom would be a good example of a top in the markets.

You need to know this fact. *It never feels good*. There is *always* bad news on TV. I know some of you out there got out of the market in 2008 and you haven't been back since. Well that has turned out to not be a good decision on your part, if true. I know what you are thinking, "Well Rick, you got out of the market in 2008 and stayed out for six months. Why can't I do the same?" The difference is that I am a trained professional and you are not! Plus, that time period was a rare occurrence. Yet, everyone thinks that another 2008 is just around the corner.

Since 1970, the S&P 500® has declined more than 30% just once. This was in 2008. Interesting tidbit. However, it has made a *double digit* return *30 times* out of the last 44 years. Nevertheless, everyone still thinks that another 2008 is right around the corner. The reality is that it may not happen again anytime soon. I believe that this is a once in a generation type event.

From 1970 through 2014, it only happened once where the S&P 500® (i.e., the stock market) lost more than 30% in a year. One time out of 44 years! If you had invested $10,000 back then in the S&P 500® and left it alone, it would be worth $587,600 today. Let's kick that up a bit, shall we? If you had invested $100,000, then it would have been worth $5,876,000 today! Yet, you want to get in and out of the market? This is not smart people. You miss out when you are out of the market.

The moral of the story is that having a plan, a process and a professional (the three P's), then you will be absolutely fine staying fully invested at all times. The only problem with this strategy is that it is boring. It is very boring. The financial gurus on TV are always telling you to jump in and out of the market and you believe them! Instead, be a bored investor. It will pay off more than you can ever imagine.

You may be wondering how come I am not on TV, if I am so damn smart. I am an introvert, remember? Besides, why do I want to be on TV for two minutes at the most and explain why the stock market is up or down? I'll leave that activity to the Wally Streets who need to stroke their own egos and make themselves feel important.

I will however, go on TV to promote my book. Any takers?

Chapter Summary

What did we learn in this chapter?

- We learned that investing is boring, not exciting.
- We learned not to show Rick any charts or news articles from the internet.
- We learned our investor tools are no comparison to Rick's tools.
- We found out that Rick knows technical analysis better than we ever will.
- We learned that bull markets never feel good.
- We found out that 2008 was a once in 44 year occurrence.
- We learned that being fully invested since 1970 would have given us a 70% success rate or a .697 batting average which would easily put us in the Hall of Fame for Boring Investors.
- We learned that it is essential to know about the three P's, having a plan, a process and a professional.

Notes

Chapter Twenty-Four

Volatility Matters

"Anyone who doesn't take truth seriously in small matters cannot be trusted in large ones either."

~ Albert Einstein

[This page intentionally left blank]

Volatility Matters

In my last book, no need to buy it by the way, I disclosed my 20/65% rule. This rule says that do not put more than 20% into any one asset class (except cash) and do not put more than 65% in the stock market. Both rules apply at the same time.

I have squeezed this rule a little tighter here recently. There are more assets classes that I want to be in and if I was limited to only 20% per asset class, then I could theoretically only invest in five things. I rarely ever put close to 20% into any one asset class anyway. However, today I have modified this down to about 10% per asset class on the equity (stocks) side and no more than 15% on the fixed income (bonds) side. In reality, I invest in about 12 to 14 different asset classes, so a lot of them are as low as 2.5% in any one particular asset class.

My partner Stan twisted my arm and asked me to stretch out my 65% limit to 75%, but only for younger people with extremely long time horizons. I agreed, but we do not have many young clients who are that risky. I can count on one hand the clients we have with 75% equities. Most fall in the 65% or less category.

You may be wondering, "Why do you have these assets class limits Rick?" It is because I like to limit the volatility in a portfolio to reduce the range of ups and downs. Every now and then, I will get a panicky call from a client where they watched something on TV (imagine that), and called me about their account losing money. Typically, they will see something like "the stock market has dropped 7% in the last three weeks" on TV. I will pull up their account and take a look see. In most cases, because of the diversified way I invest for clients, with the asset class and equity limitations, they might be off 2 or 2.5% compared to the market's 7% drop. Usually, I get an "Oh, that's not as bad as I thought."

This is the thing with financial advisors who are worth their salt. They explain how they invest in the beginning of the relationship, but then they have to re-educate their clients on the three P's all along the way, because of those financial television shows. Financial advisors have to remind their clients that they have a plan, a process and that they are a professional. This is what we do. We are professionals.

Boy, I would like to take those TV's and chunk them out a ten story window. They are the source of a lot of my headaches. Stay away from the TV. Learn a new language, read a book, take a trip or do something more worthwhile, will you? Thank you.

What you have to understand about investing is that volatility matters more than anything. If you invested in 100% stocks, then you would have the widest swings in prices you can get. The markets gyrate around all the time. Up and down and up and down. It is enough to make you dizzy.

Now, I want to give you a little simple math, so you can understand how volatility works. Instead of being 100% in the market, what if you were only 80% in it? You would have 80% of the volatility. If you were 70%, then you would have 70% of the volatility. If you were 60% in it, then you would have 60% of the volatility. Simple logic would tell you that if the market made 10% and I had 60% of the volatility, then I would make 6%. Wrong. It doesn't work like that. Although, I agree it seems logical.

With a properly diversified asset class portfolio, a 60% equity mix may actually perform at 80% or more of the market's return. Why? Because the asset classes chosen really matter. In addition, the percentages that you choose to weight towards each of those asset classes matters, too. A skilled portfolio manager can actually overweight certain assets classes expected to outperform and underweight those asset classes that he or she expects to underperform. Or, they may eliminate an out of favor

[346]

asset class and replace it with one that they think is poised to do well in the future. By making these kind of decisions, or tweaks if you will, it is possible to do well with even a 60% equity mix. If the market makes 14%, then wouldn't you be okay making 11% without all the same gyrations? I thought so.

Volatility also matters on the downside. If you took statistics in college, then this will make sense to you. If an investment of the S&P 500® goes up and down, it has a standard deviation range of expected returns. You take the standard deviation and double it. This means that roughly 98% of the time, the S&P 500® will perform within that range. For example, it may have a range of 25% on the upside and minus 28% on the downside. So, 98% of the time, the return of the S&P 500® will fall in this range somewhere. I know what you are thinking, "Rick, what about the other 2% of the time?" I'm glad you asked. This is known as tail risk. Come again?

Tail risk is best thought of with a bell curve. A bell curve looks like a bell, thus that's why they call it a bell curve. Think about the Liberty Bell in Philadelphia. The chart would have a line that starts on the bottom left, rises to a curved top, then descends back down to the right. Underneath that bell, is the 98% of the stock market's returns. The 2% outside of the bell is the chance that it will fall outside of that range. The left side representing the extreme 1% of the time *losses* possibility and the right side representing the other extreme 1% of the time highest *gains* possibility. I am just generalizing these percentages to make it easier to understand, so don't beat me up about the tail risk being 1.2709876% or something. I'm on to you engineers. I know how you think.

The year 2008 was a tail risk year. It fell outside the two times standard deviation range. It was in essence a fluke from a statistical standpoint. An expensive fluke for some, but nevertheless a statistical fluke. You follow me?

As a professional money manager, if you can limit the possibility of tail risk, then you are doing a good job. I limit it with the three P's. I have a plan which is 12 to 14 asset classes diversified across multiple asset classes which are monitored and re-evaluated periodically as conditions warrant. I have a process which means I do research on new or existing ETF's and decide which to include or remove from a portfolio. Then, I shift the percentage weights of each of those assets classes to either a more conservative or aggressive mix to match a client's needs. I will include more dividend paying ETF's to help generate needed income, or I would include more growth oriented ETF's to generate more growth. After all, my final of the three P's is that I am a professional. That means don't try this at home.

Chapter Summary

What did we learn in this chapter?

- We learned about asset class limitations and equity percentage limitations.
- We learned how volatility matters and how we can reduce it.
- We now understand that good asset class selections can improve our performance.
- We learned about tail risk and standard deviations.
- We reiterated our understanding of the three P's and how all three work together to design a well thought out strategy for our benefit.

Notes

Chapter Twenty-Five

Keep it Public

"A word to the wise ain't necessary. It's the stupid ones that need the advice."

~ Bill Cosby

[This page intentionally left blank]

Keep it Public

Just for fun, I like to watch American Greed: Scams, Scoundrels and Suckers on CNBC. I am simply amazed and astonished how many people give money to crooks without a second thought. In almost every case, these crooks are using securities and I use the term "securities" very loosely here, because most of the time there are no securities at all. These crooks create these investments out of thin air. The investors are writing checks to them personally or their "company." That is usually a big freaking mistake to write a check out to Wally's company. Can you say Bernie Madoff?

I took one look at one of those made up statements from Bernie Madoff's firm and knew right away it was fake. Although, I fail to understand why the regulators could not see the same thing. I spotted it instantly. If you want to read more about the fiasco of Wall Street, then I recommend Larry Doyle's book, "In Bed with Wall Street." You can find it here: http://www.senseoncents.com.

One time a few years ago, I actually caught a Ponzi schemer. This Wally Street was promising an outlandish return (12%) on an investment that did not exist and several people lined up to buy it. I still do not understand how people fall for Wally Street hawking an investment that pays 12%. Luckily, we caught this crook after he had only stolen a few million dollars of his "clients" money. These clients made the mistake of buying into "securities" that were not publicly traded and falling for that fictitious 12% return.

All these crooks have to do is promise 12% returns. You would be surprised how many crooks promise 12% returns. I don't know what it is about that number, but it seems like on every one of the American Greed television shows, the crooks promised investors a 12% return. That must be the magic number or something. Apparently, that is all investors need to hear to make themselves totally stupid.

Of course, the American Greed producers like to put a face on the victims. They seem to always be able to find someone who "lost everything." I am conflicted about these people. On the one hand, I think, "Why didn't they come see me?" Especially, the local people *in my county* who were on this show! On the other hand I think, "How could they be so gullible?" Every time the gullible side wins out. These people are gullible! I'm sorry, but that is the sad truth.

Here is the mistake these people made. They invested in something that is not publicly traded and also something that is not regulated. As an investor, this needs to be one of your criteria for investing:

Never invest in anything that is not publicly traded, nor regulated. Also, never invest in something that guarantees 12%!

This is not the only thing to watch out for mind you, but it is a good start. All of these Ponzi scheme crooks sell phony investments. It is likely to be phony if it is not publicly traded. More often than not, they are using phony investments created out of thin air. You have to be smart and understand that there isn't any investments that pay 12% guaranteed! None. Nada. Zilch. Zero.

If someone tells you that you can get 12% guaranteed, then you are talking to a Ponzi scheme salesman!

Worse than that, this crook is after all of your money! Go back and read the Wally's Products chapter. In it you will find the investments that crooks use to steal your money. Perhaps, it would be a good idea to diversify your financial advisors, too. That means do not give all of your money to one advisor. This is what the smart people do, by the way. Oh,

I almost forgot, I'm available in case you want to diversify your assets among financial advisors. Although, I have no idea why you would want to continue to do business with Wally now that you know the truth.

Let's see. You can buy a portfolio of ETF's through an *independent* registered investment adviser who uses a reputable brokerage firm with a proven reputation and get your money within 3 business days if needed. Or, you can buy a *Promissory Note* with a "12% guaranteed return" from Wally Street. Which would you rather do? If you answered the latter, then you have fallen victim to Wally's reality distortion field.

People, you have to be smart when it comes to investing. Wally Street is good at blowing smoke up your skirt, but when it comes to a plan and a process, he will fall woefully short. Wally cannot explain any plan with a Promissory Note. All he can say is "it pays 12% guaranteed" over and over again until he dulls your senses. Nor will Wally be able to explain his process either. He will give you some vague story about real estate, or a business plan, but it will be nothing concrete. It will all be BS. He is trying to draw you into his reality distortion field where reality is non-existent. Do you want to be on American Greed? If not, then stay away from Wally, especially when he is guaranteeing a 12% return.

Another point that you might want to consider is to go to an *independent* registered investment adviser and have your account statements reviewed. This is how I found that Ponzi schemer! One of his "clients" brought me their bogus account statements and then he was caught. If you are currently doing business in Wally World, then I would definitely seek out a second opinion from someone like me who is an independent registered investment adviser. I know how to catch those stinking crooks. If you have any concerns, then call me immediately.

Keep it public and stay away from Wally's esoteric investments. That way you will not end up as a Ponzi scheme victim.

[355]

Chapter Summary

What did we learn in this chapter?

- Ponzi schemes generally happen with non-public investments that pay 12% guaranteed interest.
- People foolish enough to invest in non-public investments deserve what they get.
- We learned not to give all of our money to one financial advisor and Rick is always available to help diversify our assets among financial advisors.
- We learned that getting a second opinion from an independent registered investment adviser might be a very good idea.
- We realized that we never want to fall into Wally's reality distortion field.
- We learned that we never want to be on the television show American Greed talking about that 12% guaranteed return that we never got from Wally.

Chapter Twenty-Six

Keep it Liquid

"Learn to enjoy every minute of your life. Be happy now. Don't wait for something outside of yourself to make you happy in the future. Think how really precious is the time you have to spend, whether it's at work or with your family. Every minute should be enjoyed and savored."

~ Earl Nightingale

[This page intentionally left blank]

Keep it Liquid

Wally loves to put you in investments with penalties or restrictions against early withdrawals. Things like Variable Annuities, Non-Publicly Traded REIT's/BDC's, Promissory Notes, Regulation D Offerings, and Structured Products. All those make Wally a lot of money. The longer he can sock away your money, then the more money he makes. Answer me this question:

Why would you invest in anything that is not publicly traded and on top of that is not liquid?

Go ahead. Please tell me. I'm waiting on your answer. I'm going be here a while, because you cannot look me in the eye and give me a good answer to that question. Rather than me waiting on you to try and come up with something, I am going to move on.

Liquidity is another all important thing when it comes to investing your money. Wally wants to lock you up into his products *that make him money*. If you put $100,000 in a Non-Publicly Traded REIT, then he will likely make 6.5 - 8.5% on it. That is $6,500 - $8,500 stinking dollars! Wally gets that for saying "sign here." Remember, it takes a lot of skills and training to say "sign here."

What do you get in return? No liquidity, risk of principal loss and a slim chance of making a nickel, a possible roll up to another crappy thing and a fat chance of getting your money back.

A Promissory Note is worse. You give Wally your money and it is gone bye-bye. There is no liquidity on those at all and you can forget about getting your principal back.

Most Variable Annuities have surrender charges of 10 years or more when dealing with Wally Street. Okay, maybe your version of Wally sells you one with only a 6 year surrender charge. Whoop-de-frigging-do! Isn't that nice of old Wally Street?

You are getting an investment with expenses north of 3%, someone who is more than likely not trained in how to properly invest the damn thing, plus you are stuck in it. That means you have to take a loss to get your money back. This is so idiotic!

Hey, I wonder. Did Wally tell you that you can buy a Variable Annuity with _no surrender charges and no commissions?_ That's right. You can get a Variable Annuity without any surrender charges and no commissions! Interesting. That is something Wally forgot to mention I'll bet.

Did Wally also tell you, if you really wanted a Variable Annuity that you can get one with expenses of _$20 per month_, instead of 3% per year or more? This means that instead of investing $200,000 and paying $6,000 per year or more in annual expenses on Wally's "recommended" Variable Annuity, you can get one that only charges $240 per year. This also means that over that 10 year period that you are waiting for the surrender charge to go away, then you will have paid $60,000 in expenses or more. This is instead of $2,400 in expenses on the no surrender charges and no commission Variable Annuity over the same 10 year period.

Think about this fact. Suppose you are in year two of Wally's Variable Annuity. If you sold out of it, it will cost you about 8% of the $200,000 in my example. This is $16,000. You have already paid $12,000 in expenses for the first two years you were in Wally's Variable Annuity. If you choose to stay in it, then each year it will cost you another $6,000 in expenses, if not more. By getting out now, you are saving another $48,000 in expenses. Unfortunately, it is likely to be more than that.

Is it smart to wait another eight years until the surrender charge goes away? Staying in Wally's Variable Annuity is going to cost you at least another $48,000. Getting out is only going to cost you $16,000. You need to accept the fact that you screwed up by putting your money in a Variable Annuity with Wally, in the first place. Get out of the damn thing! Go see an *independent* registered investment adviser who will put you on the right path making smarter decisions with your money.

Did your "trusted advisor" Wally tell you these things about Variable Annuities? I wonder why? Perhaps, he was only thinking of himself and making a big commission. Damn it man. I got you again, didn't I?

Silly you. You thought Wally was looking out for you. I just proved to you that he is not looking out for you. If he was looking out for you, then **_you would know_** all about these no surrender charges, no commissions and only $20 per month Variable Annuities. You still think Wally is someone you can trust? If so, then you are a fool. Sorry, I had to break out the hickory switch again, because there are so many of you sitting out there with Variable Annuities. You cannot hide from me. I know you are there. I also know that this is the number one product sold by Wally Street. The odds of you having one is very, very high.

I know. I know. Some of you will say that your adviser is a good person and they would not do that to you. Have you ever owned a Non-Publicly Traded REIT? How about a Variable Annuity? Perhaps a Unit Investment Trust? How about Class A, B or C share mutual funds? Have you ever owned any of these? If so, then guess what? Your financial advisor's name is Wally Street. It doesn't make any difference if he is a good person. He is still taking advantage of you, because of the business model he works under. That is the brutal reality that you need to deal with. It's the business model that is the culprit!

Liquidity is king. Keep it public and keep it liquid.

Chapter Summary

What did we learn in this chapter?

- For God's sake, keep it liquid.
- Wally Street wants to tie up all of our money for a long time.
- Most everything that Wally sells has liquidity restrictions, so he can make more commissions.
- We are pissed off that Wally didn't tell us about these no commission, no surrender charge Variable Annuities.
- We realized that the business model is the problem and nothing will ever change as long as we keep doing business with Wally.
- You learned the hard way that you are a victim of Wally Street and you are finally seeing the light. Finally!

Notes

Chapter Twenty-Seven

The New Normal

"Imagine for yourself a character, a model personality, whose example you determine to follow, in private as well as in public."

~ Epictetus

[This page intentionally left blank]

The New Normal

I did not come up with the saying, "The New Normal." I believe it was Mohamed A. El-Erian, who recently announced his retirement from PIMCO Funds that originally coined it in 2009. He said in article back then and I am paraphrasing here, that "The New Normal would be where we see continued slow growth, persistently high unemployment in the U.S. economy and debt and deficit concerns where the Federal Reserve Bank tries to manage it by purchasing securities." He said this back in 2009. That was a little more than four years ago.

If you look at what has happened since, I'll be darn, we have slow growth, persistently high unemployment, debt and deficit concerns and the Federal Reserve Bank trying to manage it all by buying securities on the open market. It actually wasn't that hard to forecast. All you had to do was look to Japan as an example. Economies are built on supply and demand. When there is ample demand, then there is ample growth. When there is a lack of demand, then there is a contraction, recession or depression.

I know what you are thinking. "Well Rick, how do we invest in "The New Normal"?" You know that screechy sound that comes across your television sometimes that says, "This is a test of the emergency broadcast system. This is only a test."? Well, this chapter is a test, too.

I wanted to see if you were paying attention. Did you fall into my trap of wondering about slow growth, high unemployment, debt and deficit concerns and what the Federal Reserve Bank was going to do at their next policy meeting? If so, then you just lost a letter grade for my course my dear pupil.

Remember when I said that bull markets never feel good? All of that kind of junk is always going on, so why should you be worrying about it? Let me worry about it for you. I am the professional with 27 plus years of dealing with these issues, not you. This is one of the reasons that you pay me a fee. Besides, even if you worry about my judgment, we still can kick it upstairs to one of our billion dollar plus money management firms to take care of things for you. They know what to do in "The New Normal," too.

The best thing you can do is to remember, despite "The New Normal," is that you have the three P's. A plan, a process and a professional that takes care of things for you. Got it? Good.

If however, you have Wally Street as your financial advisor, or you are a do-it-yourself investor, or a technical analysis guru, then you will need to worry about slow growth, high unemployment, the debt and deficit and what the Federal Reserve is going to do next all the damn time!

The choice is all yours.

Chapter Summary

What did we learn in this chapter?

- We learned that we lost a letter grade in class, because we slipped back into thinking stupidly.
- We learned that one of the reasons we pay Rick is so he can worry about the markets, the economy and the government and how to navigate our portfolios as a result.
- We learned that if we decide to invest on our own, or with Wally, then we have to worry about all that junk related to the economy, the debt and deficit, the government, and what the Federal Reserve is going to do next all the damn time!
- We can see clearly how hiring an independent registered investment advisor with the three P's is worth every cent. Especially since we don't have to worry about all that junk related to the economy, the debt and deficit, the government, and what the Federal Reserve is going to do next all the damn time!

Notes

Chapter Twenty-Eight

Social Security Options

"To know, is to know that you know nothing. That is the meaning of true knowledge."

~ Socrates

[This page intentionally left blank]

Social Security Options

There is a new seminar program offered up by Wally Street. It is based on Social Security and when you should take it. A lot of insurance companies have jumped into the market with Microsoft PowerPoint® presentations on the subject of Social Security and are giving them to Wally Street for free as long as he sells Variable Annuities with their firm to you. There are even some software firms that are selling computer programs to Wally Street to help him help you with your Social Security decisions. Remember, Wally Street is looking out for you. He is so concerned about you that he wants to "help you."

The first thing that you ought to know is that you can go to this web site and do a retirement estimation on your potential Social Security benefits.

https://secure.ssa.gov/acu/ACU_KBA/main.jsp?URL=/apps8z/ARPI/main.jsp?locale=en&LVL=4

In case the web site changes, please note that you can find it at www.socialsecurity.gov. Web addresses change and you can start here to find the Retirement Estimator calculator, in case the above link no longer works. They are not mailing out those Social Security statements any longer, in case you did not realize it.

Wally Street's seminar is going to give you the Social Security basics in his PowerPoint® presentation, but also tell you about Delayed Retirement Credits, File and Suspend for married couples and what is known as the Restricted Application Strategy.

Let me save you the trouble of going to Wally's seminar. I'll explain them for you right here. By the way, I don't think Wally likes me too much.

[373]

[This page intentionally left blank]

Delayed Retirement Credits

Delayed Retirement Credits are for people born in 1943 and after, who can get a yearly increase of 8% on their Social Security benefit for each year they wait after their normal retirement age. Or, they can get 2/3 of 1% for each month they wait after their normal retirement age. That is simple enough to understand, but what planning opportunities are there by delaying your Social Security benefits?

The first thing that jumps out at my avid pupil ought to be the fact that you get an 8% per year increase in benefits. I can understand those who have no other income or assets and need to turn on their Social Security benefits as soon as possible. However, when you may not really need the Social Security benefits, or you have other assets that you can draw on for a year or two, then this can be very beneficial.

For example, if your normal full retirement of Social Security was going to pay you $2,000 per month, but you have $24,000 in a CD earning less than 1%, then it would make more sense to use the CD for income. The income from the CD would be primarily principal and would not have much of any taxes due on it. In addition, that pool of money would need to be compared with your Social Security pool of money. This CD makes a 1% return versus an 8% comparison. If you took the Social Security benefit, you will be spending that money, but miss out on the 8% growth you could have earned by waiting, plus it is taxable too.

It is the same process if you used the CD. You would be spending the CD money. However, the CD money if saved would only net you less than 1%. While the Social Security delayed would net you an increase in your benefit of an additional 8%.

That is not too tough to follow. I'm not sure why Wally needs to do a whole PowerPoint® presentation on it. Oh yeah. He is "concerned" about you. I almost forgot.

File and Suspend Strategy

The File and Suspend strategy was originally used in the past for married couples where one spouse was the primary earner. However, it is used a little differently today with two income households.

Suppose the husband was at the full retirement age of 66 and was entitled to $2,000 per month. However, he chose to file and suspend his benefits. The wife could then file for spousal benefits of 50% of the husband's and receive $1,000 per month. At the time of filing for the spousal benefit, the wife suspends her own benefit which would have been $2,400 a month at her full retirement age of 66. As a result, the husband's $2,000 per month benefit continues to grow at the rate of 8% per year and so does the wife's $2,400 per month benefit. Of course, all that is coming in from Social Security is $1,000 per month. Generally, we are assuming that both spouses want to continue to work a few more years and are using their work income to make up for the shortfall from Social Security. Or you can use dead CD or money market funds instead.

If the wife or husband was only 62, then it creates a penalty in the amount that you can get. After you know the reduced benefit and her husband has filed and suspended his benefit, then ordinarily, she would be entitled to 50% of his benefit at her full retirement age. However, by jumping the gun at age 62, she is only entitled to 65 – 75% of her husband's full benefit depending on the year she were born. This is opposed to $1,000 per month, if she waited until her full retirement age.

It all hinges on your health. If you are healthy and still working, then it may be better to wait until full retirement age which depends on the year that you were born. There is also another alternative known as the Restricted Application Strategy that is a different strategy to consider.

[This page intentionally left blank]

The Restricted Application Strategy

The Restricted Application Strategy is where both spouses are at full retirement age. One spouse has a better Social Security benefit than the other. Let's say that the husband has a $2,400 a month benefit and the wife has a $2,000 a month benefit. The wife can apply for half of her husband's which would be $1,200 per month, then delay taking her own Social Security benefit until age 70 which grows by 8% per year. So, at age 70, she switches to her own benefit which will grow to $2,721 a month.

The couple would be getting $3,600 per month from age 66 to age 70, then at age 70, this would jump to $5,121 per month with this Restricted Application Strategy. This is an extra $721 per month as opposed to them both just taking their $4,400 total benefits at full retirement age.

I know what you are thinking. "Mr. Rick, what about the $800 per month difference that we did not take for those four years between age 66 and 70. That would mean missing out on $38,400."

Well, at age 70, you would be getting that extra $721 per month. If you _both_ live another 10 years, then that will net you an additional $86,520 as opposed to just taking your normal full retirement benefits.

Without the Restricted Application Strategy, assuming that you just took your normal full retirement benefits of $4,400 a month total, then at the end of that life expectancy (age 80 or 14 years), then you will have been paid $739,200.

However, Wally you see, he has got this nifty little PowerPoint® presentation on Social Security and he is all full of piss and vinegar. Remember, what is Wally's ultimate goal? To sell you something that makes him a commission. With the Restricted Application Strategy of taking $3,600 per month for 4 years, then switching to the $5,121 per month that is a grand total of $787,320 in benefits paid. Sounds great and wonderful, except the problem is that you have to be certain that *both of you* live to age 80. How sure are you about that? That is just a minor detail. You know Wally doesn't like to worry about minor details.

Congratulations. You just discovered how actuaries think. Yes, the government has this as an alternative, but is it worth it in your case? Perhaps, not. You have to pull out your trusty HP 12C calculator to find out. Plus, if one of you dies, then it all goes up in smoke. Those actuaries have this all figured out. Too bad Wally doesn't.

There are some other things to consider, too. If you did take the $3,600 for those four years and pulled out the $800 a month shortfall from some of your other investments, then that portion could be taken strategically. In other words, that $800 could be taken out of dead CD money earning nothing where you would not owe any taxes on it. Social Security income is taxable in most cases up to 85%. If you can shelter taxes on that $800, then you would have to factor that into your analysis. Damn it man. Just when I thought this was going to be easy, it gets complicated.

The main problem with the Restricted Application Strategy is that both spouses need to wait until full retirement age and be close to the same age. You cannot do it if one spouse claims their benefits *before* their full retirement age. If they do that, then they cannot switch to a higher benefit later. They are stuck. Also, if there is a big age difference, it is definitely not going to work for you. The reason being that you cannot pull both Social Security benefits at the same time if there is a big age difference.

The moral of the story is that you need to know these rules, because it depends on each of your benefits, your difference in age, when you take them and how you take them. You have to do the calculations and consider health issues, too.

I have given you enough information to research your Social Security options. Believe it or not, the www.socialsecurity.gov web site has a lot of easy to understand tools and calculators to help you decide. The main thing you might want to remember is, if you take benefits at age 62, then this could hurt you. Further, if both spouses have good benefits, then the Restricted Application Strategy might be a plausible way to go if you both are in excellent health with long family life expectancies.

In addition, if you have other assets that are not making anywhere near 8%, then delaying your Social Security benefits could be beneficial. Every situation is different and you really just have to run the numbers. There is no cut and dried answer that works for everyone, unfortunately.

Wally loves seniors. People who need help with their Social Security benefits are seniors and that plays right into Wally's wheel house. Our good friend Wally Street will gladly give you this Social Security information as long as you do business with him. Of course that means buying a Variable Annuity or two, a Non-Publicly Traded REIT, some UIT's, some Municipal Bonds and perhaps a handful of class A, B or C shares mutual funds. You would not mind that, would you?

Chapter Summary

What did we learn in this chapter?

- The Social Security web site has some good information and tools to help us with our decisions on Social Security benefits.
- We learned that Wally Street is on the prowl promoting his expertise as a Social Security expert with his PowerPoint® presentation.
- We learned about Delayed Retirement Credits and the strategies related to them.
- We learned about File and Suspend and whether this is beneficial or not.
- We learned about the Restricted Application Strategy and why this method is popular for married couples who are close to the same age.

Chapter Twenty-Nine

Elder Care Planning

"Obstacles are those frightful things you see when you take your eyes off your goal."

~ Henry Ford

[This page intentionally left blank]

Elder Care Planning

At some point, in almost everyone's family, they are faced with a crisis involving their parents or their spouse or other close relative. Sometimes, you can anticipate it like with Alzheimer's or Parkinson's disease, but other times you cannot. Usually, it strikes suddenly like with a debilitating stroke and you are woefully unprepared to deal with it.

In our extended families, we have had Alzheimer's, Lou Gehrig's disease, and disabling strokes. Don't think it will not happen in your family. That would be foolish on your part.

Typically, with an older couple, usually the healthier of the two spouses takes care of the one needing the help. However, what happens when the healthy spouse dies first? Then, what? Usually, if there is an adult child that lives nearby, then they are thrust into the role of taking care of mom or dad. However, what if that adult child is not the best one to jump into that role? Should other children have to move to where mom or dad lives? Should they move mom or dad to their town? Will they have to quit their job to help mom or dad?

What kind of firm do you hire to help the person who has the crippling disease that requires long term care? Do you even know where to start looking? How about assisted living centers and nursing home choices? If you are from out of town, how will you pick one? Usually, mom and dad have moved to Florida or some other retirement state to live out their lives and their adult children may be in totally different states. This complicates matters. Most likely, you have no clue about the firms offering these type of services.

This is where an Elder Law Attorney comes into play. You want to get a referral to an Elder Law attorney from a trusted source, such as another attorney or CPA, or me for example. I would look for an Elder Law attorney that is a member of the National Academy of Elder Law Attorneys. They have a search engine at their web site located at: http://www.naela.org.

Here are the <u>cold hard facts</u> when it comes to paying for Elder Care services.

1. You can pay for it with all of your own money. Yikes!
2. You can use Long Term Care Insurance to pay for it, if you have any.
3. You can avoid going to an Elder Law attorney because you are penny wise and pound foolish (i.e., stupid) and spend all of your money down to $2,000, and then go on Medicaid.
4. If you are a Veteran or spouse of a Veteran and meet certain qualifications, then you may get some benefits to help, but generally this will be limited in scope.
5. You can go see an Elder Law attorney and do pre-crisis and post-crisis planning to stave off spending all of your assets on Elder Care expenses.

The best choices in that list are when you can combine choices 2, 4 and 5 together. Alas, most people will not buy Long Term Care Insurance and not everyone is a Veteran that meets the qualifications, so the next best choice is number 5. An Elder Law attorney knows how to protect your assets pre-crisis by starting the clock and post-crisis when you need urgent help, plus how to get you qualified for Veteran's benefits, if applicable to your situation.

It used to be in the good old days that all you had to do was give away your assets in order to qualify for Medicaid. The government got wise to this and put in a 3 year look back rule. Then, they changed it to a 5 year look back where it stands today. This means that if you give away any assets, even assets to your church, then Medicaid will not pay for your care, until you pay that amount that you paid to your church, towards your own care first. This look back period is during the last five years that *any and all gifts* are looked at by the states running their Medicaid programs. By the way, you cannot hide past gifts. You took that charitable tax deduction, didn't you? That's how they know. You have to tell them everything and prove it to them. There is no loophole here.

Some states, like Florida allow you to keep the principal of your IRA while other states like Kentucky make you sell it as part of the required spend down process. If you have to sell it, then you have to pay the taxes on it, too.

It is ironic isn't it? The fact that you save all your life in an IRA taking out only the required minimum distributions only to find later that you have to liquidate the whole IRA and pay the taxes in order to pay for your Elder Care expenses, because you thought that it would not happen to you. Sad, but true.

My partner Stan Rosenthal is an expert in this area of Elder Care Planning and he has taught me a lot about it along with my Elder Law attorney friends.

Elder Care Planning is a complex area and a very specialized niche of expertise. I could write literally for days and days on all the ways to plan for pre-crisis and post-crisis care. However, that would be rather pointless, because I do not want to leave you with any impression that you can navigate these waters on your own. Once you tried, then you would soon realize how difficult it would be to try and figure out all the rules involved in Elder Care Planning, Medicaid, Medicare, Long Term Care Insurance, Veteran's Benefits, spend down requirements and many, many more confusing rules.

Here is what you need to really understand. *Pay very close attention.* Think ***critically*** now, my avid pupil.

The Elder Law attorney may charge $5,000, $10,000 or even $15,000 depending on whether it is a pre-crisis plan or a post-crisis plan. At first glance, you may think that is too high, but you would be sorely mistaken. The Elder Law attorney is the only person who can design a plan to keep as much of your assets as possible. The truth is that you are going to pay that $5,000, $10,000 or $15,000 whether you realize it or not. Are you doubting me? Never doubt me, or I might have to take away another letter grade my dear student.

Here is how you will pay the $5,000, $10,000 or $15,000 like it or not. If a nursing home costs on average about $6,000 a month, then if you do not hire an Elder Law attorney, then you will spend $6,000 a month, like it or not, every month. Three months from now, while you thought the Elder Law attorney's fee was too high, guess what? You have spent $18,000 on the nursing home and probably more, yet you are no closer to protecting the rest of your assets. *Do you get that?* You are going to pay that $5,000, $10,000 to $15,000, like it or not. Either you will pay it to an Elder Law attorney who can help you, or you will give it to the nursing home owner to benefit his family and not yours. Okay Kemosabe?

If you are dumb, then you will decide in the fourth month, after paying $24,000 to the nursing home, to *then hire* the Elder Law attorney who still might cost the same $5,000, $10,000 or $15,000. At this point, it may have cost you up to $39,000 to protect the rest of your assets. This is when you could have only paid the $5,000, $10,000 or $15,000 instead in the first place! Or, you could just say to hell with it all and let the nursing home guy have all of your money. Trust me. A lot of people do.

If you are smart, then you will hire the Elder Law attorney _as fast as humanly possible_ and let him have the chance to save as much of your assets as possible. The Elder Law attorney is the best friend that you have in this situation and I mean your absolute best friend, too. Here is some really good advice:

Hire an Elder Law attorney as fast as humanly possible.

The moral of the story is that you _cannot delay_ hiring an Elder Law attorney at all. If you do, then all you are doing is making the guy who owns the nursing home get off with your money while your family suffers. The nursing home owner doesn't mind. You are helping him and his family, not yours. This is called being bull headed. My partner Stan Rosenthal calls it "going broke in a nursing home."

It is kind of like that idiot who used an online legal document web site to buy a living trust and where his family found out the hard way what a mistake that was for them. You cannot be bull headed when it comes to Elder Care Planning. The money that you pay the Elder Law attorney means more money that is saved for your family. That's a fact, Jack.

It is very important that you understand how this works. I hope my frank explanation got through to you. You have to involve an Elder Law attorney and you have to do it today, especially if you are facing a crisis. No hesitation, please.

Of course, the really smart people are the ones who plan for all of this ahead of time with pre-crisis planning by starting that 5 year clock. Pre-crisis planning is not as expensive as it would be with waiting until a crisis actually hits. With pre-crisis planning, the Elder Law attorney can effectively shelter possibly 100% of your assets if you are married, or a little bit less if you are single, with their Elder Law expertise. Otherwise, you can be stupid and go broke in a nursing home.

[389]

By the way, Wally wants to help you with spending down your assets to qualify for Medicaid. His recommendation will be to buy a Medicaid compliant annuity. This is where you take your assets and buy this annuity and it pays an income stream with no deferral or balloon payments. The theory is that since your assets are off the balance sheet and turned into an annuity income stream, then it means those assets disappear from your balance sheet as an asset.

Each state has specific rules around these type of Medicaid compliant annuities. In fact, some states disallow the strategy altogether. The point that I wanted to make is you cannot just go to Wally Street for Elder Care Planning *without* having the Elder Law attorney in the mix. Odds are that Wally is not keeping up with the complexity of Medicaid rules and regulations. You do not want to take Wally's advice, unless the Elder Law attorney has advised you to do the Medicaid compliant annuity strategy.

One more thing. I had a guy come to me for help with his 20 plus accounts, because his wife was in a nursing home and he was out of options. The Elder Law attorney advised him what to do. Moving everything around and re-titling assets was going to be a huge time drain for both the Elder Law attorney and myself. There was one problem. The guy didn't want to pay the Elder Law attorney or me for help. This was not a good decision on his part. He paid the $10,000 he didn't want to pay the Elder Law attorney to the nursing home owner instead, after his wife spent the next two months in the nursing home. Not smart at all.

The choice is all yours. You can be bull headed and think the Elder Law attorney's fee is too high and watch your assets disappear into the hands of the nursing home owner, or you can shelter your family's assets. It is not that tough of a decision once you *think critically* about it. Sadly, some people still give their money to the nursing home owner, instead of hiring an Elder Law attorney. This is not very smart, unfortunately.

Chapter Summary

What did we learn in this chapter?

- We learned that someday we will need an Elder Law attorney and Rick can help us with a recommendation.
- We might want to reconsider buying Long Term Care Insurance.
- We know what to do if we are suddenly faced with a crisis with our parents or other family members who need long term care.
- We found out that the smart people hire Elder Law attorneys to plan in advance to protect family assets and potentially shelter most of their assets by starting the five year clock.
- We found out that bull headed people who don't want to hire an Elder Law attorney is the reason why the nursing home owner makes so much money.
- We realized how foolish it would be to go broke in a nursing home.

Notes

Chapter Thirty

Gaining Control Debt Plan®

"I am in favor of cutting taxes under any circumstances and for any excuse, for any reason, whenever it's possible."

~ Milton Friedman

[This page intentionally left blank]

Gaining Control Debt Plan®

Take heart people in debt. I have a debt solution that is fun and will get you out of debt in no time. I am calling it the Gaining Control Debt Plan®. It is the updated version of The Taking Control Plan® for those of you who have been through my process for getting out of debt.

What most Wally Streets in Wally World will tell you about getting out of debt is no fun at all. Further, if you are in debt, then Wally does not want to talk to you. Remember, he has that $5,000 per person revenue quota he has to reach. If you are in debt, then you are wasting Wally's time.

Wally's debt relief advice is a cursory glance at your expenses, then he will tell you to quit eating out at restaurants. That's it. That is the extent of his advice. A more accurate way of explaining this is that, "You are spending too much money on discretionary expenses, so you need to stop." See what I mean? That is no fun.

My advice to get out of debt is better, builds confidence and it is fun, too. It consists of six buckets:

1. Fixed expenses.
2. Special one-time expenses.
3. Under control expenses.
4. Savings accounts.
5. Retirement accounts.
6. Investment accounts.

There is a method to the madness if you will. Each bucket has to flow correctly in order to make this work, so keeping everything in the proper funding order is very important.

[This page intentionally left blank]

Fixed Expenses

Fixed expenses are where you know what the payments are every month and there is not a lot that you can do to change this fact. I do not mean fixed in the literal sense, but rather figuratively. In other words, a fixed expense example would be your utility bill. It is not a fixed amount each month, but it is a certainty each month. Therefore, it is a fixed expense in my book.

Some examples of fixed expenses are:

- *Mortgage/Rent*
- *Home Equity Loan*
- *Auto Loans*
- *Personal Loans*
- *Credit Cards*
- *Utilities*
- *Alarm Systems*
- *Groceries*
- *Gas/Fuel/Oil Changes*
- *Property & Casualty Insurance*
- *Internet*
- *Life Insurance*
- *Health Insurance*
- *Charities*
- *Real Estate Taxes*
- *Estimated Income Tax Payments*
- *Provision for Unexpected Expenses*

These are examples of monthly expenses that you pay every month with some variations. With my Gaining Control Debt Plan®, I want you to categorize these expenses into the fixed expenses bucket. These expenses are paid out of a specific checking account that you have with bill pay on it. Any of these fixed expenses that you can put on automatic pilot via bill pay, then that is what you do. I suggest setting up bill pay so that all of these fixed expenses are paid every other Friday. Listen to me now. I am trying to make your life easier.

You should be able to do this for most everything in this list with the exception of groceries and gas for you vehicles. You use your debit card from the checking account to pay for those variable fixed expenses.

You probably need to sit down with a spreadsheet or with a software program that does it for you and figure up these expenses. A spreadsheet program will do the trick, so there is no need to go out and buy any budget software. However, if you already have some of this type of software, then you should be able to categorize all of your fixed expenses with it to match my version of fixed expenses. Don't use their version of fixed expenses, because this will not match my strategy.

I will describe how to do it with a spreadsheet in just a little bit.

Special One-Time Expenses

You may have some expenses that you pay once per year. I want you to categorize these expenses into the special one-time per year bucket. These expenses are paid out of a totally separate savings account. You create a savings account for these special one-time expenses. Every pay period, you make a deposit into this savings account to cover the upcoming special one-time expenses.

You are basically pre-funding these special one-time expenses in advance. This is better than getting hit with them all at once and then scrambling around trying to figure out how to pay it.

What you do is if you have a flood insurance bill that comes due in January for example, then depending on what month it is, you calculate out how much you need to pay that flood insurance per pay period. Then, you set it aside in the special one-time expenses savings account. You repeat this same process for all of your special one-time expenses.

If it is October, then you have a limited amount of time until January rolls around, so at first, the amount that you are saving for these type of special one-time expenses may seem high. However, once you pay it in January, then you can divide next year's flood insurance by the 52 weeks remaining until the next payment is due. Got it? Good.

[This page intentionally left blank]

Under Control Expenses

Here comes the fun part, especially if you are married, but this works equally as well if you are single. You create an under control account for each of you. This is your own checking account with a debit card and check writing. The husband has his own under control account and so does the wife. You can do this even if there is only one breadwinner. Just because you are a spouse who is not working, doesn't mean that you are not spending money on discretionary items. You probably want to use a credit union or other bank checking account with minimal account fees and free checking.

You tally up your discretionary expenses for the last six months and average that out. Here is the kicker, however. You break that down further to match your pay period. If you are paid bi-monthly, then you figure out how much goes into your checking account for your 1st and 15th pay periods. If you are married, then you split it in two and fund each checking out accordingly. If you are single, then you put that full amount into your under control checking account.

Here is the picture. For example, let's say you're spending on lunches, dry cleaning, clothing, shoes, haircuts, health club dues, sporting events and other discretionary items $900 a month. If you are paid bi-monthly, then take $900 times 12 to get your annual figure, then further divide by 24. So, $450 goes into your under control account if you are single and $225 goes in it if you are married. For that pay period, you can only spend $450 on discretionary items during that pay period, or only $225 per person if married. You cannot go over your allotted amount. That is the rule.

Typically, with married couples, what you will find is that one spouse is a better discretionary spender than the other. For one of you, making it to the next pay period without blowing your entire $225 will be a piece of cake. Also, your under control account will grow! However, the other spouse may run out of money. Here is the penalty. No money for you! If you spend your allotment, then tough luck. You have to wait until the next pay period comes around. I am trying to get you out of debt, remember?

Keep in mind, that with the under control account, you can choose to spend your $225 per pay period *on anything* that you want to spend it on. So, if you want to eat out every day, then go for it. Wally Street's advice was to tell you to quit eating out. My advice is to spend your under control account in any manner that you wish. The major difference is that you have the freedom to spend your discretionary dollars on whatever you want, as opposed to Wally's brilliant suggestion.

As a married couple, you both agree to tally up all your fixed and special one-time expenses and make mandatory pay period deposits into those two accounts to take care of those expenses without any worries. The last thing on my list above was a provision for the unexpected. You add a little extra to fixed expenses to make sure that you have plenty of money to cover everything, just in case your utility bill goes up or something similar.

If you are married, then you basically have four accounts setup to cover expenses and discretionary spending and possibly more depending on whether you want a separate savings account for each one-time expense.

- A fixed expenses checking account.
- A savings account for special one-time expenses.
- Two separate checking accounts with debit cards for the discretionary and under control expenses, if you are married, or one checking account if you are single.

Once you have all of these accounts in place, then you begin the process of tackling the debt.

Let's start with the credit cards, because those are always the debt that never seems to go away. If you have two or three credit cards, then pay extra money on the one with the highest interest rate and pay the minimum on the others. You build into your fixed expenses account the extra money you need to pay on the credit cards over and above the minimums.

For example, let's say you had 3 credit cards with the minimum payment required on all three totaling $500. Credit card number one has a minimum of $200. Credit card number two has a $200 minimum and credit card number three has a $100 minimum. You pay an extra $250 on top of the $200 minimum for credit card number one for a total of $450 per month. The other two you just pay the minimums for now.

Once credit card number one is paid off, then you take the $450 and put it on top of the $200 minimum for credit card number two. Now you are paying $650 on credit card number two. Before you know it, you will have credit card number two paid off. At that point, you take the $650 and add it to the $100 minimum on credit card number three. This means that now $750 is going towards credit card number three. You would repeat this process until you have eliminated all of your credit card debt.

Once your credit card debt is eliminated, then you can take the amounts that you were paying into those and put those on the next thing that needs to be paid off. This could be a car loan, perhaps. You would pay an extra $750 towards the car loan. Before you know it, that car loan will be paid off.

[403]

You basically continue this same process by using the $750 to pay down another debt item, and then when that is paid off, you take the former payment from that and add it to the $750, then look for the next debt item to pay off. If you were paying $400 a month for the car, then you now have $1,150 per month to go towards the next item that needs to be paid off.

The beauty of this strategy is that your fixed expenses are pretty much the same every month, except your debt is disappearing until it is finally all gone.

If I had to list an order of things, then I would start by paying off credit cards first. Pay off personal loans second if any. Pay off any car, boat, RV, Jet Ski and motorcycle loans next. Home equity loans would follow those items.

Once you reach this point, then the only thing that should be left is your mortgage. If you have paid off all your credit cards, personal loans, vehicle loans and your home equity loan, then by golly, I guess you deserve to go ahead and pay off the house. Uh oh, there is that screechy sound again. You know the one when you hear, "This is a test of the emergency broadcast system." You cannot pay off your house just yet, my friend.

The thing to keep in mind is to keep the cash flow of payments the same into your fixed expenses account. Every time you pay something off, then you take those former payments and add on top of the next debt item. You continue this process until you are completely debt free.

The fun part of the under control accounts is that you can ask your sweetie to loan you $20 until the next pay period if you run out of money. Of course, you may have to give them a little non-monetary reward of some kind, if you know what I mean. Regardless, you have the freedom to spend your discretionary account in whatever manner that you wish.

I know what you are thinking, "What about my 401k?" Keep your shirt on, will you? I will get to that soon enough. Savings accounts for specific goals come first, however. Remember, I am trying to make you the smartest person in the neighborhood.

[This page intentionally left blank]

Savings, Retirement and Investment Accounts

You thought I forgot about your 401(k), IRA, Roth IRA, and 403(b) didn't you? Well, I didn't. There are some more buckets that have to be taken care of first. These are the savings buckets. The retirement and investment buckets come later. You have to fund these in the proper order, too.

The first thing you do is setup a separate savings account for vacations. Every pay period, you put something in it. You plan for it first thing. Then, you set up separate savings accounts for other goals such as home improvement, or a new car. You put those amounts towards those goals each pay period.

Once you get those setup, then you come to an agreement on an emergency fund amount and establish a savings account for that, too. You automatically put money in it every pay period until you reach the agreed upon emergency fund amount. Oh by the way, now that you have paid off your debt, then that same fixed amount of money goes to the emergency fund to get it built quickly. Once you reach that point, then you can take the money that you were putting in this emergency fund and shift it over to your Roth IRA account, if you are eligible to do so. If you are eligible, then you can fully contribute to your Roth IRA account and get it maxed out before you know it.

If you make too much money, because your AGI is too high, then do not forget about my backdoor loophole idea with the non-deductible IRA to Roth Conversion. This is assuming you do not have an existing IRA in place. Don't forget about this quirky rule on this backdoor loophole idea. Remember to file IRS form 8606, too. By the way, use a professional tax preparer, preferably a CPA will you? You do not want to do this backdoor loophole idea without consulting a CPA. Got it?

The Roth IRA has the ability to always get your cost basis out without any penalties, no matter what age. Remember, I talked about the importance of liquidity. With a 401(k), in an emergency, you may or may not be able to get a loan. It depends if your 401(k) allows it or not. If you have an old 401(k) at your former employer, then you cannot take a loan, so your only option is a withdrawal. If you take a withdrawal, then it will cost you possibly a 10% penalty to get the money if you are under 59 ½, plus you will have to pay the taxes on it, too.

With a Roth IRA, you have liquidity with the cost basis at any age. If you have some emergency and your emergency fund gets tapped out, then you need to be able to go to a liquid source, i.e., enter the Roth IRA.

What we are doing here is doubling down on your liquidity. You have the emergency fund built, plus the Roth IRA's cost basis liquidity. Now, isn't that a smart idea? Lots of liquidity. That's what I like to see.

My avid pupil should be getting the picture by now. The money goes into the emergency fund until fully funded. No money is put away into any 401(k) or 403(b) until the emergency fund is fully funded and the vacation, home improvement and new car savings accounts are also funded. Next you fully fund the Roth IRA's. Nothing to the 401(k) or 403(b) at all until you reach this point. That is the rule.

Once the emergency fund is fully funded, then you take the money that you were using to build it (which includes the amount you were paying on debt) and put it towards a Roth IRA. Since you have paid off all of your debt and funded your emergency fund and have built up your savings accounts, then you now have that cash flow to shift over to the Roth IRA. Once the Roth IRA's are fully funded each year, then you can go to the 401(k) or 403(b) and start working on fully funding those. You see how this works?

Nothing goes into these 401(k) or 403(b) accounts until all debt is paid off, except the house, then the emergency fund and then your vacation, home improvement and new vehicle savings are funded. The cash flow from your former debt will fund your emergency fund fairly quickly. Next, you will get those savings accounts funded in a hurry. Further, you will have fully funded Roth IRA's, if your income level allows it. Finally, you will even have fully funded 401(k)'s and 403(b)'s as applicable to your situation.

Once you reach this point, you can then turn to putting money into a taxable investment account to build up your net worth. Keep in mind however, that Wally will want to sell you a Variable Annuity at this point.

At the end of all of this, you will be one of the smartest people in the neighborhood with an emergency fund, no debt, vacation savings, home improvement funds, new car savings and possibly a fully funded Roth IRA and a fully funded 401(k) or 403(b) plus regular contributions to your investment accounts. What my friend could be better than that?

Remember, it is absolutely pointless and brutish to have a lot of debt, no emergency fund while at the same time putting money into a 401(k) without any liquidity. Let me repeat that. It would be brutish. My way is a much better way. In fact, it is a plan and a process to not only get out of debt, but to build up emergency funds and contribute to your important savings accounts, then build your net worth and liquidity with Roth IRA's, then fund your 401(k)'s or 403(b)'s and other investment accounts.

Don't forget the non-deductible IRA backdoor loophole idea, if you make too much money to contribute to the Roth Conversion account which may be the case with those low AGI limits that I mentioned earlier. The liquidity of the Roth Conversion account is very important.

You cannot omit the Roth IRA or Roth Conversion and jump straight to the 401(k), because the 401(k) does not give you the added liquidity of the Roth IRA or Roth Conversion. Stay in the proper order. There is a method to the madness, if you will.

If you have a spreadsheet program, then you can easily figure all this out by making a line item spreadsheet broken down into these main sections:

1. Wages and Income – Sum per pay period.
2. Fixed Expenses – Sum per pay period.
3. Special One-Time Expenses – Sum per pay period.
4. Under Control Expenses – Sum per pay period.
5. Savings – Sum per pay period.
6. Emergency Fund – Sum per pay period.
7. Retirement – Contribute only after 2 – 6 above are funded.
   a) Roth IRA or non-deductible IRA to Roth Conversion.
   b) 401(k) or 401(b) or 457 – After Roth is funded.
8. Investments – After retirement accounts are funded.

This will allow you to figure your cash flow and know what you can do towards savings and investments. You have to do it all in the order that I say to make it work. No cheating! This is a good, fun way to get completely out of debt and fully fund your savings, retirement accounts and investments. I hope you like my idea and better yet, if you are currently in debt, then I hope you will implement it. Of course, you can always call me for help.

Did Wally every give you an idea to get out of debt like this one? That's what I thought. Do you still think that I am just another Wally Street?

Chapter Summary

What did we learn in this chapter?

- We learned a fun way to get out of debt.
- We found out how to setup checking and savings accounts to take care of all of our expenses.
- We found out how we could spend our discretionary money on anything that we wanted.
- We learned that it is never a good idea to invest in a Roth IRA, 401(k) or 403(b) without first being completely out of debt and with a fully funded emergency fund.
- We learned how this plan flows, multiplies and feeds into always improving our situation.
- We learned that if we don't blow our under control account and our spouse does, then we might be able to negotiate a little non-monetary reward here and there.

[This page intentionally left blank]

Chapter Thirty-One

Family Trees

"In every conceivable manner, the family is link to our past, bridge to our future."

~ Alex Haley

[This page intentionally left blank]

Family Trees

Before it is too late, tell your story and build your family tree. Get it down on paper. Tell the story about your grandparents, your parents, your aunts and uncles, siblings and cousins. You will find it liberating on one hand and realize how important it will be to your family on the other hand.

Making a family tree can be educational and fun. Do a little genealogy for the benefit of your family. There is a free web site at www.familysearch.org that will provide a lot of publicly available information. The thing that you have to remember is back in the day, when the census people came around, a lot of people would just give them their first and middle initials instead of their first and middle names. I suppose that they distrusted the government back then. Imagine that. Also, some of those census people were either hard of hearing or could not spell very well. One or the other. Names can be misspelled. If you keep these things in mind, then you may be able to find the information that you are seeking.

I have used the familysearch.org web site and discovered that my dad (Hillman) had three uncles and two aunts that we never knew about, because his dad died at a young age. His mom remarried and she never told us about them.

I had always thought that my great-grandparents on my mom's side came from Portugal. They did but, they actually came from the island of Madeira which is out in the Atlantic Ocean. Google it and you will see how far it actually is from mainland Portugal.

I would have never known about Madeira and its factor in my family tree, if I didn't do the genealogical search.

My grandmother on my biological father Bill Allison's side always said she was closer to the Ridgeway family. I never could understand this since her maiden name was Utley until I found out that her father, Francis Utley, died while her mom Nancy was pregnant with her. As a result, my grandmother Ollie never knew her father. Her mom Nancy was born on a Cherokee Indian reservation and of course, her mother, Martha Parsons was part Cherokee Indian. Nancy (my great-grandmother) soon remarried to Sam Ridgeway and my grandmother Ollie grew up with all the Ridgeway kids. It finally clicked for me.

My grandmother Ollie once received a letter from the Cherokee Nation offering her land in Oklahoma if she wanted it. She was living in California at the time and didn't want to leave California, so she declined it. I would have never known all of this without starting the genealogical search and discussing this with my aunt Nancy.

My aunt Nancy (named after her grandmother Nancy Ridgeway) told me that her grandfather, John Washington Allison had remarried and had more kids, but she didn't know any of them, but knew of them. That got my curiosity up and I found out that I have a lot more Allison relatives in Arkansas than I thought. It turns out that my great-grandfather John had eight kids. Before I went on this search, I thought that he only had two kids, one of which was my grandfather Terry Allison. I may have to go beat on some doors the next time I visit Arkansas to introduce myself to my Allison relatives.

I have discovered several parts of my family tree going back into the 1700's. However, I am still working on filing some holes.

What are your family surnames? You have a story to tell. Believe me. It is a good thing for your family to know who you are and where you came from. Build that family tree. It is fun what you can find out. I found it fascinating.

Another web site that is helpful in understanding more about your family surname is located at: www.houseofnames.com. They have a lot of good information about surnames.

I also highly recommend www.23andme.com and their DNA test. They have a really neat web site with a lot of DNA information related to your health. Of course, it makes it more beneficial if other family members also take the DNA test. All you have to do is spit in a little vial and mail it off. Again, I highly recommend it.

The Food and Drug Administration (FDA) recently approved the DNA test from the www.23andme.com folks. Apparently, some people freak out if they find out they might get diabetes or cancer or something. I suspect that the FDA may require them to put in some kind of medical professional in between the release of the DNA and the person who bought the DNA test. I surmise that www.23andme.com will get this all worked out, one way or another. Ancestry has a DNA test, too. I am sure that they will have this same issue with the FDA.

The web site www.23andme.com has information on where you came from (your DNA ancestry) and a place to build family trees. There is a ton of other information on their web site for members who take their DNA test. Personally, I like their family tree graphics and its capabilities. But, wouldn't you know it. They transferred their trees to My Heritage which caused a little bit of a learning curve. You can add notes and pictures to each person's record, too. Ancestry has a similar service.

My family surnames in alphabetical order are Allison, Bailey, Bridges, Kennedy, Loving, Morte, Parsons, Simon, and Utley. Who knows? I could be your fourth cousin once removed!

I saw one of the stars of the Big Bang Theory on that show about genealogy, called "Who do you think you are?" His name is Jim Parsons. He plays the character Sheldon on The Big Bang Theory. While they were showing him his Parsons family tree, I noticed a lot of similar Parsons family names in my family tree. I jokingly thought that perhaps I might be related to him in some way. Maybe we are fourth cousins once removed!

The point is that someone with these last names got on a boat, crossed the Atlantic Ocean and came to America, got married and had kids. If they didn't, then I would not be here. If that doesn't tell you that God meant for you to be here on this earth, then I do not know what will. Whether you think you are or not, God believes you are a unique and special individual.

My DNA test showed that I am primarily Irish-Scottish, also British and from Portugal and the Basque region of Spain. Amazingly, my family surnames came from Britain, Ireland, Scotland, Portugal and the Basque region of Spain. I also have that little bit of Cherokee Indian in me, too. My DNA test was right on the money. Even the Cherokee Indian part showed up in my DNA test results. My family tree genealogy matches the DNA test precisely. Truly amazing.

You can use www.ancestry.com, or www.familysearch.org for your search and then www.23andme.com for DNA information and to keep up with it all. You will be glad you did. This is a good activity for you especially if you are retired and bored to tears. It beats watching financial shows on TV!

Chapter Summary

What did we learn in this chapter?

- Family trees are helpful to family members with black holes about loved ones that they never knew.
- Family tree information can be found at http://www.familysearch.org for free, or http://www.ancestry.com with a paid subscription.
- Information about family surnames can be found at http://www.houseofnames.com.
- We found out something to do to keep us from being bored in retirement.

Notes

Chapter Thirty-Two

My Personal Story

"Perhaps I am stronger than I think."

~ Thomas Merton

[This page intentionally left blank]

My Personal Story

Our lives are a series of significant emotional events. Each time we experience a significant emotional event, it affects us in some way. Most of the stories that follow happened long ago, but they are vivid memories to me. They changed my life, my thinking and my view of what is important.

My friends call me Rick, or RJ. I was born in Little Rock, Arkansas to Billy and Donna Allison. Unfortunately, Bill and Donna divorced shortly after I was born. Both spouses remarried and coincidentally each had three kids. I am however the only child of Bill and Donna.

Donna gained custody of "Little Ricky" and remarried when I was only about 2 years old. My mom still calls me Ricky, even though I am in my fifties. Go figure. So, does my sister Sharri. My mom married Hillman Johnson of Sardis, Mississippi, but they lived primarily in Little Rock. Although, I did spend a little time in Nashville, Tennessee as a toddler.

Bill joined the Air Force when he was 17 years old. He was a paratrooper and a Korean War Veteran. He was both in the Army and the Air Force. When he left the service, he went to work as a policeman initially in Midland, Texas. Later on, he moved to the Central Coast area of California and took a job as a policeman in Grover City which is now called Grover Beach. Bill lived there with his kids and his immediate family. His parents, Terry and Ollie, plus his sister and brother-in-law, Betty and Jim Clark lived there too. Jim was also a police officer. His sister Nancy was not far away in Las Vegas.

After working as a policeman in Grover City, California, the Chief of Police job came open in nearby Arroyo Grande. Bill applied for it and was awarded the job. While Bill was building his family in California, Donna and Hillman were doing the same in Little Rock.

Hillman was six foot six inches tall and believe it or not, he was a dance instructor early on in life for Arthur Murray Studios. Can you imagine a guy 6' 6" giving ballroom dancing lessons? One day in walks Donna, my mom, with her free dance lesson that she had recently won. Hillman and his dance instructor friend, Ray Powers, took bets on who was going to get a date with Donna. Hillman won the bet. They ended up being an amazingly fluid dance couple, especially when you consider the fact that he was 6' 6" and my mom was only 5' 2". Let me tell you, they could float across a dance floor together. It was fun to watch.

Hillman had a superb personality. Later on, he went to work as a career agent for Southwestern Life Insurance Company. He spent the rest of his life as a life insurance agent and was very successful. He was extremely extroverted and loved to kid around with people. He gave everyone nicknames. It depended on who he was talking to, but he always managed to come up with a nickname for everybody. In fact, his friends couldn't wait to find out their nicknames. Some of the ones that I remember were "Reverend", "Francois", "Frank and Jesse James" for a pair of brothers, "Stevie Wonder", "Stonewall", "All Bad", "Wheels", and "Hollywood". He called me "Ricardo Montalbon" and sometimes "Hollywood" when I would wear sunglasses.

All of these nicknames were for his friends and clients with whom he interacted with on a weekly basis. Imagine dropping by and hearing "Stevie Wonder!" This was his nickname for Steve Burk, who was also in the insurance business. Steve graduated as the Valedictorian from Vanderbilt University. I have never met a guy any smarter than Steve Burk. He studied for several professional designations at the same time and passed them all. He doesn't really promote himself in that manner, but I think he has at least 10 financial designations. I'm not sure if he still uses them all or not, but it doesn't matter. He still is smarter than anyone that you will ever meet. Although, he is very humble about his intellectual abilities. To Steve, it is all about helping others.

Steve Burk was my mentor when I went into business with my dad, Hillman in 1984. Between the two of them, my dad and a few other influential fellows named Frank Dueschle and Greg Dunseath, I learned the life insurance business.

I remember a funny interaction that Hillman had with Greg Dunseath. My dad and Greg both worked at Southwestern Life and the other agents, including Greg looked up to Hillman. One day, Greg asked my dad if he thought he would make it as a life insurance agent. My dad said, "Yes, you will make it, because you have four kids! You got no choice. You have to make it!" I can still remember my dad laughing about that one.

Frank Dueschle took me under his wing when I first got into the financial services business. He helped me with the importance of being ethical. Frank was a Catholic as I am, but he was a much more devout Catholic. He set an outstanding example of what it is like to be a good, ethical person in the insurance industry. A lot of my ethics about this business are a result of Frank being a mentor to me. My dad always called him "Francois." Frank and my dad were very close.

Hillman had a bad temper sometimes. It was usually when he had two cups of coffee. He would start cussing after two cups of coffee. Most of the time it was some insurance company making him mad. These life insurance companies were always changing their products. They typically would come out with a great product and guys like my dad would sell the crap out of it, then later, they would pull the product off the market. My dad had a saying for this. "That was the old deal. This is the new deal." Of course, the new deal was not as good as the old deal, so what my dad would do was find another life insurance company with a better deal. He was always trying to do the best for his clients by being independent and looking for the best policies he could find. This is why he used Stevie Wonder, because Steve had relationships with all the top life insurance companies in the country and he deciphered the best ones for my dad to sell.

Hillman had some great years selling life insurance. In 1988, he was one of the top agents in the country for one company. I acted like his right hand man at the time and went with him on his big cases. We ended up winning a trip to Hong Kong that we would take in December of 1989.

The year 1988, was a good year as I married my wife Natalie and we sold a lot of life insurance, too. It was love at first sight with me and Natalie. I saw her when she was on a date with another guy. Once I saw her, I knew that I wanted to be with her. Now, being an introvert like myself, that presented a major problem. How was I going to garner up enough courage to ask her out? Lucky for me, my friend Rob's little brother knew who Natalie was at the time. I found out that she worked at Allstate Insurance Company. I found out where her office was and walked right in there and asked to see her. Of course, her desk was right in the middle of the office where there was about 50 other people working. I felt like everyone in the place was looking at me. Nevertheless, I walked in there and asked her out. Lucky for me, she said "yes." The rest as they say is history. We recently celebrated our 25th wedding anniversary.

We had our first child, Reese on Labor Day in 1989. Unexpectantly, he came a month early. Natalie had read one of those baby books and she had a focal point of a Reese's Peanut Butter Cup wrapper pinned to the wall while she was in labor. After hours and hours, Dr. Reid Henry finally agreed to do a C-section. I was there when Reese was born and boy was I a babe in the woods. After Reese was born, Dr. Henry said,

"See you later." I was like "What? Wait a minute. Where are you going?" Silly me, I didn't realize that the pediatrician was taking over at this point.

Natalie was out of it and did not realize what was going on, but I was concerned. Reese was under an oxygen tent and his little chest was sinking in and out. I was petrified out of my mind. No one was there with me. There was no Dr. Henry and no pediatrician, because it was Labor Day. The pediatrician was called, but he didn't want to come in. He just told the nurses to tell me not to worry. He wasn't the pediatrician we picked out, but instead was his partner who was on call.

All week, Reese was in the hospital under that oxygen tent in the neonatal ICU. I was scared out of my mind that week. Then, after five days, our pediatrician bursts through the door of Natalie's room and said, "He's fine. Treat him like a normal baby. You can take him home." Then, he proceeded to start to walk out of the room, but I protested. I thought wait just a darn minute. He has been under an oxygen tent all week in neonatal ICU and now he can just go home? Of course, we wanted to take him home and we wanted him to be a normal baby, but being a parent for the first time, I had my concerns.

This is the thing about me that has always been true all of my life. I never take anyone's word for something without first looking at both sides of an issue or doing a little research on my own. It was like when somebody from a life insurance company came by and told us about their policy. My dad would say, "Yeah, yeah I know. You're the best and to hell with all the rest." All of these guys hawking their company's insurance products were full of it. Stevie Wonder was the great equalizer. He knew which ones really were the best and he told us why.

Natalie and I were married in 1988, but decided to renew our vows at the same time we baptized Reese into the Catholic faith. Natalie gave me a gift of a gold crucifix that I still wear to this day. I have a picture of Natalie, Reese and myself hanging in my office wall of this very special day. Father Hebert, our priest was holding Reese and pointed out that he thought he might have had an accident. Yes, Reese had pooped his pants at his baptism!

A couple of weeks later, my mom, dad, Natalie and I were all going to Hong Kong to meet with Stevie Wonder. It was a reward for selling life insurance in 1988. We left Reese in good hands with Natalie's mother Barbara who agreed to take care of him for us while we were gone. Of course, Barbara had a job during the day so, we took Reese to a couple who watched about a dozen kids at their house. They had taken care of my brother David's daughter previously, so we trusted them.

Sometimes you just know things are going to change and there is not a thing you can do about it. Natalie and I had a great time in Hong Kong and in fact we won a little recognition for being the cutest couple. After about a week in Hong Kong, we went to bed in preparation for an extended trip to Thailand. However, I was awaken about 5 a.m. with a horrible phone call. It was Barbara telling me that Reese had died from Sudden Infant Death Syndrome. Of course, I had no idea what this was other than healthy babies go to sleep and do not wake up.

As you can imagine, Natalie and I were devastated. We had to fly back and it took 30 hours before we got home. We had a picture of Reese made with some baby clothes that my friend Dale Lindon and his wife Pam had sent us. Reese looked cute as a button in those baby clothes. This is the picture that I keep on the wall by my bed to this very day.

Before I got on that plane to Hong Kong, I felt as if Natalie and I might get killed in a plane crash or something. It was an eerie feeling. Perhaps, in some strange way God was trying to prepare me for what was to come.

[428]

How on earth was I going to handle this? Now here I was, faced with a horrible tragedy and I had to deal with it like or not. There are several things you learn when life hands you a tragedy. You learn who the people are that are really important to you. The ones that were there when Natalie and I got off the plane after that 30 hour flight from Hong Kong like my brother Gary and sister Sharri. The guys from my baseball team that showed up at my son's viewing. My friend Kevin Alexander who gave me a hug at Reese's grave site that I will never forget. My brother David who came by my house after he got off work. The same brother who had a daughter and helped me to be a dad to my son Reese. A Little Rock policeman and one of my baseball buddies, David Hudson who came over to our house to lend his support. My best friend Mike whose strong Catholic background was of immense support. These are the people who mean a lot to me and whose act of kindness I will never forget. These people stepped up and offered their support to Natalie and me.

As Natalie and I worked through the stages of grief, we focused our efforts on joining a group of parents who had also lost their kids. When you lose your parents, you lose your past, but when you lose a child, you lose your future. Eventually, after a year of going to this group which was called the Compassionate Friends and then later the Bereaved Parents, we volunteered to help lead the group meetings. All the horrible murders that you hear about on the news, or read in the paper, we would later meet those parents. There is a difference between parents whose children were murdered and those who died of an illness. It is harder on the parents of murdered children, because almost all of the time, it is totally senseless.

I finally quit feeling sorry for myself when a lady came to one of those meetings who had lost her three boys in a house fire. That was a slap in the face to me. How can I feel sorry for myself when this poor lady lost all of her kids in one day? This was the turning point for me where I was able to begin the process of moving forward.

You never get over losing a child. Never, ever. In addition, you are never the same person either. My view of the world is vastly different from most people. Fame and fortune are nothing compared to your family. Not a day goes by when I don't think of my son Reese.

As far as I knew, Hillman was my dad. In fact, most people who know me never knew I had another dad. Only a few very close friends. I never knew Bill Allison. If no one had ever told me that I had a dad named Bill Allison, then I probably would have never known otherwise. However, when I was a senior in High School, I learned that my father Bill Allison had died. Bill had recently moved from Arroyo Grande, California to a small town in south Arkansas called Camden. He got the Chief of Police job there. I was told he moved back because he wanted to have a relationship with me once I turned eighteen. Sadly, we never got that chance. Oh, how I wish things were different.

Bill was chasing a criminal down the railroad tracks and was running atop one of the rail cars when he jumped off and the butt end of his shotgun smashed into his chest. Later that day, he was taken to a hospital in Hot Springs and died. He was only 39 years old. They did an autopsy, but this was 1974 mind you. I cannot say that I can put a lot of credence to a pathologist's results back in 1974. Blunt force trauma to the chest can kill you. However, the autopsy said he had clogged arteries. It was probably a little bit of both. He did smoke cigarettes and you know back in those days, the cigarettes were stout. Camel's, Marlboro's and Pall Mall's ruled the day. The Allison family always believed that his death had more to do with him landing on the shotgun like he did. There has never been any history of early heart attacks like that in the Allison family going back generations.

It kind of tells you what kind of guy he was back then. He was a former paratrooper who served in the Korean War. So you know that a guy who jumps out of airplanes is a little braver than most.

As the Camden, Arkansas Chief of Police, here he was chasing down a criminal himself, running on top of a railroad car with his shotgun in hand. Obviously a guy who wasn't scared of anything. How many Chiefs of Police do you know who would do that today?

I have learned a lot about my father Bill over the years from my aunts, uncles, and my half siblings, Tami, Jon and Kelly. However, it is never enough information for me. It is still a black hole in my heart. I am sure that it was even harder for Tami, Jon and Kelly since they grew up with him. If only things were different for all of us.

I went to college at the University of Arkansas at Little Rock where I majored in Criminal Justice. I enjoyed taking the Criminal Justice courses. I found them very fascinating. When I was in college, my parents never really pushed me in any direction at all. Recall that my real dad had just died about 6 months prior to me starting college, so my head was not in the right place. I was pretty much left to fend for myself. I got involved in the Sigma Alpha Epsilon Fraternity and really enjoyed it. This is where I met Greg Brownlow.

Greg was a year ahead of me and he was such a great guy. His dad owned a Gulf Oil gas station in town. One night, all of us fraternity brothers found out that Greg had cancer. My mom knew about it before me. I remember her telling me that he was eaten up with it. He only had a short time to live. We all took it pretty hard, but Greg was only interested in having fun and keeping everyone else's spirits up. He didn't want nobody sitting around moping over him. He literally walked in the door about fifteen minutes after we found out he was dying. He straightened our asses out real quick. Greg wanted to hang out and have fun with the time he had left and that's precisely what we did.

About a month or so later, I was at the Frat House one night and Greg came in and asked me if I would take him to his dad's gas station. He had run out of gas and needed to go get some. So, I took him down there and we milled around the station for a bit, then he got some gas in a can and we went back to his car. Greg was so polite and thankful for me helping him that night and I was like honored to do it. He made a huge impression on me. Here he was dying of cancer and I did a little no nothing thing and he thought it was the greatest favor he ever had. I'll never forget him. Greg had tremendous courage. He only lived to be 22, but what a guy. Greg is buried in the same cemetery as my son, Reese and my dad, Bill. Whenever I go visit the cemetery, I also make a point to say "Hi" to Brownlow.

One of my best friends in high school was Mike Rowland. He was a scrawny little guy like me in high school. I think we might have weighed 140 pounds each. We met during gym break where Mike and I were both shooting basketballs. Mike could shoot basketballs from the foul line like you wouldn't believe. He could stand there and shoot a hundred shots and make over 90 of them. This is what he did to practice. Every time he did this, his goal was to always shoot 100 shots at the foul line and see if he could up his made free throws. After we met, we stuck together like glue.

Mike and I joined the same fraternity, Sigma Alpha Epsilon (ΣAE.) Our fraternity had a Leadership School event at Northwestern University north of Chicago every year and Mike and I got in his car and drove up for it. Chicago is a great city and we had a blast. The Leadership School taught us some good values and how to be great leaders. It must have worked its magic on me, because I ended up as the ΣAE fraternity President for the Arkansas Beta Chapter at UALR.

Mike and I ended up being roommates in an apartment. Neither one of us had much of anything. Not much furniture. Mike had a bed, but I sleep on the floor with just a mattress. I had the stereo system and he had the records. Stevie Wonder, the real Stevie Wonder was big back then. We listened to Stevie Wonder more times than I care to admit. We had a lot of fun, me and Mike. Probably too much fun.

Imagine two guys going to college and coming from an all boy's high school. We didn't see any girls, much less know any, because we went to an all boy's high school. When we got to college, they were everywhere. There was a sorority house right across the street.

Mike quickly picked up a sorority girlfriend from across the street. It was one of those love-hate relationships. They were crazy about each other, but they fought like cats and dogs. My buddy Mike was all about having fun and he was going to have fun one way or another.

I lived in West Little Rock and Mike lived over in Dog Town as we called it. Dog Town was across the river in North Little Rock. It was all of about 15 minutes away, but seemed like another planet for some reason. I used to go over to Mike's house which was right by his parents' house. While we were in college, his dad was dying of emphysema. He was on one of those oxygen machines. His dad was funny. He had a great attitude. His dad used to quip that he was taking a Breathalyzer test when he was getting oxygen, or he was on the "drunk-o-meter" as he liked to call it. Not long after that, his dad passed away. We both had something in common losing our dads, except Mike knew his dad.

Mike had a sister with Juvenile Diabetes and her name was Kelly. She was going blind because of it, but she was the sweetest thing on earth. When I went over to their house, Kelly would hold my arm and walk with me. She liked to talk and boy what a wonderful girl. Kelly ended up going to the local deaf and blind school. One day, these two redneck thugs kidnapped Kelly. They raped and murdered her and literally threw her in a ditch. They were a couple of horrible people. At the trial, the prosecutor botched the case by giving one of the murdering bastards' immunity from prosecution for telling on the other killer. Well, the one given immunity was such a liar on the stand that the jury could not convict the other killer. Both of these jerks got off. It was tough on Mike and his family. Mike's mom is one of the most devout Catholics that I have ever known and she brought her kids up the right way. I hated to see her go through all that. She forgave those killers as a strong example to all of us. She taught us how to forgive back then and trust me, we all paid attention to her forgiveness lesson that she wanted us to learn.

While Mike and I were living together in that apartment, on one particular Sunday, Mike overslept and missed the morning mass. He was real disappointed that he had missed mass. I will never forget the look on his face that day. Sometimes, I think God sends you little messages. This particular day, it was a message really meant for me. That one thing is something that I will never forget. Anytime that I get lazy about going to mass, I think of Mike and his dedication to going to mass.

My brother David was the first in our family to have a child. He had a girl and they named her Natalie like my wife's name. We all called her "Little Natalie." Dave lived on the same street as me. He had the best lawn in the neighborhood. Dave drove a truck for Coca-Cola and then the local beer distributorship later on. He was a big hunter like my dad Hillman.

Dave had a Kawasaki 900 motorcycle and he let me drive it every now and then. Dave and I both had several motorcycles when we were growing up. They were mostly dirt bikes. I have always been a fan of motorcycles, but also know how dangerous riding one can be. Dave had a bad wreck on his bike one day and ended up in the hospital for a day or two, but ended up okay. That was the end of his motorcycle days. He got rid of the Kawasaki after that.

Dave and his wife ended up getting a divorce. They met when they were young, like 19 years old and had been together for a while. Dave took it really hard and I mean really hard. One night he called me up and was threatening to kill himself. I talked him out of it. I told him that things would get better in the future once he got past it all. He had several guns in the house and I knew he was serious. I don't know why he called me, but I guess he thought that I could help him. Luckily, he got through that rough time in his life. He really loved his wife and simply did not want to be without her. After the divorce, he ended up gaining custody of his daughter Natalie. That tells you something about him right there. How many fathers do you know that can get custody of their little daughter?

My sister Sharri's first son's name is Jake and she was having everyone in the family over for cake and ice cream to celebrate his first birthday. David was down in south Arkansas that morning hunting deer. When he showed up, he had already had a beer or two. Dave was about the last to leave Sharri's house. He wanted to let some time lapse before driving home. Rather that make Little Natalie stay up too late and drive home with her in the car, he asked my mom and dad to take her home with them and he would pick her up tomorrow. It was already past 11 p.m.

It was about 3 a.m. when I received another one of those calls that you never want to receive. David had been killed in an accident with an 18 wheeler on his way home. This 18 wheeler had just recently pulled over to the side of the road and they were at the on ramp on Exit 29 on I-40 going towards Little Rock. One truck driver was training another driver how to drive. It was at this very moment that this truck driver trainee got behind the wheel for the first time during their trip. While he was driving down the on ramp to get onto I-40, he was having trouble shifting gears. Unbeknownst to him, he drifted right out into the highway and was in front of Dave before he could do anything about it. The Arkansas State Trooper speculated that there was a vehicle to Dave's left and he had nowhere to go to avoid the truck. Dave's Toyota truck slammed right into the back corner of the 18 wheeler. He died that night as a result. Dave wasn't wearing a seatbelt and the drinking didn't help either.

Not wearing a seatbelt was a bad habit that he modeled after Hillman. Hillman didn't like to wear seatbelts either. Every time I saw Dave driving without his seatbelt, I would get on him about it. I don't know if he would have survived this accident, but at least he would have had a chance. I wish they could have made the mandatory seat belt laws a few years sooner. Dave died of blunt trauma to the chest as a result of hitting the steering wheel. This is another stage of grief. Denial. If only this, that and the other was done, then he would still be alive. I went through denial with Reese. If only we didn't let him stay with that couple. If only we didn't go to Hong Kong and on and on.

As a family, we were all so thankful that Dave had the foresight to ask mom and dad to take Little Natalie with them. Otherwise, we might have lost her too. In my mind, he saved her life that night.

Dave had a 1978 Camaro that he took really good care of it. He added some nice exhaust pipes to it. Every night, I knew when he was coming home because I would hear those pipes roar up my street. My son Marshall owns it now. We had it repainted and fixed it up. You can see a picture of it at www.pinterest.com/rjadviser.

After Dave died, we had to go clean out his house. Oh man, did I hate this task. This was awful. This was something with finality attached to it. I knew my brother was gone and I did not want to be there cleaning out his stuff. It just wasn't right. This was one of the hardest things that I have ever done in my life. I hated it.

[436]

Several times I went to Dave's house because a boxing match was on TV. He was a big boxing fan and so am I. He would invite a bunch of guys over to watch boxing and we would all scream at the TV and have a few beers. Occasionally, he would throw one of his buddies a bachelor party at his house. We will not talk about those any more.

I have a picture of Dave holding my son Reese in his arms in my office. His daughter, Little Natalie is also in the picture. I am glad that I have that picture. It helps to think that Dave is holding onto Reese for me in heaven.

My dad Hillman was a big chicken when it came to going to the doctor. He never liked to go and he was afraid of needles. You would think a guy six foot six inches tall would not be afraid of anything, much less needles. As a result of his irrational fear, he let something go on way too long. He was sick, but he didn't want to go to the doctor. I think he knew that he might have cancer. We all went to the hospital where he was having exploratory surgery to see if he did have cancer. Sure enough, he did. Hillman had about six months to live. Hillman said, "I'm a dead man walking." He tried chemotherapy for a time, but puked so much that he finally said to hell with it. He was only 57.

I had moved my financial planning business away from his office about seven years earlier, but I decided to move my office in with his when we found out about his cancer. I tried to help his clients while serving mine, too. Hillman was a trooper. He was a fighter and he was never hospitalized or anything until his very last weekend.

I was at work that last week when in walked Father Hebert. He walked straight back to see my dad. I asked my mom what he was doing there and mom said that my dad thought a lot of how Natalie and I were good Catholics and he wanted to follow our example and become a Catholic.

Right there in my dad's office, he became a Catholic. Father Hebert asked me to come back to my dad's office. Father Hebert then told me that my dad said he didn't have many sins, but that I probably did. We all laughed over that. He was a funny guy, let me tell you.

After that, I had planned on going to Tampa Bay for a business meeting that weekend. My mom and dad were going to go to Orlando to see the NASCAR Café and also to take Little Natalie to Disney World. Dad was a big NASCAR fan and he wanted to see it, so we made plans to meet in Orlando. Dad had a friend that supplied the gasoline to the NASCAR tracks and he got to go and be in the pits with the drivers. He met several of them and went to a lot of NASCAR races. One time he met Cale Yarborough. They were standing by his car and my dad asked Cale, "How do you fit in there?" Cale said it was not too tough. Then, my dad quipped, "I meant how do you fit in there with the big balls you must have to drive as fast as you do?" They all laughed of course. That was my dad. A very funny guy.

I drove down to Tampa with a friend of mine, Jim McKnight. Jim was one of my baseball buddies and he wasn't working, so I asked him if he wanted to ride down to Tampa with me. He said he would and I am glad he did, because that is about 900 plus miles to Tampa from Little Rock.

We were probably about a couple of hours away from Tampa when my cell phone rang. We had just pulled up to a gas station, so we were stopped. It was one of my fraternity brothers, Martin Northern. He told me that Mike Rowland, my best friend had just been murdered by a crack addict. Mike was working late at his mom's drapery business and had just called his girlfriend and said he was on his way home. He walked out of his building and opened the door to his car when a crack addict attacked him from behind with a hammer. Mike had three dollars on him, a ring, a watch and a bracelet. The killer had just knocked on the door at a neighbor's house and asked to borrow a hammer. This was at about 10 o'clock at night mind you. This neighbor knew who he was giving the hammer to. This crack addict was the son of a preacher. Everyone knew this guy. He was in and out of trouble all the time. Yet, he still gave him that damn hammer. Here I go again with the "what if's" and the denials.

Mike was rushed to the hospital. His family was there with him, but Mike was already gone. The machines were keeping him alive long enough for the family to get there, that was all. His girlfriend told me that she wished she had never seen him like that. It was real hard on her and Mike's family.

Being a criminal justice major, I knew that his funeral would not be right away, because of his murder and the fact that it would require an autopsy. Jim and I talked and talked about Mike the rest of our trip and we decided to go ahead and go to Tampa. It was just a one day meeting anyway. About an hour later, when we were almost to Tampa, I got another phone call. My dad was in the hospital. He had fallen down and they took him to the hospital. He didn't want to go, but my mom made him go.

Jim and I decided to stay the night in Tampa, then get up and drive back. Another 900 plus miles to go. Periodically, I would get calls on my dad's condition, then it seemed like the calls stopped for a while. I was all shook up over Mike's murder and luckily for me, Jim was with me and he was driving. Funny how God puts people in your life to help you. Jim was a big help to me during this time.

Several hours into our trip back, I called to check on my dad. He had died. That is why the calls had stopped. Everyone was there with him except me. I looked at this like God was protecting me. He knows how I cry when I watch no-hitters in baseball and he didn't want me to be there at Mike's or my dad's hospital bed. Believe me, I would have been there at both of their bedsides, if at all possible. God had other plans.

Now my thoughts turned to attending two funerals in one week. Mike had a girlfriend and he had just told me that "She is the one." This was the one he was going to marry. Mike was over at my house a few days before he was murdered. His girlfriend lived in my neighborhood. So, Mike would drop by every now and then. That day he was at my house, Mike was so happy. He was always positive and happy, but on this day, he was all smiles. He was standing there next to me and I had a thought that Mike looked taller than me. Mike wasn't taller than me, but on that day, he looked taller than me. I knew there was something special in that moment, but I could not quite put my finger on it. God was giving me one last joyous moment with my best friend. That is what I realized later.

Mike's mother told me that right before he died, an elderly lady he knew that lived nearby did not have a bed at her house. She was on a fixed income and could not readily afford a new mattress set. Mike loaded up his mattress set and took it to this elderly lady. He slept on the couch at his house and sacrificed his bed to that lady. That act of kindness tells you who Mike was as a person. When he helped people, he didn't want or need any recognition for it. He simply knew it was the right thing to do.

Mike's funeral was at his Catholic Church in North Little Rock. There were seven priests at that funeral. Seven! That fact alone speaks volumes about who Mike Rowland was a person. I thought about his mother. Here she was with her daughter Kelly murdered and now Mike was murdered. Two of her four kids were murdered. Another one of those little reminders from God that there are always people worse off than you.

One of the priests who was there was Father Hebert. He was Mike and my high school English teacher. In addition, he was the same priest that baptized Reese, made my dad a Catholic and he was doing my dad Hillman's funeral. After the mass for Mike, Father Hebert saw me and came up to me and started crying. Yes, priests cry too. He wanted to know why I was there since my dad had just died. I told him that Mike was my best friend and there was no way that I was missing this celebration of his life.

Of course, Mike was the best friend to more than just me. I'm sure about a half dozen other guys considered him to be their best friend, too. Kenny Stroud and Mike Wrobleski come to mind. Mike was a really popular guy. He knew he was a best friend to more than one guy. He was a rock star in his own way.

At the gravesite, I went up to Mike's girlfriend and told her about how Mike had just been over to my house and how he told me that she was the one. She appreciated me telling her, but I knew deep down in my heart that this was similar to me cleaning out Dave's house. There was a finality to it. She was going to have to move on in her life without Mike whether she wanted to or not. She was a strong girl and I watched from a far as she was able to get past Mike's murder. A few years later, she found someone new and got married to him, so I felt better about it. People make choices in life when faced with decisions like this one. Either you can choose to be a victim and sink into despair, or you can choose to move forward. She made the right choice. She moved forward.

My dad Hillman had a visitation before his funeral. Two of his friends, one a dentist, the other an attorney could not go in and see him. It was simply too hard on them. I had a moment alone with my dad's body. It was just me and him. I looked at him and he looked as if he had a smile on his face. I felt a strong feeling that he was okay.

[441]

Hillman joked most of his life about religious people. He always said to "hold onto your wallet when you are around people claiming to be religious." His words always seemed to come true around this issue. He witnessed firsthand all those crooked people who stole money from people via television pledges. My dad's mom, Alberta had gotten kind of senile in her old age and fell for these pleas. One time my dad went home to find out that she had given them like $60,000. Her P.O. Box was a foot deep in Urgent FedEx looking envelopes where they had to have money immediately otherwise all the world's children were going to starve. The truth is that these thugs sold their donor lists to other preachers and they bombarded any old lady who was foolish enough to send in a check. It is easy to see why Hillman did not like religious people after having seen what happened to his mom.

On the last weekend of Hillman's life, he became a Catholic. Jesus said it was never too late. Dad had committed to the Lord on the last weekend of his life. That kind of matched his style. As I looked at his body that day, I really felt that he had done it. He made it. He was in Heaven. Supposedly, I had a small influence in his decision. I think probably it was more the Holy Spirit working on his heart. He was given a great gift of time. My brother David or my friend Mike didn't have that same gift.

After Mike died, I would go by and see his mom. For five years after Mike's death, we would have a memorial golf tournament called Circle of Friends. After five year's Mike's mom didn't want to do it anymore. We raised money for the Arkansas School for the Deaf and Blind where his sister Kelly went to school. I believe that they were able to build a special playground area for the kids as a result of Mike's Circle of Friends golf tournaments.

Recently, I was digging through my closet and I have a box of old hats. It is up high in my closet and I had to kind of knock it down to see what was in it. When I knocked it down, a bunch of hats fell out. I put them back in the box and put it back up high on the shelf. As I looked down on the floor, there was a Mike Rowland Circle of Friends hat. Coincidence? I do not think so. I believe that Mike's spirit was talking to me and he wanted me to put his hat on the shelf by itself, so that is precisely what I did.

I have this small narrow drawer in the kitchen and between my wife and I, we often get free can wraps to keep cold drinks cold. We had so many of these that they overflowed the drawer and dropped down to the cabinet below. I was pulling out the overflow of these can wraps when I stumbled upon one from the Mike Rowland Circle of Friends golf tournament. Another coincidence? I do not think so. Okay Mike, I put a picture of the hat, the can wrap and some Circle of Friends golf balls up on my Pinterest web site for all to see. I hope you are happy. Go to www.pinterest.com/rjadviser to view the pictures. They are under the Sigma Alpha Epsilon Fraternity Board. Pictures of my family are also there under the Family board section.

I always send Mike's mom a Christmas card and she does the same. One time, a few years back, she told me that her son Charlie had ALS. Charlie had helped run the golf tournaments in Mike's honor. Now, he had Lou Gehrig's disease. My uncle Dennis had that and we all know it is a death sentence. I hated it for Mike's mom. Three of her four children are now gone. She recently moved to Dallas to live near her remaining daughter and grandkids. I was kind of glad to see it. North Little Rock had not been kind to her. Here it was again, a message telling me that there are always people worse off than you.

After Reese was born and died, Natalie and I decided that there was no reason to wait on trying to have another child. Marshall was born in 1990. His middle name came from the doctor who delivered Reese. He was kind of a quirky doctor who liked to wear Birkenstocks to work, but we liked him a lot. He was a good guy so, we gave Marshall his middle name. When Marshall was born, we were all on pins and needles about having another SIDS baby, because he was born within a week of Reese's 1st year death anniversary. By now, we knew what SIDS was and the signs of it. As I mentioned before, I am one of those guys who prefers to learn on my own. I spent a lot of time at the University of Arkansas Medical School library. I poured over all the journals related to Sudden Infant Death Syndrome. If you want to know anything about it, then ask me. I can tell you all about it.

In my research, I found out some things that I didn't like. SIDS babies tend to have similar characteristics. Of course, I wish I knew these facts in advance. SIDS babies are often left alone in a bedroom crib when they die. All babies should sleep on their back. Reese was found not breathing on his stomach, face down. SIDS babies tend to die soon after having a bottle. This was also the case with Reese. SIDS babies tend to be premature infants. Reese was about a month premature. SIDS babies tend to have some type of cold or respiratory infection prior to their death. Reese did, too. We took Reese to the doctor when he had the cold, but the pediatrician told us not to worry about it. SIDS babies tend to die more in the winter months. Reese died in December. SIDS babies tend not to grow at the same rate of more normal babies. In other words, their growth percentages tend to lag other babies in the first few months. Those are some of the factors related to SIDS.

Since Reese died, people are a little more educated in regard to Sudden Infant Death Syndrome. The American Academy of Pediatrics instituted a successful "Back-to-sleep" campaign in 1994 to inform parents to keep their babies on their backs when they are in their cribs. A San Diego study from 1991 to 2008 showed that the incidence of SIDS decreased from 85.4% to 30.1% as a result of newborn parents who were made aware of this issue. Apparently, babies sleeping face down after having a bottle was a major factor in SIDS deaths. Please make sure the people in your family who are having children are aware of this issue. You might save a life.

In order to keep a special eye on Marshall, we put him on a monitor. Well, he set that thing off 28 times in the first 30 days. Talk about freaked out parents. I cannot tell you how many 100 yard dashes I ran to his room in the middle of the night. Thankfully, Marshall would be a non-SIDS baby. He is a special son, a perfect kid and way smarter than me, too. I always tease him about being "all knowing and all powerful." We are blessed to have him as our son.

After a couple of years, we wanted to have another kid. However, Natalie miscarried. As a Catholic, this is a life to me. I felt like I had lost another child. We tried again, but we had another miscarriage, then yet a third. I can still remember looking at the fetus on the ultrasound and at first being excited that this third one was going to work, then suddenly realizing that there was no heartbeat. I even had some names picked out. Grant and Olivia. All Natalie and I could do was just hug each other and cry. These miscarriages were very disheartening. They take the wind out of your sail. We thought about giving up, since we were getting close to 40 years old.

One night we were watching this little B rated movie called "Rudy" about a short guy who wanted to play football at Notre Dame. He never gave up and finally achieved his dream despite what seemed like immovable obstacles. We related to this movie. This was God's way of telling us not to give up. Natalie decided, she decides a lot of things in my life by the way, that we would name her Rudi if it was a girl and Rudy if it was a boy. The next time we tried, we made it all the way and our daughter Rudi was born. She had red hair no less, like her mom. She is my sweet pumpkin love. She illustrated my Wally Street character for this book. I think she portrayed the character pretty well.

Looking back, we had three children who were born, only to lose one and then we had three who never were born. Six children in all. I see other families who have no trouble having kids. I often wonder if they know what a truly special gift that they have been given. I hope they never take it for granted.

When faced with the tragedy of others like Mrs. Rowland, or my own family tragedies there is always an opportunity to make a decision. The decision is always to choose between being a victim and sink into despair or depression, or to move forward. All of my life, I have endured a lot of heartache, but have always chosen to move forward. When you look at your life and the tragedies that you have faced in yours, ask yourself are you moving forward? If not, then you should. I did not say "get over it." I said simply to move forward. When you look back, think of the good times and the blessings that you were given by having shared your life with that person. You will be reunited one day with them. Think how joyous that moment will be when it happens.

I have not forgotten any of the tragedies in my life, but they have made me into the person that I am today. It is okay to look back on your life for reflective purposes, because there is always a lesson to be learned. You do not want to dwell on the past however, because this is when victimization starts to creep in and control your life. You cannot change the past, but you can change how you live in the future. Understand that there are always people that are worse off than you. I would go out on a limb and say that I am probably one of them, too.

One more thing about personal tragedies. When someone you know is faced with a tragedy, you may find it difficult to talk with them about it. In my case, I have found that most people don't want to talk to you about it, because they do not want to upset you. However, what you may not realize is that people like me, like to talk about it, because it helps us in some small way. Although you may find it difficult to find the right thing to say, what is more important is just to let people like me talk about the person they lost. Got it? Good.

In regard to your financial life, it is much better to admit your mistakes and try not to repeat them. If you have Wally Street for a financial advisor, then I already know the mistakes that you have made. It is time to move on now from Wally, even though it may be very hard to do. Wally World and its business model is the major culprit and the source of the problem. You have to understand that if you continue to do business in Wally World, then you will continue to be sold products that generate revenue for Wally Street. Realize that this is of absolutely no benefit to you. That's a fact, Jack.

You really need to _think critically_ about this one issue. If your financial advisor is working for a bank, insurance company or a Wall Street firm, then what does that say about their ethics and integrity? It should tell you that their ethics and integrity are not quite as strong as independent registered investment advisers. It also means that your Wally Street is okay with the business model that generates revenue for his firm and himself at your expense. Do you see this critical difference? I hope so, because in my mind, it is a _major_ difference.

Before you read this book, Wally Street was the reason that you were stupid. That is a weakness you can now overcome by making the smarter decision to move to an _independent_ registered investment adviser who truly does things in your best interests.

One more thing. If you go to your Estate Planning attorney, Elder Law attorney, or CPA for a referral to a financial advisor and they refer you to Wally Street, then give them a good talking to, will you? After you do that, then tell them to buy a copy of this book. We can't allow them to continue referring their clients to Wally Street. That would be pretty stupid on their part.

On the other hand, if your Estate Planning attorney, Elder Law attorney, or CPA refers you to an **_independent_** registered investment adviser, then my friend you have found one smart cookie, who like me, is looking out for your best interests.

Hopefully, by writing this book, this little peon has made a small dent in the Wall Street machine and pointed out why you should never do business with the likes of a Wally Street. With your help, perhaps we can turn the tide against Wally World and our friend Wally Street.

Will you do me a favor? If you live in the Florida area, then reach out to me for help with your financial life. Tell others about "The Introverted Advisor" in St. Johns, Florida that just might be able to help them with their financial situation. I would appreciate it.

Tell your friends to buy this book, too! I need all the help I can get. Or, as my dad would say, whenever anyone did him a favor, "I'll dance at your next wedding."

You have finally passed my class and I am proud of you. You are no longer stupid Kemosabe. Sorry about the hickory switches and the few crude words here and there. Please forgive me. I meant no disrespect. Really, I didn't.

Keep moving forward my avid pupils. Or, as my dad would say, "Hit the ground in high places!"

God Bless you and yours.

Richard Allison Johnson *aka* Richard Mark Allison
The Introverted Advisor

Sources

The primary sources for this book was obtained from freely available information in the public Internet domain via a Google search.

Internal Revenue Service – www.irs.gov
Social Security Administration – www.ssa.gov
The U.S. Mint – www.usmint.gov
Morningstar® - www.morningstar.com
Lipper® - www.lipperweb.com
Wikipedia® - www.wikepedia.org
Rockefeller Trust Co. – www.rockefellerfinancial.com
Pensco Trust Co. – www.pensco.com
Equity Trust Co. – www.trustetc.com
Charles Schwab & Co., Inc. – www.schwab.com
23 and me – www.23andme.com
Ancestry – www.ancestry.com
Family Search – www.familysearch.org
Brainy Quote – www.brainyquote.com

Organizations providing continuing education that assisted in some of the ideas presented in this book:

Estate Planning Council of Northeast Florida - www.nefepc.org
Alliance Bernstein Wealth Management – www.alliancebernstein.com

The author's company web sites:

Marian Financial Services, Inc. – www.marianfs.com
     An independent registered investment adviser firm.
First Coast Planning, LLC – www.firstcoastplanning.com
     A licensed insurance agency.

Comments on social media:

Do you think that I sit around looking at social media web sites all day? Not hardly. Only Wally Street does that.

Generally, I do an occasional blog post and that feeds into these other web sites automatically. Of course, if you want to follow me on all these crappy, time wasting web sites, then go right ahead.

The author's social media web sites:

Blog – http://rjadviser.blogspot.com

LinkedIn – http://www.linkedin.com/in/rjadvisor

Twitter – http://twitter.com/rjadviser

Facebook -   http://www.facebook.com/kyatma
                http://www.facebook.com/firstcoastplanningllc

Pinterest – http://www.pinterest.com/rjadviser

The author's newsletter:

I send out a monthly newsletter via email on the 15th of each month. Let me know if you want to be added to the list. Send me an email to: rick@marianfs.com.

[THE END]

(Hopefully of doing business with Wally Street.)

www.ingramcontent.com/pod-product-compliance
Lightning Source LLC
Chambersburg PA
CBHW051202200326
41519CB00025B/6978